Verdura

ALSO BY VIANA LA PLACE

CUCINA FRESCA
(with Evan Kleiman)

PASTA FRESCA
(with Evan Kleiman)

CUCINA RUSTICA
(with Evan Kleiman)

Verdura

VEGETABLES
ITALIAN STYLE

Viana La Place

Illustrations by Ann Field

William Morrow and Company, Inc. New York

Library of Congress Cataloging-in-Publication Data

La Place, Viana.
    Verdura: vegetables Italian style / Viana La Place;
illustrations by Ann Field.
        p.   cm.
    Includes index.
    ISBN 0-688-08764-7
    1. Cookery (Vegetables) 2. Cookery, Italian. I. Title.
TX801.L3   1991
641.6'5—dc20   90-49304
                                                                              CIP

Printed in the United States of America

First Edition

1 2 3 4 5 6 7 8 9 10

BOOK DESIGN BY RICHARD ORIOLO

To my father, Pierre

ACKNOWLEDGMENTS

I would like to thank my editor, Ann Bramson, for her warm and generous spirit and guiding hand. To my agents, Maureen and Eric Lasher, I express my deepest gratitude. From the beginning they were a source of encouragement and support. Loving thanks to my husband, Jim Krupka, for many happy hours shared at the table. Others have contributed to this book, both directly and indirectly, and I want to take this opportunity to express my appreciation. Thank you to Kathy Ternay who helped test recipes; to Terry Joseph, for her technical expertise; to Evan, for the three books that came before; to my sisters, Maria and Michelle, for always being there for me; to Aileen and Harry Krupka, for their enthusiasm; and to Ann Field, for capturing the essence of the book in her lively illustrations. Most of all, I am indebted to my mother, Antonietta Cammarata La Place. Her beautiful and evocative stories about life in Italy and her poetic spirit have shaped my sensibilities and enriched my life beyond measure.

CONTENTS

Verdura

INTRODUCTION

Verdura means vegetables. It is a word that at its root means green, and which conjures up images of green fields, freshness, and the natural world. To me, *Verdura* represents a style of eating directly related to nature, with vegetables at the center. It reflects my own personal style of eating and the tastes I most love.

The first few years of my life were spent in a small town in southern California where the backyard was a tangle of fruit trees, vegetable garden, and berry vines. My earliest memories are of ripe apricots and persimmons and the wild greens my grandfather collected. A move to a nearby suburb changed the source of our food from garden to supermarket, but our way of eating did not change—fresh vegetables and salads at every meal and simple roasted chicken or fish. As a child of Italian parents, I acquired a taste for vegetables early in life. I badgered everyone at the table for the tasty heart of their artichoke, ate tomato sandwiches spiked with oregano after school, and dipped my bread into the vinegary juices in the bottom of the salad bowl.

When I moved to Berkeley to go to college, I had to learn to cook. Cookbooks were my guide and inspiration—from Richard Olney's *Simple French Food* to the works of Elizabeth David. Trips to relatives, the first when I was twelve, and later, during my college years, revealed to me Italy in all its wonder and the deeply satisfying traditions of eating and time spent at the dinner table. I majored in art, but cooking and Italy soon became my all-consuming passion. After college, I moved to Los Angeles and worked as a chef in the city's vanguard Italian restaurants. There I developed a repertoire of recipes that led me to teaching and writing cookbooks. From the beginning and all during my years of cooking, I have always found my greatest pleasure and truest expression through vegetables.

Italians have an enormous love and respect for vegetables, not surprising given the range and quality available. Fruits and vegetables are part of the fabric of Italian life. Luminous umbrellas form canopies over market stalls. Bright green fava beans, groupings of fragile lettuces, blood oranges, and masses of sharply aromatic onions glow softly in the filtered light and perfume the air. In spring, the countryside alternates farmland—squares of feathery green fennel and astonishing rose-colored artichokes—with fields of keenly fragrant wild mustard flowers and thickets of prickly-pear cactus. Soft grassy meadows are dotted with chamomile, and orchards bloom with fruit trees colored white, cotton candy pink, and lavender. During the hot summer months, basil flourishes on city terraces and kitchen gardens abound with zucchini flowers and plump, spicy-scented tomatoes. Fall colors turn to burnished purple and pale green as grapes ripen in vineyards, and in winter, the dark earth is brightened by groves of citrus trees bearing golden fruits.

As we turn our focus away from meats and heavy meals and move toward the fresh flavors and beauty found in nature, we can learn from the Italian style of eating, where vegetables play a leading role. We can learn from their ingenuity in creating an extraordinary range of vegetable dishes. In America, artichokes are traditionally prepared in one way only—boiled and served with butter. In Italy, artichokes are braised in herbs; the hearts are breaded and fried; they appear in pasta sauces and are made into a pesto to spread on bread. Raw artichokes are thinly sliced and served with slivers of Parmesan cheese, or the tender heart of an immature artichoke is dipped in olive oil and salt and enjoyed as the season's first tender offering. There is adventure and exuberance in this style of cooking, a respect for the seasons, and a passion for freshness.

Verdura celebrates vegetables in all their remarkable variety in antipasti, salads, sandwiches, soups, main dishes, and more, with a special chapter on fruit desserts. *Verdura* offers a complete approach to cooking that is based primarily on fruits, vegetables, herbs, lettuces, edible flowers, and lean cheeses. Strong, fresh seasonings—olives, capers, red chile peppers, lemon juice, and saffron—are used to bring out flavors and add piquancy.

The spirit of Italy is in the pages of this book, but the applications are for us and the way we want to live. *Verdura* offers simple, lively recipes that look to nature for inspiration. Our task is to reconnect with that verdant and mysterious force. We can start by relearning, or learning for the first time, the order and progression of fruits and vegetables that come with the subtle shiftings of earth and sun, a knowledge dulled by modern life. It is this knowledge, this closeness, that can renew our bond with nature and, in the process, guide us to a new way of eating.

A Guide to Vegetables and Herbs

*T*oday the variety and quality of American produce have improved dramatically. Many supermarkets and most specialty stores carry a wide range of unusual vegetables and fresh herbs. Health food stores usually stock a selection of organic fruits and vegetables, and they always seem to taste better than supermarket offerings. Farmers' markets have cropped up across the country selling the season's best fruits and vegetables. Seek out the one closest to you and you will be amply rewarded as you return home with shopping bags exuding fresh, sweet smells. Ethnic markets are another good source for interesting produce. Or drive to the countryside in search of stands selling local fruits and vegetables. Above all, a lovingly tended home garden is the most gratifying way to supply yourself and your family with the very best produce.

This section is a practical guide. Refer to it as you cook for any technical information you need or if you want to learn more about a particular vegetable or herb.

ARTICHOKES

An artichoke is the flower bud of a large, silver-green thistlelike plant that can grow to a height of five feet. The edible portions of the artichoke bud are the heart, the tender leaves, and the flesh at the base of its tougher leaves. When left on the plant, the bud blossoms into a spiky purple flower.

Select small or medium-sized artichokes. Large artichokes have tough, more developed fibers and tend to be less flavorful. Baby artichokes are artichokes picked at an immature stage and are uniformly tender. Fresh artichokes have a rich, meaty flavor that leaves a clean aftertaste on the palate, whereas old artichokes can taste dull and lifeless. Buy artichokes that have tightly clenched leaves that snap off crisply when bent back, a sure sign of freshness. An artichoke that is heavy for its size means that its heart is large.

A properly trimmed artichoke is completely edible from the heart to the tender leaves. When trimming, rub the artichokes with a cut lemon to prevent darkening. Squeeze the juice of half a lemon into a big bowl of water. Keep cleaned artichokes in the water, referred to as acidulated water, to prevent discoloration.

To prepare an artichoke for cooking, snap back the tough leaves and pull down, working your way around the layers. Stop when you get to the pale yellow, tender leaves. Cut off the tops of the remaining leaves, leaving about one inch of leaf. Use a paring knife to trim away the dark green areas along the base. Trim off the base of the stem end, and cut away the tough fibers around the stem, leaving just the light-colored, tender center portion. Cut the artichoke in half lengthwise. Use a paring knife to carefully cut away the fuzzy choke, trying to cut just at the point where choke and heart meet. Baby artichokes generally do not have developed chokes, but they do have a layer or two of tough leaves that must be removed, and the base needs to be trimmed as with larger artichokes. Keep all trimmed artichokes in acidulated water until needed.

There are many more ways to serve artichokes than the one that usually finds its way to the American table with only the thorny tips of the artichoke leaves clipped. Artichokes are still considered something of an oddity here, even though they have been cultivated along the California coast since Italian farmers settled there decades ago. In Italy artichokes are inexpensive and abundant, and many varieties are available. Italians prize their flavor and tenderness and serve them in hundreds of different ways both raw and cooked. The American variety lends itself to the same wide range of recipes. A misconception about artichokes is that they take a great deal of time to cook. A trimmed artichoke, cut into wedges and braised in herbs and olive oil, cooks in fifteen minutes or less. Artichokes are delicious served hot, but are even more rich tasting when served at room temperature. You can prepare many artichoke dishes in the morning and serve them that evening with no loss of savoriness.

There are many recipes for artichokes throughout this book, from Risotto with Baby Artichokes to Artichokes Braised with Thyme. If you've never cooked artichokes other than to boil them, you will be amazed at their versatility.

ARUGULA

Arugula, a member of the mustard family, is a bitter green that is at its best eaten raw in salads. It has a tender, deeply toothed leaf with a flavor that is highly pungent. Like any other green, arugula can also be cooked but then loses much of its wonderfully assertive edge.

Although arugula has acquired a trendy reputation, its origins are as humble as can be. Arugula grows wild in the Italian countryside, and traditionally was gathered by families who looked to seasonal edible wild plants to augment their diet.

Look for arugula with fresh, springy green leaves and use it soon after buying as it fades quickly; lifeless, pale arugula is not worth buying. To prepare arugula, discard any leaves that are yellow, bruised, or wilted. Cut off the tough stem ends. The small, tender leaves can be used whole. Cut the larger leaves crosswise into strips.

Arugula is becoming increasingly appreciated in America. Specialty produce markets carry it all year round, and it has even begun to appear in some supermarkets. As more people discover its unique flavor and ask for it at their local markets, its availability should improve. Or you can bypass the markets and grow arugula very successfully in your garden. If all else fails, peppery watercress makes an excellent substitute.

Arugula can form part of a mixed salad, or it can be served alone dressed with extra-virgin olive oil and lemon juice, as in Arugula Salad as Served at Fiaschetteria Beltramme. It is delicious sprinkled raw over pizza in Potato and Arugula Pizza. Milan-Style Zucchini calls for lightly cooking the arugula.

ASPARAGUS

The asparagus is a member of the lily family. It has been cultivated for centuries, but can still be found growing wild. Select asparagus with bright green stalks that are crisp and firm. Avoid stalks that look withered. The tips should have tightly closed scales that are shaded from green to mauve. The scales are leaf buds, and any that exhibit signs of producing foliage should be avoided; it is an indication that the asparagus is past its prime. When the asparagus in your garden has grown tall and spindly and produces feathery leaves, it is a sign that the season is over.

Markets usually offer the shopper several thicknesses of asparagus. Select the thickness based on your needs or preference, since all the stalks have the same flavor. To prepare asparagus for cooking, snap off the tough, pale green or white portion at the base of the stalk. It will break off approximately at the point where the stalk turns tender. Use a vegetable peeler to peel about halfway up the remaining stalk. You will end up with a completely tender asparagus stalk without any traces of tough skin or fiber. For very thin asparagus, simply gather up the stalks in a bundle and cut them crosswise along the base of the stems at the point where the stalks turn intensely bright green. There is no need to peel the stalks. To cook tie asparagus in a bundle and plunge in abundant salted boiling water. Or place it in a large sauté pan, in one layer, in a small amount of salted boiling water. Grilling or broiling asparagus without precooking it intensifies its flavor.

Asparagus can be served at room temperature, simply drizzled with olive oil and lemon. Asparagus with Anchovy and Lemon Wild Style is traditionally made with wild asparagus, but the recipe works wonders with the less intense flavor of the cultivated stalks. In Spring Vegetable Stew, asparagus and other tender vegetables are served in butter-enriched vegetable juices.

DRIED BEANS

Dried beans play an important role in Italian cooking and turn up in antipasti, soups, pasta, and salads. The dried beans that are most commonly used include borlotti beans, cannellini beans, chick peas, and fava beans. All of the beans can be purchased in the equivalent of one-pound bags from Italian specialty stores, and some are found in supermarkets. Substitutes are suggested for some of the harder-to-find varieties.

I always have on hand cans of cooked imported Italian beans. They are of very high quality, packed without the additional seasonings and preservatives found in many brands of American canned beans. With high-quality canned beans in your pantry you can prepare satisfying and nutritious dishes in a few minutes.

All dried beans must be soaked before cooking. The night before you plan to cook the beans, place them in a big bowl and add water to cover by two to three inches. The next day drain the beans in a colander. Place them in a heavy pot and add enough water to generously cover the beans by several inches. Bring to a very slow simmer. Cover and cook the beans until they are tender but hold their shape. The slow cooking prevents the beans from bursting. Reserve the cooking liquid to use as a flavorful and nutritious broth for bean soup. If using beans for salads, drain them in a colander, gently run cool water over them, and dry them on a clean dish towel.

Borlotti

Related to cranberry beans, borlotti beans are medium-sized tan beans mottled with deep magenta. When cooked, their skin turns a rosy brown and they become creamy and slightly chalky, a texture that I find irresistible. Borlotti beans are used in soups, risotti, and pasta dishes, but I like them best in salads. Their addictive texture and lightly sweet, nutty flavor make for the ultimate bean salad, Roman Summer Borlotti Bean Salad, which teams them with slivers of raw yellow pepper, celery, and onion. Markets that specialize in Italian foods stock imported dried and canned borlotti beans.

Cannellini

Slender, elongated, and medium-sized, cannellini beans or white kidney beans, are a warm, satiny white color. Their texture is creamy and the flavor mild and light. Strongly aromatic herbs, such as rosemary and sage, are often paired with cannellini. The mild beans become permeated with their perfume, as in Warm Cannellini Bean and Herb Salad. To achieve a lighter, equally delicious, herbal flavor, try cooking the beans with basil or with celery stalk and celery leaves. Markets that specialize in Italian foods stock imported dried and canned cannellini beans. If you cannot find a source for cannellini beans, any medium-sized white bean makes a fine substitute.

Canned cannellini beans tend to be a bit mushy. If you have the time, cook the dried beans and drain them when they are tender but firm. This is especially important when making white bean salads.

Chick Peas

Chick peas are beige, irregular-shaped globes that turn gold when cooked. Their distinctive warm and nutty flavor can easily carry a simple soup of pasta and beans. Chick peas are wonderful in a salad dressed with fruity olive oil and red wine vinegar, but are at their best served warm, drizzled with fine olive oil, and topped with freshly ground black pepper. Dried and canned chick peas are available in most supermarkets and in all markets specializing in Italian food products. Chick Pea and Escarole Soup with Grilled Bread contrasts the rich flavor of chick peas with the clean, refreshing flavor of escarole.

Fava

Large and flat, dried fava beans are shaped like lima beans and are light brown in color. They look like smooth stones from the bottom of a river that have dried to a dull, soft finish. Fava beans have a very tough peel that does not soften sufficiently in cooking to make it edible. To make a rough puree, as in Dried Fava Bean and Fresh Fennel Soup, the beans are cooked peeled. To serve favas whole, make a cut in the skin at one end to prevent splitting, and when the beans are tender, serve them with the peels still on. In this very rustic style of cooking, each diner sucks the creamy flesh from the beans. Dried fava beans can be purchased peeled or unpeeled. Or you can buy the cooked unpeeled beans in cans. They are available in markets specializing in Italian or Middle Eastern foods.

Spagna Bianchetti

These are large, white, kidney-shaped beans. Spagna Bianchetti beans have a delicious, creamy texture that I find best suited to salads. The beans can be purchased dried or canned in markets specializing in Italian foods. Or you can use dried or canned butter beans, available in most supermarkets, or any other large white bean.

FRESH BEANS

Fava

Fresh fava beans are very popular in Mediterranean countries. They are sold in the pod and must be shelled. The young beans are tender and green with a clean, sweet, yet lightly bitter flavor. The peel has a more pronounced bitter quality. Each bean is peeled if the dish is to be mild and sweet, but the beans are cooked unpeeled if a more assertive flavor is desired. As the beans mature, they lose their bright green coloring, turn pale green or yellow, and become starchy (see Dried Fava Beans, page 12). Tender fava beans are also eaten raw, often accompanied by cheese.

Look for fava bean pods that are bright green, tender, and ideally about 5 inches in length. Avoid yellowed, blemished, or withered pods. Fava beans are available in the produce sections of markets in Italian or Middle Eastern neighborhoods and in specialty produce markets.

I love fresh fava beans and they appear frequently in this book, in stews, side dishes, salads, or eaten raw in antipasti. Try Roman-Style Raw Fava Beans, Scamorza, and Fresh Onion or Rustic Spring Stew, which features fava beans, peas, fennel, and artichokes.

Fresh fava beans have such a wonderfully distinct flavor that they are worth the extra effort it might take to find them, and the time it takes to shell and peel them.

Snap

Snap beans include a wide range of varieties, the two most commonly available being Blue Lake and Kentucky Wonder. Slender, bright green haricots verts and tender, pale-hued yellow wax beans can be found in specialty produce markets. Snap beans were once called string beans because of a tough string that ran the length of the bean, but modern varieties of snap beans are stringless.

Select snap beans that are small, tender, and firm. They should be fresh enough that they make a snapping sound when broken in half. Avoid large, pale beans with swollen pods and big, developed seeds. Mature beans lose their sweetness and become tough and fibrous.

Cook snap beans until just tender in abundant salted boiling water.

Cooking times vary according to age and variety. To set the bright green color of freshly boiled beans, run cold water over them immediately after draining them. Snap beans can also be braised, as in Green Beans in Coral-Colored Sauce. Braising is particularly effective when cooking older snap beans, as it sweetens and tenderizes them. For a light main dish, try Sautéed Green Vegetable Platter, with lightly sautéed haricots verts, tiny zucchini, and fresh spinach.

BEETS

Fresh beets have bulbous dark red roots, red stems, and dark green leaves with crimson veining. Both the roots and the fresh leaves are edible. Beets are not as popular as they deserve to be, considering their intensely sweet, earthy flavor and brilliant ruby color. Canned beets, which have a flabby, lackluster texture, are probably partly to blame for this.

Select small, smooth beets of approximately the same size with tender leafy tops. Cut off the tops, leaving attached an inch of stem and their root ends to prevent the beets from bleeding while they cook. Reserve the leaves, since they make choice eating. Cook the beets in abundant boiling water until they are tender but slightly resistant, or bake them wrapped in foil. Baked beets are especially sweet, with a deep, concentrated flavor. Slip off the peels while the beets are still warm.

When serving beets keep in mind that their color can bleed into other foods. I prefer to serve them separately as a first course or in salads, such as Beet and Radicchio Salad. Beet and Beet Greens Salad is a great way to utilize both the roots and leaves of fresh beets.

Beets that are deep gold in color are available in specialty produce stores and are just as sweet as the red variety. Golden beets are among the mix of brightly colored diced vegetables featured in Russian Salad.

BROCCOLI

Broccoli, originally derived from wild cabbage, was introduced to the United States in the 1920s by Italian farmers who settled in California. Although today it is quite common, then it was considered a delicacy and commanded high prices.

Broccoli has a large, central flowering head, growing on a single stalk, that is bright green but can also be tinged with blue or purple. The central head is composed of groupings of densely clustered flower buds called "flowerets." Both the flowerets and fleshy stalk are edible. When broccoli is tender and young, its flavor and texture are quite delectable. Older broccoli has coarse, pale yellow stalks and the delicate, sweet flavor is missing.

Select broccoli with slender, brilliant green stalks and tightly closed blossoms. Avoid those with woody stalks or with yellowed or blossoming flowerets.

To prepare broccoli, use a paring knife to strip the peel, starting at the base and stopping where the flowerets begin. Cut the peeled broccoli as directed in the recipes. Cook broccoli in abundant salted boiling water until tender but firm. Undercooking broccoli does the flavor as much of a disservice as overcooking it. To set the color of cooked broccoli, run cold water over it immediately after draining.

Broccoli deserves its reputation for possessing health-giving properties. Since its flavor and color are so vibrant and appealing, it's not hard to make broccoli a regular part of your diet. Broccoli and Tomato Salad is particularly bright and bracing. Polenta with Broccoli Sauce features highly flavorful braised broccoli.

Romanesco Broccoli is a variety of broccoli with a chartreuse head composed of clusters of flowerets that form spiral patterns. Its flavor resembles that of cauliflower.

CARROTS

Carrots have a brilliant orange color, a crisp, juicy texture, and a sugary flavor. Although the most common varieties are long and slender, carrots come in a range of shapes and sizes.

Select firm, smooth, medium-sized carrots with fresh, leafy tops. Deprived of the leafy tops, there is no way to gauge the freshness. Larger carrots tend to lose their sweetness; sometimes they are almost bitter, and often they contain a hard, woody central core. Standard carrots picked when immature will not have had a chance to develop sweetness. Sweet miniature varieties can be found in specialty produce stores.

Raw carrots add a delightful flavor and texture to antipasti and salads such as in Vegetable Carpaccio and Shaved Parmesan Cheese.

The flavor of carrots mellows when they are cooked, but they still retain a good deal of their sweetness. For an unusual side dish try Carrots with Porcini Mushrooms.

CAULIFLOWER

Cauliflower is a member of the cabbage family. The white "flower," technically called the "curd," must be shielded from the sun to remain white. Since this step involves extra work for the grower, the price of cauliflower is higher than that of other vegetables in the cabbage family.

Select cauliflower with white, unblemished heads and fresh green leaves. Avoid any heads that are yellowed, bruised, or rough and bumpy. Newly available in specialty produce markets is a purple variety.

When properly cooked, cauliflower is delicious and healthful. The cauliflower head can be boiled whole. Simply remove the green leaves and trim the stem end. Plunge in abundant salted boiling water and cook until tender but firm. Or break the head into flowerets and cook in boiling water to cover. Do not overcook. If boiled too long, cauliflower becomes soft and loses its fresh, sweet flavor. Braise it for a richer taste. Never serve cauliflower totally raw; a light cooking is necessary to soften its texture and bring out flavor. Cauliflower with Lemon Dressing highlights its fresh, pure flavor. Pasta with Cauliflower and Sun-Dried Tomato Paste features the developed taste of braised cauliflower.

A hybrid of cauliflower and broccoli is new to specialty produce markets. It has a large head like cauliflower, with rounded clusters of flowerets, but is colored a brilliant pea green.

CELERY

It is the Pascal variety of celery, with its light green stalks, that is most commonly available in markets. Select celery with firm, crisp stalks and fresh leafy tops. Avoid celery with limp stalks or those that have a spongy texture. Do not purchase celery packed in plastic bags.

Raw, the tender stalks of celery are crisp and juicy and have a delightfully fresh herbal flavor, as in Lady in White, which features raw celery, fennel, and fresh mozzarella. Cooked, the flavor turns mild but is equally delicious. Celery is an important component in the fragrant, finely diced vegetables that form the basis of many pasta sauces, braised dishes, and risotti. Celery can be braised and served as a delicate vegetable side dish. Or, when cool, it can be dressed with olive oil and red wine vinegar.

Celery leaves have an intense bracing flavor when used raw in salads, and they add a clean herbal quality to cooked dishes such as Pink Risotto with Celery.

EGGPLANT

The most common type of eggplant sold in the United States is the large, dark purple, globe-shaped variety. Japanese eggplant, which is smaller and more elongated, is becoming increasingly available. And small white eggplant also appears in some specialty produce stores. Other varieties range in color from green to mauve streaked with white. Eggplant can be as small and round as cherries, egg-shaped, or very slender and tapered. Most varieties have the same flavor except for a bitter, dark orange Thai eggplant that is sold in Asian produce markets.

Look for eggplant that is firm and has a smooth, shiny skin and fresh, green stem end. It should be heavy for its size, an indication that the flesh is solid and without an excess of developed seeds. Smaller varieties tend to be sweeter and have fewer seeds and thinner skin. Avoid bruised eggplant with soft spots or any that have shriveled skin. Mature eggplant with dull skin and dark seeds may have flesh that has turned bitter.

The skin of a large eggplant can be tough: It is sometimes necessary to peel the eggplant before cooking. Braising or boiling usually softens the skin sufficiently so that peeling is not necessary. At one time eggplant was salted before cooking to draw out the bitterness in the flesh. Since modern varieties are free of bitterness, the only reason to salt eggplant is to remove excess moisture. This step is optional.

The flesh of cooked eggplant is creamy and mild. Sautéeing it in olive oil adds richness to the flavor. If eggplant is grilled, fried, or broiled until the surface of the flesh turns golden, the flavor intensifies and deepens. Try Eggplant and Zucchini Platter, where both vegetables cook until golden. In Lemony Grilled Eggplant, the vegetable takes on the smoky taste of the grill.

FENNEL

Fennel somewhat resembles celery, but has a large, white edible bulb or swollen leaf base and fine, feathery green leaves. The bulb, when eaten raw, is crisp and juicy with a flavor hauntingly reminiscent of licorice. When fennel is cooked, it turns meltingly tender and the licorice-like flavor softens and blurs. Fennel may be braised, sautéed, or grilled. Cooking the vegetable until its surface turns golden brown concentrates its sugars and brings up its sweetness. Fennel is gaining in popularity and becoming increasingly available in markets.

Select small, tender bulbs. A sign of juicy flesh is a white pearly glow to the outer layers of the bulb. Trim off the stalks and feathery leaves right above the bulb. Reserve stalks and leaves to flavor soups and pasta cooking water. Discard any tough or blemished outside layers of the bulb. Cut the bulb in half or in quarters. You can also slice the fennel into fans by cutting it vertically through the bulb. To julienne, completely cut away the core to free the layers of fennel, and cut the layers lengthwise into slivers.

Raw Vegetable and Mozzarella Salad features crisp, raw fennel, and Butterfly Pasta with Fennel and Balsamic Vinegar teams fennel with tomatoes and rich, mellow vinegar.

WILD FENNEL

Wild fennel does not develop an enlarged bulb as does cultivated fennel. It is the tender stalks, feathery leaves, and aromatic seeds that are highly prized for imparting a potent, licorice-like flavor. Although it is not available in markets, if you live near the California coast you can find it growing on hillsides, in empty lots, and along country roads. Use it only if you are sure it is completely untainted.

Wild fennel is used extensively in the cooking of southern Italy and its surrounding islands, where the tall, feathery sprays of green leaves fill the air with their strong scent.

To approximate the flavor of wild fennel, use a combination of fresh fennel and fennel seeds. The finely chopped, feathery tops of the cultivated bulb add color to any dish and a trace of licorice-like sweetness. Wild fennel is called for in Fried Zucchini Blossoms on Wild Fennel Branches, where the tops form a fragrant bed for fried zucchini flowers.

GARLIC

Garlic is so important an ingredient in cooking that it is worth taking the time to select good, fresh bulbs. Look for firm, unsprouted bulbs with large cloves tightly wrapped in white or mauve parchment-like skin. Avoid bulbs that are bruised, yellowed, or soft. Store the garlic in a cool, dry place with good ventilation and never refrigerate it. To peel, squeeze both ends of a clove of garlic toward the center. If the garlic is fresh and crisp, the skin will split open and slip right off.

To add flavor with a little bit of bite, use finely chopped raw garlic in tomato salads or in raw tomato pasta sauces. Finely chopped garlic, gently cooked in olive oil, imparts a wonderful perfume, but loses much of its pungency in cooking. If it is cooked until lightly golden, a stronger garlic flavor emerges. Whole garlic cloves, roasted or sautéed until golden, become creamy, rich, and sweet. For very hot-tasting garlic, peel the cloves, then mash them or put them through a garlic press to release the juices. A clove of raw garlic, cut in half and rubbed onto grilled bread, infuses the bread with a strong flavor and a heady aroma. When the bread is drizzled with olive oil after being rubbed with garlic, it is called "bruschetta." See Simple Bruschetta with Oregano for the basic recipe for bruschetta.

GREENS

Bitter Greens

Bitter greens range in flavor from lightly tangy escarole and curly endive to very assertive-tasting mustard greens, collards, kale, turnip greens, and dandelion greens. Select these greens with tender, fresh leaves and avoid any that are yellowed or that have coarse, overdeveloped veins and stems.

The very tender leaves of many of these greens can be added raw to salads. For example, you can use the creamy yellow and pale green central leaves of escarole and curly endive, young leaves of dandelion, and tender mustard greens.

Collard greens and kale as well as the tougher leaves of other strongly flavored bitter greens must be cooked.

Mixed Greens with Black Olives calls for both bitter and mild greens sautéed with black olives. Salad of Greens and Cheeses features raw escarole teamed with romaine and arugula, tossed with tangy cheeses.

Mild Greens

SPINACH AND SWISS CHARD   Succulent, dark green spinach grows in clusters of long-stemmed leaves. The light, mineral flavor of spinach is at its most appealing when the leaves are picked young. Select spinach with small, crisp green leaves. Avoid spinach with overdeveloped, yellowed, or drooping leaves. The stems of the larger leaves must be removed before cooking. Snap them off individually, or gather the bunch together and cut across the base of the leaves. Spinach is often filled with grit and dirt and must be washed carefully. Place the spinach in a basin of cool water and agitate the leaves to release the dirt. Let the dirt settle to the bottom of the basin and carefully lift out the spinach. Drain and clean the basin. Repeat the above steps until the basin is free of grit.

Spinach is so tender that it cooks in only the water that is left on the leaves after washing. Select a large, wide pan. Cover and cook over medium-high heat until the spinach wilts. Check frequently to make sure there is enough moisture. If the spinach appears to be drying out, add a few tablespoons of water to the pan.

Small raw spinach leaves are delicious in salads such as Salad of Field Greens. Green Risotto with Cream and Herbs features fresh spinach enriched with a touch of cream.

Swiss chard is a delectable herbaceous plant with tender, ruffled leaves and succulent white ribs or stems. When buying Swiss chard, look for fresh leaves with white, firm stems. Avoid any with torn or ragged-looking leaves and blemished or limp stems. Nothing compares to young Swiss chard straight from the garden. Both the leaf and stem are incredibly sweet and tender.

Swiss chard leaves are tender enough to cook in the water that clings to them after being washed. Slender Swiss chard stems can be sautéed, but thick ones require a preliminary brief cooking in salted boiling water to cover.

Try Swiss chard dressed simply with olive oil and lemon juice, to highlight its light, vegetal flavor. Fettuccine with Swiss Chard and Mushrooms pairs two vegetables enriched with butter for a savory pasta dish.

Salad Greens

Many specialty produce markets carry a wide variety of tender, small salad greens, often referred to as baby lettuces, whose flavor ranges from sweet and mild to very hot and peppery. The lettuces tend to be milder tasting than the more assertive chicories, and have a more tender leaf. Colors range from pale green, chartreuse, and deep green to rose, russet, and ruby red. Leaves can have softly ruffled or jagged edges or be smooth and tapered, and textures vary from soft and buttery to crisp and slightly resistant. You can select just one leafy green or a complex and fascinating mix.

Even if you do not have access to a specialty produce market, supermarkets carry a wide selection of lettuces and other greens. You can create wonderful salads by selecting tender romaine and butter lettuces, red-leaf lettuce, the buttery yellow central leaves of escarole and endive, peppery watercress, herb leaves, and even the young leaves of radishes. Many markets carry succulent radicchio and Belgian endive, and arugula is gaining in popularity and appearing in more and more markets.

MUSHROOMS

Captured in the flavor of mushrooms, especially those that grow wild, is the rain-soaked essence of leaf, wood, and earth. Although technically not vegetables, since they grow without producing leaves, roots, flowers, or seeds, mushrooms belong in the repertoire of vegetable dishes. Their deep and resonant taste gives added dimension to vegetable flavors.

Button mushrooms are cultivated on a large scale and are the ones most commonly found in supermarkets. Their mildness requires careful cleaning and cooking to maximize what little mushroom flavor they contain. Many specialty markets and some supermarkets now carry a selection of true wild mushrooms, such as porcini, chanterelles, and morels, and cultivars like shiitake, oyster, and brown, or Italian field, mushrooms. Look for firm, fresh mushrooms. Avoid bruised, blemished, or slimy specimens. Button mushrooms should look white, smooth, and firm, and have tightly closed caps.

Mushrooms absorb water like sponges. As they cook, they release any excess water into the dish and dilute the flavor. The mushrooms steam in this excess water, rather than absorb the butter or olive oil in which they are cooking, and they become limp rather than golden and crusty. To prevent mushrooms from absorbing water in cleaning, wipe clean the caps and stems with a damp cloth. If the mushrooms are very dirty, place them in a colander and very briefly run cool water over them, then wipe clean. Trim the stem ends and discard. In the case of shiitake mushrooms, discard the entire stem.

If wild mushrooms or interesting cultivated varieties are not available, use dried porcini mushrooms. Porcini retain the flavor of the fresh ones to a remarkable degree. A few dried porcini mushrooms imbue button mushrooms with a deep, woodsy flavor. Dried porcini mushrooms are sold in Italian markets and specialty food shops. Look for packages containing large, creamy white pieces, which are slices of the mushroom caps.

Fresh, crisp button mushrooms are used to great effect in Grilled Bread with Raw Mushroom Salad, featuring thinly sliced mushrooms marinated in olive oil and lemon. In Grilled Wild Mushrooms with Oregano, the taste of shiitake mushrooms comes close to capturing the intensity of true wild mushrooms.

ONIONS

There are many types of onions on the market, from tiny pearl onions to large, globe-shaped onions. They can be white, red, brown, or yellow in color. When buying any variety, look for firm bulbs with brittle, shiny skins. Avoid any that are soft and those that are sprouting. Store onions in a cool, well-ventilated place and do not refrigerate them.

Sweet, juicy red onion is especially delicious served raw in salads, as in Bread Salad Sienna Style. I enjoy the bite of raw onions in salads, but if you prefer a milder flavor, slice the onions and soak them in cool water to cover. Change the water several times over a thirty-minute period. Drain and dry well. Cooked onions become incredibly sweet. Roasted onions are featured in Salad from the Vucciria Market, the roasting turning the onions deep gold and sugary, to become a sauce for Pasta with Caramelized Onion and Crystallized Ginger.

Scallions, also referred to as green onions, are used very effectively in springtime dishes that call for a light, fresh onion flavor. They add a lively bite to Raw Vegetables in Pinzimonio with an Olive Oil Dipping Sauce.

SWEET PEPPERS

Beautiful, glossy, and colored fire red, deep gold, green, or purple, peppers are one of the joys of vegetable cooking. Select firm varieties with a smooth, regular shape and an even color. Avoid overripe peppers with soft spots. Feel the weight of the peppers and choose those that are heavy for their size, an indication of thick flesh. This is especially crucial when roasting the peppers: Thin-fleshed peppers cannot tolerate the intense heat of roasting, become difficult to peel, and turn flabby rather than remaining crisp and succulent.

Yellow peppers are the sweetest of all, followed by red peppers. As peppers cook, they release lightly syrupy, honeyed juices that flavor such dishes as Peperonata with Potatoes and Black Olives. In Fried Yellow Peppers with Mint, yellow peppers are matched with equally sweet fresh mint.

Green peppers are unripened red peppers. They have a pleasing tart flavor that is at its best when they are served raw, sliced thinly in salads. A delicious contrast of tart green peppers and sweet grapes is featured in Salad from the Gran Rialto Market.

Purple peppers have green flesh beneath their eggplant-colored skin; the skin turns green when cooked. They are best served raw and unpeeled, cut in slivers to dip into olive oil—a good way to highlight their unusual coloring.

To serve peppers raw, I prefer to peel them first because I find that the tough, waxy skin interferes with enjoying the crisp, juicy flesh. To facilitate peeling them, select those that are smooth and evenly formed. Cut the pepper into sections and remove the seeds and white membranes. Use a vegetable peeler to peel away as much of the skin as possible. This step is optional, but highly recommended.

To roast peppers, place them on a gas burner or under the broiler. Roast on all sides and use tongs to turn them often. Do not use a fork; it will puncture the skin and release the juices. When the peppers are lightly charred on all sides, but before they turn ashy, use the tongs to transfer them to a paper bag. Close the bag tightly and let the peppers cool. Peel the peppers by rubbing off the skin either with your fingers or by rubbing them in a clean dish towel. Working over running water makes the job easier and cleaner, but sacrifices some of the flavor. Cut the peppers in half lengthwise, cut out the core, and remove stray seeds and white membranes. Yellow peppers require less roasting than red ones to loosen the skin.

POTATOES

Potatoes fall into two categories. Thick-skinned, brown russet potatoes have a dry and fluffy texture and are used for baking and frying. Thin-skinned potatoes include round and long whites and round reds, and are used primarily for boiling. Their texture is fine, firm, and waxy. Thin-skinned potatoes are also called new potatoes. This refers to the fact that they go directly from field to market, as opposed to russet potatoes, which are kept in storage.

The once lowly potato, scorned as fattening, is acquiring cachet. New varieties such as yellow-fleshed Yukon Gold or Finnish yellows or a purple variety have captured the imagination of cooks. Potatoes have a mild, lightly sweet flavor and a soft, seductive texture. Their mild flavor is what makes them so versatile. They become permeated by the flavor of herbs, take on the foresty flavor of mushrooms, the tart-sweet flavor of tomatoes, or become impregnated with the tang of red wine vinegar.

Select potatoes that are firm, smooth, and without sprouts. Avoid any with green areas or overall green coloring. Keep potatoes in a cool, dry place that is well ventilated. To prevent peeled potatoes from discoloring, immerse them in cool water until ready to cook.

In Diced Potatoes with Arugula and Herbs, boiling potatoes are diced and combined with a shower of chopped herbs and arugula for a delicious side dish. Potato and Artichoke "Cake" features layers of creamy riced russet potatoes, sliced artichokes, and tomato-basil sauce.

RADICCHIO

Radicchio is a spectacularly pretty leaf chicory with a mottled magenta and white coloring, a crunchy texture, and a refreshing, bitter flavor. Popular as an addition to mixed salads, radicchio is also delicious cooked. Its color darkens, its texture softens, and its bitterness becomes somewhat muted.

The Verona variety, small and cabbage-shaped, is available in many supermarkets and all specialty produce markets. Other varieties available to the home gardener include Treviso, with an elongated leaf, and Pallo Rossa and Rouge di Verona, which have red and green coloring.

Look for compact heads with fresh leaves. Avoid heads that have brown spots or that have decay at the root ends.

Radicchio leaves are delicious in a salad of assorted lettuces and add color and drama. Radicchio, Gruyère, and Grilled Bread Salad shows off the color, crunch, and bitterness of the leaves against nutty cheese and country bread. Grilled Stuffed Radicchio contrasts mozzarella with tender cooked radicchio. An elegant side dish is Radicchio with Cream and Parmesan Cheese.

RAPINI

Rapini, a member of the flavorful *Brassica* family, is much used in rustic Italian cooking and is enjoyed for its bracing, bitter flavor. Rapini has a central stem out of which grow small leaves and flowerets of tightly clustered buds that resemble broccoli. The stem tends to be fibrous and must be peeled.

Look for rapini with slender green stems and tightly closed buds, and avoid any that have begun to flower. Rapini is available in markets in Italian neighborhoods and speciality produce stores. In Rapini with Garlic Bread Crumbs, stalks of rapini are served sprinkled with crunchy bread crumbs.

SUMMER SQUASH

Summer squash is picked before it is fully mature. It has tender skin and edible seeds; its flavor is mild and light; and the texture is tender and moist. Included in this category are zucchini, both the dark green and golden types; English zucchini, a very pale, slightly swollen-looking version of regular zucchini; scaloppine squash, small, rounded, dark green, with a scalloped edge; pattypan squash, similar to scaloppine squash, but colored green, white, or gold; and yellow crookneck squash with a narrow neck and swollen body. Very small, immature summer squash are sometimes sold with the flowers still attached; these are considered choice eating. Squash blossoms that do not bear fruit are highly prized for their brilliant coloring and delicate flavor. The blossoms can be fried, stuffed, or lightly braised, mixed with eggs in a frittata, or used in risotto or pasta dishes.

When selecting summer squash, look for firm, glossy squash with smooth, tender skin. It should be heavy for its size, a sign that it is full of compact flesh. Small to medium-sized summer squash have the best flavor and texture. Bigger squash begins to develop larger seeds and has a higher water content; it will not cook to as fine a texture and the flavor may become attenuated.

Do not peel summer squash. Simply wash it well and rub with a clean dish towel. Run your fingers over the surface to make sure the skin is completely clean and free of grit. Trim the ends except if you are cooking it whole in boiling water. If it is cut, the squash will absorb too much water in cooking.

One of the loveliest recipes using tender, sweet summer squash, perfect for warm-weather eating, is Summery Stuffed Zucchini, served at room temperature.

WINTER SQUASH

Winter squash has a hard, thick shell and large, developed seeds. The flesh ranges in color from yellow to a deep orange-red, and the texture from smooth to fibrous. The flavor can be quite mild, or be sweet and nutty. Because of its thick shell, winter squash can be kept in storage for months.

The varieties of winter squash include pumpkin, large, fibrous, and mildly sweet; banana squash, large, medium sweet, and fairly creamy; and Hubbard squash, large, medium sweet, and rather creamy. Butternut squash is small with creamy flesh and a sweet, nutty flavor. Other varieties are Golden Acorn, Sweet Dumpling, Chinese, and Delicata.

Select squash that feels heavy for its size and has a hard, firm shell. If buying already cut pieces of squash, look for good, deep color and moist flesh. Banana squash is commonly sold already cut and seeded.

To prepare, cut the squash in half or in pieces and scrape out the seeds. Use a vegetable peeler or paring knife to peel the squash. Or bake the squash with the skin on, then scrape the soft flesh from the shell.

Winter squash's sweet flavor, brilliant color, and soft, yielding texture are featured in soups, risotti, and side dishes. An unusual recipe calling for winter squash is Lentil Soup with Red Squash and Fennel.

TOMATOES

There are so many varieties of tomatoes that the home gardener can really have a field day. Not only are tomatoes red; they can be pink, gold, yellow, white, or striped. They can be as tiny and sweet as a variety called Sweet 100's. One mysterious nameless tomato being talked about over fences by home gardeners weighs up to three pounds and is said to be flavorful and full of flesh. Tomatoes come in a range of shapes from pear-shaped or oval to round or square. Many specialty produce stores now carry unusual varieties such as yellow cherry and pear tomatoes.

Tomatoes play an indispensable role in vegetable cooking. Not only are they wonderful sliced raw in tomato salads, or baked or grilled as side dishes, but they form the basis of hundreds of other dishes, such as pasta sauces, rice dishes, soups, and tarts.

A good salad tomato should be firm, plucked from the vine just before it is fully ripened, and heavy with the spicy scent of its foliage. A blazing red tomato streaked with green and with firm, crisp flesh makes an ideal salad tomato. The red skin means the tomato has had a chance to develop some flavor; the green indicates the flesh is tart and crisp. A fully ripened tomato that is still firm is also highly desirable for tomato salads. For cooking, select vine-ripened tomatoes heavy for their size, with a deep red color and firm, yielding flesh. Pear-shaped Roma tomatoes have a high proportion of flesh to seeds, but they can sometimes be dry and woody. Larger tomatoes can vary in terms of the proportion of flesh to seeds and water content.

Supermarket tomatoes sadly leave much to be desired. To maximize their flavor let them ripen fully at room temperature. Never refrigerate tomatoes since this stops the ripening process. The extreme cold also destroys the texture of the tomato, turning it soft and mealy.

To peel tomatoes, plunge them in abundant boiling water for about ten seconds. Test one tomato by piercing the skin with the tip of a sharp knife. The skin should immediately separate from the flesh. Drain in a colander and run cold water over them to stop the cooking. Core the tomatoes and slip off the skin.

Another way to peel tomatoes is to roast them. Impale a tomato through the stem end. Roast over a gas flame or over a grill, turning to expose the tomato on all sides. After the skin makes a popping sound and is lightly charred in one or two places, core the tomato and peel. Too much contact with the heat, either by boiling or grilling, will soften the tomato and "cook" it. The peeled tomato should be completely intact.

To seed tomatoes, cut them in half horizontally and gently remove the seeds with your fingertips.

Try some of the more unusual varieties of tomatoes in familiar dishes to give them a different twist. Slices of sweet yellow tomatoes and fresh mozzarella sprinkled with purple basil make a beautiful, non-traditional caprese salad. Yellow as well as red cherry tomatoes are featured in Bite-Sized Mozzarella and Cherry Tomatoes.

HERBS

Fresh herbs play a crucial role in vegetable cooking. They add a wide variety of flavor notes from light, high, and sweet to dark, deep, and woodsy.

Many fresh herbs are now available in supermarkets. Look for those that have fresh, unblemished leaves. Bruised, discolored, and wilted herbs are not worth buying, since they have lost their aromatic strength. Contact with water over a period of time will cause more delicate herbs, especially basil, to blacken. The aroma of fresh herbs begins to dissipate the moment they are picked. Strong-flavored herbs like thyme and rosemary keep their perfume longer than more fragile herbs, such as basil. Use all herbs within a day or two of purchase. Growing your own is the most pleasurable way to have a supply of intensely scented herbs on hand. They bring their perfume and beauty to the garden, both in their leaves and blossoms, and demand very little attention in return for all they give.

Basil

Select basil with fresh, bright green, unblemished leaves. Use only the leaf and discard the stem. Basil must be handled gently, since it bruises and blackens easily. Tear the leaves into fragments, as this does the least amount of damage and maintains the color and aroma. Too much chopping turns basil black and lifeless, with most of its aromatic properties lost to the chopping board. If the recipe calls for chopped basil, do it right before adding it to the dish and work quickly and efficiently using a minimum of strokes.

Green basil is the variety commonly available in markets. Purple basil, with its deep-colored leaves, is sold in specialty produce markets.

Since nothing rivals the intense fragrance of freshly picked basil, try growing it in a pot on the balcony or in your backyard. It is easy to grow and will provide you with masses of fresh basil all summer long. Basil complements the flavor of a wide variety of vegetables, from artichokes to zucchini.

Marjoram

Marjoram is the most floral of all the herbs. The small, tender leaves are so highly perfumed that they must be used with restraint. Marjoram is traditionally teamed with light, sweet foods such as zucchini and eggs. It is used in Zucchini Stuffed with Mushrooms and Marjoram, and adds a summery note to Chick Pea and Escarole Soup with Grilled Bread.

Mint

Spearmint has a large, tender leaf and a fruity aroma. It is preferable to peppermint for cooking. Use only the leaf and the most tender portion of the stem. Mint's sugary perfume is highly effective when teamed with sweet vegetables like peppers or winter squash, but also perfectly complements artichokes, eggplant, and tomatoes. Try mint instead of basil in a fresh tomato sauce for a delightful change of pace. Mint is stuffed into small eggplants in Spaghetti with Eggplant-Flavored Tomato Sauce. It brings a fresh, aromatic quality to Sweet and Sour Red Squash with Mint.

Oregano

Oregano is the only herb that is used dry more frequently than fresh. Dried oregano is pungent but highly perfumed, especially the Mediterranean variety. Mexican oregano is not as floral and therefore less desirable for the recipes in this book. Dried oregano is called for in a number of recipes, such as Simple Bruschetta with Oregano and Grilled Wild Mushrooms with Oregano.

Fresh oregano has a strong, peppery edge to its flavor that can be very effective in cooking. Use only the leaf and the most tender portion of the stem. Fresh oregano is used in Raw Zucchini with Lemon Dressing, an antipasto of thinly sliced zucchini where the slight harshness of the herb brings an earthiness to the sweet flavor of the squash.

Italian Parsley

Indispensable in vegetable cooking, parsley has a bright, bracing, fresh flavor. Italian parsley, the variety I use for the recipes in this book, has a broad, flat, extremely tender leaf. Its flavor is more finely articulated than that of the more common, less tender curly-leaf parsley. If you cannot find Italian parsley, feel free to substitute the curly-leaf variety. The leaves and tender stems of parsley can be used in cooking, but when used raw in dishes, discard the stems and use only the leaves. The coarse stems are good for flavoring soups and broth.

Rosemary

Rosemary is highly aromatic and adds a deep, resinous flavor to vegetables. Use it sparingly, for a little goes a long way. Only the spiky leaves are used in cooking; the stems are too tough and woody. Strip the leaves from the stems and chop them finely. Or cook with a sprig of rosemary and remove it when the flavor has permeated the dish to the desired degree.

Sage

The silver-gray, velvety leaves of the sage plant have a penetrating, almost musty aroma that is used most effectively when mixed with other herbs. Alone, it complements white beans, potatoes, and other mild-flavored foods.

Thyme

This is a warm, earthy-tasting herb. Its fragrance brings to mind herbs growing wild on sun-baked hillsides. Thyme goes well with a wide variety of vegetables, including mushrooms, zucchini, artichokes, and tomatoes. The stems are woody, so use only the leaves. Since the leaves are quite tiny hold the bunch by the stem ends and, with a large knife, scrape the leaves from the stems.

Menus

ANTIPASTO PARTY FOR 12

Perfumed Black Olives
Ricotta Salad with Crostini
Classic Bruschetta with Roasted Tomatoes
Roman Summer Borlotti Bean Salad
Summer Holiday Rice Salad
Eggplant and Zucchini Platter
Smoked Mozzarella Marinated in Herbs and Olive Oil

FORMAL DINNER

Black Truffle Crostini
Leeks in Pink Mascarpone Sauce
Risotto with Baby Artichokes
Smashed Salad
Golden Dream Pears

RUSTIC LUNCH FOR 4

Salad of Field Greens
Ricotta Torta with Herbs
Fresh Fava Beans with New Onions
Cherries in Red Wine on Country Bread

ELEGANT LUNCH FOR 4

Artichokes Hotel Gritti Style
Pink Risotto with Celery
Salad from the Gran Rialto Market
Coffee-Flavored Ricotta

CHILDREN'S LUNCH

Raw Vegetable Sticks
Soup from the Garden
Sandwich with Thin Herb Frittatas
Orange Jewels

FARMHOUSE DINNER WITH FRIENDS

Rustic Bread and Mushroom Salad
Artichokes Stuffed with Ricotta
and Pine Nuts
Arugula Salad as Served
at Fiaschetteria Beltramme
Orange Custard

LATE SUMMER GRILL DINNER

Grilled Stuffed Radicchio
Grilled Skewered Vegetables
Grilled Polenta
Grilled Figs with Honey and Walnuts

LUNCH IN THE COUNTRY

Simple Bruschetta with Oregano
Tomato Salad with Herbs
Summery Stuffed Zucchini
Fresh Figs with Anisette and Mint Leaves

SIMPLE DINNER

Raw Vegetable and Mozzarella Salad
Whole Wheat Spaghetti with
Fresh Tomato-Mint Sauce
Fruit Salad from the Orchard

RAINY DAY LUNCH

Winter Squash and Leek Soup

Radicchio, Gruyère, and
Grilled Bread Salad

Zabaglione with Marsala-Soaked Raisins

Anise Cookies

SANDWICH PARTY FOR FRIENDS

Raw Vegetables with Olive Oil Dipping Sauce

Green Olive Salad

Antipasto of Spicy Carrots

Herbed Goat Cheese Sandwich

Artichoke and
Black Olive Pesto Sandwich

Mozzarella, Tomato, and Arugula Sandwich

Summer Berry Salad with Maraschino/Biscotti

LUNCH IN THE GARDEN FOR 6

Roman-Style Raw Fava Beans,
Scamorza, and Fresh Onion

Fried Zucchini Blossoms on Wild Fennel

Mint Frittata with Tomato Garnish

Diced Potatoes with Raw Arugula and Herbs

Ice Cream with Blackberries

BREAKFAST FOR 1

Whole Grain Bread with Mascarpone
and Strawberries

Strong Cappuccino

PICNIC AT THE BEACH

Inflamed Green Olives

Salad from the Vucciria Market

Rice and Eggplant Timbale

Watermelon with Bittersweet Chocolate Shavings

SICILIAN SUMMER DINNER

Eggplant and Almond Caponatina with Crostini
Spaghetti Trapani Style
Prickly Pears

SPRING LUNCH

Spring Radish Salad
Asparagus with Anchovy and Lemon, Wild Style
Risotto with Romaine and Fennel
Strawberries with Lemon and Sugar

SUMMER AFTERNOON SNACK

Crostini with Ricotta and Fruit Topping
Espresso

Pantry Recipes

*P*antry recipes are those tasty morsels that are ready to be used for impromptu entertaining, for snacks and picnics, and for giving simple foods a bright touch.

They include seasoned olives, which are the work of a moment and add a savory touch to a sandwich or an informal lunch. Pestos made from black olives, sun-dried tomatoes, and brilliant green herbs fall under the category of pantry recipes. Toss them with hot pasta for a quick meal, spread them on crostini; use them to liven up sandwiches or soups.

Caponata is a recipe for the pantry since it remains rich and savory for a week when refrigerated. Spread caponata on crostini for a snack, serve it as a relish with sandwiches, use it as a stuffing for vegetables, or as part of a composed platter of little tastes.

There are recipes for two cheeses—one marinated in olive oil and herbs, another, a spread seasoned with lemon and chopped herbs. Both are perfect as sandwich fillings or picnic food.

There are two olive-oil recipes, both spicy, to toss with hot pasta or drizzle into a bowl of soup.

A basic mayonnaise is also included, a lighter, lemony version that is a fresh accent to vegetables.

Some of the recipes stay fresh and lively for a few days, others a few months or longer. The versatility of the recipes is what makes them special and unites them. With a variety of these foods on hand, you will never be at a loss for quick, savory dishes.

INFLAMED GREEN OLIVES

Olive Verdi Infocate

MAKES 2 CUPS

I first tasted these olives flavored with red chile pepper and garlic in Agrigento, Sicily. They provided a fiery beginning to my meal . . . an appetite-stimulating antipasto if ever there was one.

Serve the olives in a rustic bowl along with a basket of bread and a pitcher of cold white wine.

Select medium-sized olives with a fine, firm texture, a pleasing, not too sharp flavor, and prepared without herbs or other seasonings.

2   *cups green olives*
1   *very small fresh red chile pepper*
1   *large garlic clove*
1   *tablespoon extra-virgin olive oil*

Drain the olives if they are in brine. Place them in a shallow bowl. Stem the chile pepper and cut it in half lengthwise, remove the seeds, and finely chop. Peel the garlic clove and crush it into a paste using either a knife blade, a mortar and pestle, or a garlic press.

Add the chile pepper, garlic, and olive oil to the olives and mix well.

These olives can be served immediately. Or cover with plastic wrap and marinate for several hours. If making the olives a day or two in advance, refrigerate and return to room temperature before serving.

PERFUMED BLACK OLIVES

Olive Profumate

MAKES 2 CUPS

ark, rich black olives are marinated in fragrant orange zest, bay leaves, and crushed garlic. The sweetness from the oils in the orange zest permeates the olives and makes them as irresistible as candy.

If you do not own a zester, be sure to buy one for zesting citrus simply and painlessly. It is a big improvement over the traditional four-sided grater where half the zest seems to be lost to the grater and you end up grating your fingertips in the bargain.

2 cups black olives in brine, drained
Zest of ½ orange
4 bay leaves, broken into large fragments
2 garlic cloves, peeled and crushed
Enough extra-virgin olive oil to lightly moisten olives

Combine all the ingredients in a bowl. Let marinate, covered, at least 2 hours and preferably overnight. If marinating olives overnight, refrigerate and return to room temperature before serving.

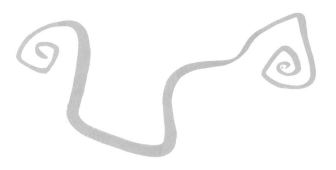

BLACK AND GREEN OLIVES WITH CELERY

Olive Nere e Verde al Sedano

MAKES 2 CUPS

These olives marinated in celery and garlic transport me to a small seaside restaurant on the Italian coast, where all that one could see out the windows was an expanse of sea lashed by winds and low clouds that had turned the water to an opaque turquoise gray.

The prickly herbal tang of the olives sharply recalls the warm smell of the bread served in the restaurant and of fish being grilled, the perfume of baskets of oranges arranged on a wooden counter, the electric, overpowering scent of iodine in the sea air as I left the restaurant, and the beautiful desolation of the sea.

To do justice to this offering, select very good-quality olives of a medium size without any added herbs or other flavorings. Try the Pelopponese brand of bottled Kalamata and cracked green olives in this dish. I've had good results using them.

1   *cup Kalamata olives*
1   *cup cracked green olives*
1   *tender celery stalk with leaves, stalk thinly sliced, leaves coarsely chopped*
1   *celery core, found at the base of the celery stalk, trimmed and thinly sliced, optional*
1   *large garlic clove, peeled and thinly sliced*
1   *tablespoon extra-virgin olive oil*
1   *tablespoon imported red wine vinegar*

Drain the olives if they are in brine. Place all the ingredients in a shallow bowl and toss well. Cover and let rest for at least several hours or overnight, tossing the olives from time to time. If preparing a day in advance, refrigerate, then bring to room temperature before serving. Lasts for several days.

GREEN HERB SAUCE WITH WALNUTS

Salsa Verde con le Noci

MAKES ABOUT 1 CUP

Chopped raw herbs combined with olive oil and lemon juice or vinegar are part of the repertoire of Italian sauces. The brilliant green color and fresh herbal flavor of this sauce add zest to thinly sliced cheeses, beef or chicken, grilled fish, potato salads, and slices of tomato. In this recipe chopped walnuts lend their creamy flavor and capers add piquancy. Increasing the proportion of parsley turns the sauce into a refreshing salad.

The flat, tender leaves of Italian parsley are best suited to raw sauces, but curly parsley can also be used. The sauce stays bright green and fresh in the refrigerator for several days. Add the lemon juice or vinegar just before serving.

1 *small bunch Italian parsley, leaves only, chopped*
Small handful basil leaves, coarsely chopped
2 *garlic cloves, peeled and finely chopped*
3 *tablespoons finely chopped walnuts*
1 *small piece fresh fennel bulb, finely chopped, optional*
2 *anchovies, chopped to a paste, optional*
Extra-virgin olive oil
Lemon juice or red wine vinegar
Salt and freshly ground black pepper to taste

Combine the herbs, garlic, walnuts, optional fennel, and, if desired, the anchovies in a small bowl. Add enough olive oil to create a spoonable sauce. Add lemon juice or vinegar to taste and season with salt and pepper. Cover and refrigerate until needed. To maintain the bright green color over several days, omit the lemon juice or vinegar before refrigerating the sauce and add it just before serving.

BASIL AND ALMOND PESTO

Pesto con le Mandorle

MAKES APPROXIMATELY ½ CUP

brilliant green uncooked herb sauce that has become a classic. This less traditional version calls for almonds rather than pine nuts and results in a sweeter, more textured pesto. Stir it into hot buttered Arborio rice (see page 226), for an intriguing change of pace from pasta. Spooned into soups, pesto adds richness and a heady perfume. It loses its bright color soon after coming in contact with heat, so add it at the last possible moment. Use this potent, unctuous sauce sparingly.

2 *cups fresh basil, stems removed*
4 *garlic cloves, peeled*
¼ *cup blanched almonds, coarsely chopped*
⅓ *cup extra-virgin olive oil, divided*
½ *cup freshly grated imported Parmesan cheese*
Salt and freshly ground black pepper to taste

Place the basil, garlic, and almonds in a food processor and process until everything is chopped to a rough or fine consistency, depending on your preference. With the machine running, add half the olive oil in a slow, steady stream. Turn off the processor and add the Parmesan cheese. Process until the cheese is absorbed. With the machine on, slowly add the remaining olive oil. Add salt and pepper to taste. Transfer to a small bowl. If you do not plan to use it immediately, cover the pesto with a thin layer of olive oil and store refrigerated in a tightly closed container.

BLACK OLIVE PESTO

Pesto di Olive

MAKES ½ CUP

*I*n its purest form, black olive pesto is a simple blend of black olives and olive oil that used to be ground to a paste with a mortar and pestle. These days it is more often prepared in a blender. You can make a rough version of this pesto or a smooth and velvety one. The flavor is strong and faintly bitter and the aroma, like wine, engulfs your senses. Although I've come up with many variations on black olive pesto, adding citrus rind, herbs, and other flavorings, I always return to this elemental version.

2 cups oil-cured black olives
Extra-virgin olive oil

Pit the olives by cutting around the diameter and twisting the two halves in opposite directions. Place the olives in a blender with enough olive oil to moisten them lightly. Process olives until a rough or finely textured puree forms, adding oil as needed. Transfer the mixture to a small jar with a tight-fitting lid. Pour a light film of olive oil over the top. Cover and store in the refrigerator.

SUN-DRIED TOMATOES
PUGLIA STYLE

Pomodori Secchi alla Pugliese

*I*n Puglia in the summer, clusters of small, ripe cherry tomatoes dry in the sun as they hang from the rafters of farmhouses. When the tomatoes are only slightly dry, they are brought indoors and hung in bunches to be used all winter long.

A different drying method is used for larger tomatoes: They are cut in half, salted, and left out in the sun until they lose their excess moisture. The tomato pieces are layered in jars and covered with good olive oil. In Puglia they are seasoned with mint, oregano, and garlic, as in the following recipe.

I always make my own sun-dried tomatoes. I prefer them a little more moist than the store-bought ones in jars and I can make them at a fraction of the cost. The method outlined here calls for drying them in an oven set at the lowest possible temperature.

The craze for sun-dried tomatoes has abated somewhat, and fortunately they are no longer sprinkled indiscriminately over everything. Keep the farmhouse tradition in mind. Serve them in a very simple context, as in an assorted antipasto platter with vegetables preserved in olive oil or vinegar and with fresh mozzarella.

Ripe tomatoes
Coarse salt
Fresh mint leaves
Dried Mediterranean oregano
Peeled garlic cloves
Extra-virgin olive oil

Cut the tomatoes in half or in quarters, depending on the size. Place them, cut side up, on a baking sheet and sprinkle them lightly with salt. Turn on the oven to the lowest possible setting. Place the tomatoes in the oven and let them dry slowly for 7 hours or longer. When the tomatoes have shed their excess moisture, but before they are completely dry, remove them from the oven. In a Mason jar, layer the tomatoes interspersed with mint leaves, sprinklings of oregano, and garlic cloves. Cover with extra-virgin olive oil. Close the jar tightly and re-frigerate. These tomatoes will keep for months.

Sun-dried Tomato Paste

To make sun-dried tomato paste, place sun-dried tomatoes in a blender or food processor. Process until a smooth paste forms, adding olive oil as needed. Transfer to a small bowl. Pour a thin film of olive oil over the top. Cover and refrigerate. Sun-dried tomato paste lasts a very long time.

LITTLE TOMATO AND BASIL SALAD

Insalatina di Pomodoro e Basilico

SERVES 4 AS A SMALL SALAD

Use this small salad as an accompaniment to Ricotta Torta with Herbs (see page 263), or as a topping for grilled tuna, swordfish, or chicken. A spoonful or two makes a bright addition to a golden wedge of frittata.

For a change of pace, use sweet yellow tomatoes and purple basil.

2 *medium tomatoes, red or yellow.*
1 *garlic clove, peeled and minced*
2 *tablespoons extra-virgin olive oil*
Salt and freshly ground black pepper to taste
Small handful green or purple basil leaves, cut into julienne

Core the tomatoes and cut into small dice. Place in a small bowl and combine with the garlic, olive oil, salt and pepper to taste, and basil. Stir gently.

Eggplant and Almond Caponatina

Caponatina alla Siciliana

SERVES 6 TO 8

aponata, or caponatina, a dish made with eggplant, olives, capers, and a touch of tomato, is quintessentially Sicilian. Its very name conjures up vistas of prickly-pear cactus with swollen ripe fruit and of limpid aquamarine water. A combination of red wine vinegar and sugar produces its haunting sweet-and-sour flavor. In this recipe a diced pear adds an unexpected fruitiness, lightly echoing the sweetness of the sugar. A topping of toasted almonds sets off the glistening dark mound of eggplant, giving the finished dish the look of an exotic confection. To serve, surround the caponatina with Crostini, a perfect foil for the eggplant's rich taste. Caponatina lasts for a week refrigerated.

1 *firm medium eggplant*

Coarse salt

6 *tablespoons extra-virgin olive oil, divided*

3 *stalks celery*

1 *firm ripe pear*

½ *28-ounce can imported canned Italian tomatoes, seeded and pureed*

Salt and freshly ground black pepper to taste

2 *tablespoons capers*

20 *black olives, pitted and halved*

5 *tablespoons imported red wine vinegar*

2 *tablespoons sugar*

3 *tablespoons finely chopped toasted almond slivers*

1 *recipe Crostini (see page 366)*

Trim the eggplant and cut into ¾-inch dice. Sprinkle the eggplant cubes with coarse salt and toss well to distribute the salt evenly. Let drain in a colander for approximately 2 hours. Remove excess moisture with paper towels.

Place 3 tablespoons of the olive oil in a large sauté pan. When the oil is hot, add the eggplant cubes. Sauté over medium heat for about 10 minutes, stirring often. Lift the eggplant out of the oil and let drain on paper towels.

Remove strings from the celery stalks and cut crosswise into ¼-inch slices. Cook the celery in salted boiling water for about 8 minutes, or until tender but firm. Drain well and set aside.

Peel the pear and remove the core. Cut the pear into small dice.

Place the remaining oil in a large sauté pan and turn the heat to medium. Add the tomatoes and simmer for a few minutes. Add the diced pear and season with salt and pepper to taste. Stir well and cook for approximately 5 minutes. Add the celery, capers, olives, vinegar, and sugar. Cook for 15 minutes, or until the tomato has reduced to a thick sauce. Add the eggplant, stir to combine the ingredients, and cook for 10 minutes, or until the eggplant is tender but still holds its shape.

Transfer to a platter and mound the eggplant into a dome shape. Let cool. Cover and refrigerate. Marinate for several hours or overnight. Before serving, sprinkle the caponatina with chopped almonds and surround with Crostini.

SMOKED MOZZARELLA MARINATED IN HERBS AND OLIVE OIL

Mozzarella Affumicata alle Erbe

SERVES 4 TO 6

One day in Rome, I put together a little picnic for myself to take back to my hotel room. I bought some honey-sweet muscat grapes, a crisp tomato, a big roll, and went to Fiore, Fiore, one of my favorite food shops, on Via della Croce, and bought smoked mozzarella, marinated in herbs.

I opened my hotel windows wide, and as I ate my picnic lunch I could see before me a cubist landscape of tiled rooftops and blue sky, potted plants and trailing vines. From the window I watched the motions of daily life being enacted: a woman returning home from work; a family seated at a table eating; a child doing his homework; an old woman at her window watering plants. It was the midday break when the streets become deserted and the only sounds to be heard are the clattering of dishes, the musical singsong of Italian voices, and the soft flutter of birds in flight.

1   *pound smoked mozzarella*
1   *tablespoon dried oregano*
½   *teaspoon crushed red chile pepper*
Handful basil leaves
Handful Italian parsley sprigs
Salt and freshly ground black pepper to taste
Extra-virgin olive oil

Thinly slice the mozzarella. Place one layer of cheese in a low-sided glass or ceramic dish, and sprinkle with some oregano and red chile pepper. Tear a few basil leaves into large fragments and sprinkle over the cheese along with a few parsley sprigs. Season lightly with salt and black pepper to taste and drizzle with olive oil. Continue to layer cheese, herbs, and olive oil. Generously moisten the top layer of cheese with olive oil. Cover with plastic wrap and refrigerate for several hours or for several days.

To serve, return to room temperature. Arrange the slices on a serving dish, first removing any of the fresh herbs that have darkened, and grind a little black pepper over the top. If desired, sprinkle fresh herbs over the cheese.

RICOTTA SALAD

Ricotta all'Insalata

SERVES 6

Pure, white ricotta is mixed with green herbs, fruity olive oil, and lemon juice to spread on small rounds of lightly toasted bread. The ricotta is garnished with lustrous black olives, crisp radishes, and tender fava beans for a light, healthful antipasto. Ricotta salad also makes a tasty, nourishing filling for a sandwich or a fresh-tasting spread for crackers. It is also great tossed with hot pasta.

1 *pound fresh ricotta*
1 *small garlic clove, peeled and finely chopped*
3–4 *green onions, white and tender green portions finely chopped*
2 *tablespoons chopped mint leaves*
3 *tablespoons chopped Italian parsley leaves*
2–3 *tablespoons extra-virgin olive oil, plus extra for drizzling*
Fresh lemon juice to taste
Salt and coarsely ground black pepper
Oil-cured black olives
Radishes with leafy tops
Raw fava beans, shelled and peeled, if available
1 *recipe Crostini (see page 366)*

Combine ricotta, garlic, green onions, herbs, olive oil, lemon juice, and salt and pepper to taste. Mix well. Cover and refrigerate for at least 30 minutes to develop flavors. Bring to room temperature. Mound the ricotta mixture in the center of a platter. Drizzle very lightly with olive oil and grind pepper over the top. Surround with black olives, radishes, and optional fava beans. Serve with Crostini. Keeps 2 to 3 days refrigerated.

LITTLE DEVIL OLIVE OIL

Olio al Diavolino

MAKES 2 CUPS

This is spicy olive oil at its finest. The raw oil is infused with the burning quality of red chile peppers without using any heat. It looks lovely, a deep greenish gold, but it is *very* hot. Stir in a few drops just before serving to liven up the flavor of a soup or pasta.

> 2 *cups extra-virgin olive oil*
> *Small handful dried red chile peppers, crushed*

Select a Mason jar large enough to contain the olive oil. Pour in the oil and add the chile peppers. Cover jar and let rest for 1 month, or until the oil is very spicy.

OLIVE OIL FROM HELL

Olio Infernale

MAKES ¼ CUP

In this quick method of making spicy olive oil, olive oil and red chile pepper flakes are gently warmed over low heat for a few minutes. The chile pepper is strained out, and the olive oil is ready to use. A few drops of this deep-orange tinted olive oil can turn a dish fiery hot.

> ¼ *cup extra-virgin olive oil*
> 3 *teaspoons dried red chile pepper flakes*

Combine the ingredients in a small sauté pan. Warm over very low heat for 5 minutes. Strain olive oil into a small jar. Cover and use sparingly.

LEMON MAYONNAISE

Maionese

MAKES 1 CUP

Fresh mayonnaise made with fine olive oil and the citrus tang of lemon is a great occasional treat. This recipe calls for one whole egg rather than just egg yolks as in the traditional recipes and is made in a blender instead of being beaten by hand. The result: a slightly unorthodox mayonnaise that is lighter in flavor and texture. If desired, you can stir in fresh herbs, capers, or anchovies that have been chopped to a paste.

1 *egg, at room temperature*
Salt to taste
¾ *cup mild extra-virgin olive oil*
Juice of ½ *lemon*

In a blender combine the egg, salt, and 2 to 3 tablespoons of oil. Blend until the mixture is light yellow and frothy. With the blender on, add the remaining oil in a thin stream. If the oil begins to pool and is not being absorbed, stop adding oil and continue blending the mixture until the oil is incorporated. Resume adding oil until the mayonnaise thickens. Add a little lemon juice, blend briefly, and taste. Continue adding the lemon juice and taste until mayonnaise achieves the desired strength. Transfer mayonnaise to a small bowl. Cover and keep refrigerated. Lasts for several days.

Antipasti

*I*n recent years, the word *antipasto* has taken on new significance. It has come to represent not just the food served at the opening of a meal, but also a style of eating in which many small tastes are offered. The range of antipasti, however, is wide and the applications are many.

An antipasto can consist of a few stalks of celery dipped in fruity olive oil, or a more substantial offering of grilled radicchio stuffed with mozzarella. It can be a few fragrant herb fritters to munch on with drinks before dinner, or a hearty offering of scamorza cheese and raw fava beans, a meal in itself.

Antipasti have an ease and freshness that make them very appealing. Quite a few of the following recipes require only a minimal amount of cooking, others none at all. Many of the recipes can be served on their own, such as the spicy roasted peppers, accompanied with good bread and a glass of cool wine; but you can also assemble a selection of little tastes for an assorted antipasto plate, an extravagant buffet, or for an outing in the country.

The recipes in this chapter range from a picnic dish of hard-cooked eggs and radicchio leaves to an elegant presentation of thinly sliced raw vegetables and shaved Parmesan cheese. There are also combinations of raw vegetables and cheeses that are appropriate as antipasti offerings or as the focus of a casual meal. Marinated vegetables are made in advance so they are ready to use to add savoriness to a sandwich or a buffet table. Hot antipasti, fragrant from the oven or crispy and golden from quick contact with hot oil, bring an immediacy and a different set of flavors, textures, and aromas to the realm of antipasti.

Use this chapter with a great deal of flexibility. Look to it for ideas for picnics, buffets, and snacks; for casual eating; or for special entertaining. What characterizes and unites the recipes is their freshness and spontaneity: the tingle of lemon juice or vinegar, the perfume of herbs, the meadow freshness of cheeses, and the crunch of garden-fresh vegetables.

Vegetable Antipasti

RADICCHIO, HARD-COOKED EGGS, AND BREAD

Radicchio, Uova, e Pane

SERVES 4

My godmother comes from a small town in northern Italy. One day, when we were sitting around my mother's kitchen table talking, my godmother told us about outings she used to make to the *castello* up on the hill.

When the first tiny shoots of radicchio forced their way up through the cool ground, she and her friends would gather them. They would put together a picnic of tender radicchio leaves, hard-cooked eggs from the farm, crusty bread, and a small straw flask of wine, and climb up the hill, arm in arm, to spend the afternoon in the countryside high above the town.

This is picnic food as it should be, simple and unlabored; honest food to enjoy on a hike in the countryside. If you like, you can easily turn this recipe into an antipasto for an informal dinner with friends. Peel the eggs and cut them in half. Arrange in the center of a platter and season with salt and, if desired, coarsely ground pepper. Surround with radicchio leaves and serve with a basket of bread at the table.

2–3 *handfuls tender radicchio leaves*
8 *fresh eggs, hard-cooked*
1 *loaf crusty bread*
Salt wrapped in a twist of paper
1 *flask of wine*

Wash the radicchio leaves and dry well in a clean dish towel. Wrap the radicchio leaves, eggs, and bread in white cloth napkins. Place them, the salt, and the wine in a picnic basket.

To eat, peel and season the eggs with salt. Break off a piece of bread and alternate bites of radicchio leaves, eggs, and bread, all washed down with wine.

RAW VEGETABLES WITH OLIVE OIL DIPPING SAUCE

Pinzimonio

inzimonio, raw vegetables served with an extra-virgin olive oil dipping sauce, can be as simple as a few stalks of celery heart or as lavish as the season's bounty allows.

My favorite assortment includes small, juicy radishes with bright green leaves; stalks of crisp white celery from the heart; slivers of fennel; long, skinny strips of sweet carrot; and green onions, all arranged in a basket lined with a coarse white cotton napkin.

The ritual of dipping the raw vegetables in the olive oil is one reason this dish is so appealing. That, and its sparkling freshness. If desired, you can use lemon juice in place of the vinegar. For spicy oil, add a few drops of Little Devil Olive Oil (see page 52).

> *Stalks of white celery heart*
> *Crisp radishes with green leaves*
> *A fennel bulb, trimmed of feathery stalks, cut into slivers*
> *Tender carrots, peeled, cut into thin strips*
> *Green onions, roots trimmed and a little cut off the green tops*
> *A cruet of extra-virgin olive oil*
> *A cruet of imported red wine vinegar or balsamic vinegar,*
>   *optional*
> *A small dish of sea salt and a small spoon*
> *A pepper mill filled with black peppercorns*

Line a basket with a white cloth napkin. Arrange the vegetables in the basket. Place the cruets of olive oil and vinegar, the dish of salt, and the pepper mill at the table. Set each place at the table with a small plate and small bowl. Each person flavors his or her olive oil according to taste, and stirs the mixture while dipping the vegetables.

VEGETABLE CARPACCIO WITH PARMESAN SHAVINGS

Verdura Cruda al Parmigiano

SERVES 4

This makes one of the simplest and most pleasing antipasti of all, a wonderful way to begin almost any meal. It calls for vegetables found in any market—celery, radishes, carrots, a green pepper—thinly sliced, tossed with extra-virgin olive oil, and topped with thin shavings of Parmesan cheese. It is crunchy, tangy, and light, and looks especially fresh and inviting served on a simple white platter.

Careful selection of vegetables will yield the best results. All vegetables, when really fresh, give off a luminous glow, a dewiness that you can sense as well as see.

1 *bunch small, crisp radishes*
3 *long, pale green celery stalks from the heart*
1 *fleshy green pepper*
2 *sweet, tender carrots*
2–3 *tablespoons extra-virgin olive oil*
Salt
2-ounce piece imported Parmesan cheese, sliced into thin
shavings, about ½ cup
Freshly ground black pepper

Trim the radishes and cut into thin slices. Trim the tops of the celery stalks and remove any coarse strings. Cut the celery on the diagonal into thin slivers. Use a vegetable peeler to peel the exterior of the green pepper. Cut out the core and remove the seeds. Carefully trim off the white membranes. Cut the pepper into short julienne pieces. Trim and peel the carrots. Cut on the diagonal into thin slices.

Place all the vegetables on a serving platter and drizzle with enough olive oil to moisten them and salt lightly. Scatter the Parmesan shavings over the top and finish with a few grindings of black pepper.

RAW ZUCCHINI
WITH LEMON DRESSING

Antipasto di Zucchine all'Agro

SERVES 4

Nothing is easier to prepare or harder to resist than this crunchy antipasto of marinated raw zucchini. In the garden zucchini is a riot of growth—large, fuzzy leaves open like umbrellas hiding delicate tendrils in corkscrew spirals; obscured in the jungle of leaves are shots of bright gold blossoms and tiny fingers of zucchini just beginning to grow.

In this recipe, freshly picked garden zucchini no more than 5 inches long would be ideal. If they are any larger, the squash lose their special delicate flavor and release too much moisture into the salad. And zucchini that isn't absolutely fresh runs the risk of being bitter. If you do not have a source for garden zucchini, careful selection in the market can yield excellent results. Look for firm zucchini with an even color and glossy skin.

1½ *pounds tender zucchini*
½ *cup extra-virgin olive oil*
Juice of 1 small lemon
2 *garlic cloves, peeled and finely chopped*
2 *tablespoons finely chopped fresh oregano leaves*
Salt and freshly ground black pepper to taste
A few small lettuce leaves

Wash the zucchini well under cold running water until the skin feels smooth and free of grit. Trim the ends. Cut the zucchini into very thin rounds.

Place the zucchini in a bowl and add the olive oil, lemon juice, garlic, oregano, and salt and pepper to taste. Marinate for 1 hour and toss occasionally.

To serve, arrange the lettuce leaves on a serving plate. Lift the zucchini out of the marinade, using a slotted spoon. Mound the zucchini in the center of the platter.

ARTICHOKES HOTEL GRITTI STYLE

Carciofi dell'Hotel Gritti

SERVES 4

complementary trio of flavors, wedges of lightly cooked artichoke hearts, diced Parmesan cheese, and black olives are drizzled with olive oil and served with a wedge of lemon. Served in small bowls, this antipasto looks very rustic indeed. For an elegant presentation you can thinly slice the artichokes and Parmesan cheese, arrange them on a plate, then garnish with olives. I prefer the easy charm of the rustic version.

1 *lemon, cut in half*
4 *large artichokes*
1 *tablespoon extra-virgin olive oil, plus extra for drizzling*
Salt to taste
2 *ounces imported Parmesan cheese, cut into small dice*
16 *oil-cured black olives*
Freshly ground black pepper to taste
4 *thick lemon wedges*

Fill a large bowl with water and squeeze in the juice of half a lemon. Use the other lemon half to rub the cut portions of the artichokes to prevent discoloration. Clean the artichokes by snapping back and pulling away the tough leaves, working your way around the base of the artichokes. Use a paring knife to trim away the dark green areas at the base and the stem. Cut away the leaves to just above the heart. Gently open the leaves and with a small spoon scrape out the choke. Place each trimmed artichoke in the acidulated water.

Drain the artichokes and place them, stem side up, in a medium braising pan large enough to contain the artichokes in one layer. Add water to measure one third up the side of the artichokes, 1 tablespoon of olive oil, and salt to taste. Cook the artichokes, covered, over medium heat until tender but still quite firm. Drain and let cool.

Cut the artichokes into small wedges and divide among 4 small bowls. Sprinkle lightly with salt. Sprinkle the Parmesan cheese and the black olives over the artichokes. Drizzle with olive oil and grind black pepper to taste over the top. Garnish each bowl with a lemon wedge.

SPICY ROASTED PEPPERS

Peperoni Arrostiti Piccanti

SERVES 4 TO 6

*F*all is when peppers are at their peak of flavor and succulence. In Italy, market stalls are piled high with perfect glossy red and yellow peppers, and every restaurant serves them—roasted, fried, braised, in pastas, risotti, or thinly sliced in mixed salads. In American markets, this is the season when the price of peppers becomes reasonable and you can indulge in eating them often.

Roasting peppers is a sensory delight—the kitchen fills with the smoky-sweet smell of the charred skin; as you rub off the blackened peel, the pepper turns to brilliant red or yellow beneath your fingers. In this recipe, roasted peppers are cut into thick slices and drizzled with spicy raw olive oil. That is all there is to it; yet the flavors are memorable— the crisp, sweet peppers with their hint of woodsmoke and the pure fruity olive oil infused with the heat of red chile peppers. A final flourish of coarsely chopped Italian parsley adds a brilliant dash of contrasting color and a strong, clean, herbal flavor.

> 4   *big, fleshy red or yellow peppers*
> *Salt and freshly ground black pepper to taste*
> ¼   *cup extra-virgin olive oil*
> 2   *teaspoons Little Devil Olive Oil (see page 52)*
> *Italian parsley, coarsely chopped, for garnish*
> *Lemon wedges*

Roast the peppers. Peel them and cut them in half. Cut away the cores, seeds, and white membranes. Cut the peppers into thick strips.

Arrange the pepper strips on a platter and season with salt and pepper to taste.

In a small bowl combine the extra-virgin olive oil and the Little Devil Olive Oil. Drizzle this mixture over the pepper strips. Sprinkle with chopped Italian parsley. Garnish with lemon wedges.

SWEET AND SOUR RED SQUASH WITH MINT

Zucca Rossa alla Palermitana

SERVES 4

Whenever I prepare this dish and smell the flowery sweet mint and the pungent hot vinegar, I think of my grandmother, whose specialty this was, and see her frying golden half-moons of squash.

After the squash becomes nice and crusty on the exterior, it is sprinkled with fresh mint. Red wine vinegar and sugar are cooked down to a light syrup and poured over the top. This dish is ready to eat after several hours, but the flavors mellow and penetrate the squash more effectively after 24 hours.

> 1 *pound banana squash or other winter squash*
> ¼ *cup extra-virgin olive oil*
> 4 *cloves garlic, peeled and lightly crushed*
> ¼ *cup coarsely chopped mint leaves*
> ¼ *cup imported red wine vinegar*
> ¼ *cup sugar*
> *Salt and freshly ground black pepper to taste*

Cut the squash across into 3-inch-wide lengths. Use a vegetable peeler to remove the peel. Cut each piece crosswise into slices that are a little over ¼ inch thick.

Place the olive oil and garlic cloves in a medium sauté pan. Sauté the garlic over low heat until it turns a golden brown. Discard the garlic. Raise the heat to medium low and fry the squash slices in the oil on both sides until they blister and turn golden brown. Cook the squash in batches, 1 layer at a time and without crowding the pan. Use a thin wooden skewer to check for tenderness. The squash slices should be tender but hold their shape. As each batch is cooked, transfer the slices to a platter. When all the squash is cooked, sprinkle the chopped mint over the top.

Add to the remaining olive oil in the pan the vinegar, sugar, and salt and pepper to taste. Stir well and raise the heat to high. Let the mixture boil until it thickens slightly. Pour the hot liquid over the squash slices. Let cool. Marinate for at least several hours before serving. Lasts for several days refrigerated.

GREEN OLIVE SALAD

Insalata di Olive Verde

SERVES 6

This salad with green olives, celery, red onion, mint, and red chile pepper is but one variation of seasoned olives that are sold in markets across Italy.

In Mondello, a seaside resort outside Palermo, you can buy green olive salad and snack on it as you stroll along the street lined with foodstands that hugs the sparkling aquamarine curve of sea.

Select large, fleshy, unseasoned green olives.

2   *cups cracked green olives, cured in brine, drained*
½   *medium red onion, peeled and sliced*
2   *tender celery stalks with leaves, stalks cut crosswise into*
         pieces, leaves chopped
Small handful mint leaves, chopped
1   *crushed dried red chile pepper*
Extra-virgin olive oil
Imported red wine vinegar
Salt to taste

Place the olives, red onion, celery, mint, and red chile pepper in a bowl. Lightly dress with olive oil and red wine vinegar and a bit of salt. Toss and cover with plastic wrap. Let marinate for several hours or overnight. If marinating overnight, refrigerate and return to room temperature before serving.

MARINATED OLIVES
WITH ROASTED PEPPERS

Olive con Peperoni Arrostiti

SERVES 4 TO 6

*I*n this earthy antipasto, the flesh of black and green olives is cut into strips and combined with roasted peppers, piquant capers, pine nuts, and chopped anchovies. Take this along on a picnic as a filling for crusty rolls.

1 *cup brine-cured black olives, drained*

1 *cup brine-cured green olives, drained*

1 *small red pepper, roasted, peeled, and cut into small strips*

1 *small yellow pepper, roasted, peeled, and cut into small strips*

2 *tablespoons capers*

2 *tablespoons pine nuts*

3 *anchovies, coarsely chopped*

6 *basil leaves*

1 *teaspoon dried Mediterranean oregano*

2 *garlic cloves, peeled and crushed*

1 *tablespoon extra-virgin olive oil*

Use a knife to cut the meat from the olives, cutting each olive into 4 strips lengthwise.

Combine the olives in a bowl along with the rest of the ingredients. Toss. Cover with plastic wrap and let marinate for several hours or overnight. If marinating overnight, refrigerate and bring to room temperature before serving.

Vegetables, Fruits, and Cheeses

LADY IN WHITE

Dama Bianca

SERVES 4

A study in white from an Italian menu dating from the 1800s. Thinly sliced mozzarella, moist and tasting of fresh milk, is topped with slivers of crisp fennel and celery heart, then drizzled with extra-virgin olive oil and lemon juice. Accompany this simple, exquisite antipasto with a fine chilled white wine and long, thin breadsticks.

1 *pound fresh mozzarella*
1 *fennel bulb*
1 *celery heart, white stalks only*
Salt and freshly ground black pepper to taste
½ *cup extra-virgin olive oil*
Juice of 1 lemon

If the mozzarella is packed in water, drain it well. Place mozzarella on paper towels to absorb excess water.

Cut off the feathery stalks of the fennel and trim away any bruised areas. Cut the bulb in half and remove the core. Slice the fennel into julienne. Cut the leafy tops off the celery. Trim the base. Cut the celery crosswise into thin slices.

Cut the mozzarella into thin slices and arrange on a platter. Scatter the fennel and the celery over the top. Season with salt and pepper to taste. Drizzle with olive oil and lemon juice. Serve immediately.

FIGS AND GOAT CHEESE

Fichi e Caprino

SERVES 4

resh figs, either the purple or pale green varieties, have exquisitely honeyed, mauve-colored flesh. Here they are stuffed with fresh,
lemony-tart goat cheese and topped with a grinding of pepper. Utterly
simple, but the figs must be fully ripened and sweet.

8 *large ripe figs*
5 *ounces fresh goat cheese*
Extra-virgin olive oil
Freshly ground black pepper

Trim the stem end of the figs and cut figs in half lengthwise. Place
the goat cheese in a small bowl. Moisten with a few drops of olive oil
and mash with a fork. Mound a little of the goat cheese on each fig half
and grind pepper over the top.

ROMAN-STYLE RAW FAVA BEANS, SCAMORZA, AND FRESH ONION

Antipasto di Fave e Cipolla Fresca

SERVES 6

A springtime antipasto of raw fava beans and new onions. Eating tender fava beans raw is a special treat. Eat them unpeeled if you enjoy the refreshing bitter edge of the peel, or peel them first for a sweeter flavor. When buying favas to eat raw, select only tender green pods and shell the beans just before serving.

Fresh onions have a juicy crispness that cannot be matched by onions held in storage. If you have access to a farmer's market or grow your own onions, use those that have been freshly pulled; sweet red onions are particularly delicious. If fresh onions are not available, substitute trimmed green onions.

Serve this dish with crusty breadsticks, a sturdy country loaf, or black pepper taralli, a type of pretzel found in Italian specialty markets, and accompany with a pitcher of cool dry white wine.

> 2 *pounds fava beans, unshelled weight*
> *A few small lettuce leaves*
> 1 *small fresh onion, peeled and thinly sliced into rings*
> 1 *pound scamorza cheese, sliced*
> *Basket of breadsticks, black pepper taralli, or bread*

Shell the fava beans and mound in the center of a platter. Surround with the lettuce leaves and scatter the onions over the top. Arrange slices of scamorza cheese around the edge of the platter. Serve with a basket of breadsticks, taralli, or bread.

RICOTTA SALATA, TOMATO, AND ARUGULA ANTIPASTO

*Antipasto di Ricotta Salata,
Pomodoro, e Rucola*

SERVES 2 TO 4

Creamy, lemony ricotta salata, a firm, moist sheep's milk cheese, is cut into chips and arranged over a bed of peppery arugula and diced tomato. Black olives are sprinkled over the top, and the antipasto is moistened with golden olive oil. Simple yet absolutely delicious, this antipasto can also be served as an informal luncheon dish followed by oranges and perhaps a few cookies.

1 *bunch arugula, coarse stems trimmed*
2 *large tomatoes*
Salt to taste
3 *ounces ricotta salata, cut into chips*
12 *black olives cured in brine, drained*
Freshly ground black pepper to taste
3 *tablespoons extra-virgin olive oil*

Cut the arugula into thin strips. Core the tomatoes and cut into medium dice. Make a bed of arugula on a serving platter. Place the diced tomatoes over the arugula and season with salt to taste. Distribute the chips of ricotta salata over the tomatoes and scatter the black olives over the top. Grind black pepper to taste on the antipasto and drizzle with olive oil.

GOAT CHEESE WITH RAW FENNEL AND RED CHILE PEPPER

Caprini ai Finocchiai

SERVES 4

This dish of lemony goat cheese and slivers of crisp fennel looks fresh and pure. Sprinkled with crushed red chile pepper, drizzled with gently warmed extra-virgin olive oil, and garnished with feathery fennel and herb sprigs, this makes a simple, elegant antipasto or first course.

1   *fennel bulb*
A variety of herb sprigs
8   *ounces fresh goat cheese without seasonings*
Dried red chile pepper flakes to taste
4   *tablespoons extra-virgin olive oil*
Salt to taste

Cut off the stalks of the fennel bulb and reserve the feathery tops. Trim the fennel bulb, removing the coarse outer layers and any tough strings. Cut the bulb into quarters, cut away the core, then cut lengthwise into julienne.

Arrange a few of the feathery sprigs of fennel tops and the herb sprigs on each of 4 plates. Cut the goat cheese into 4 pieces. Place 1 piece of cheese in the center of each plate. Scatter the julienned fennel around the goat cheese and sprinkle with red chile pepper flakes and salt to taste. Warm the olive oil in a small sauté pan over low heat. Drizzle the olive oil over the cheese.

PEARS, PARMESAN, AND CELERY

Pere, Parmigiano, e Sedano

SERVES 4

lovely and intriguing blend of flavors and textures—buttery pear, crisp celery, tangy Parmesan, and slivered walnuts—combine for a special cool-weather offering. Use pears that are ripe and fragrant, but still very firm. And splurge on the finest Parmesan cheese, Parmigiano-Reggiano. Its lovely pale-straw coloring and rich flavor elevate any dish in which it is used.

Serve this as the first course of a holiday meal. It is the perfect complement to fall dishes.

3–4 stalks of celery heart
3 ounces Parmigiano-Reggiano
Small handful walnut halves
3 large pears, ripe but firm
Extra-virgin olive oil
Lemon juice
Salt and freshly ground black pepper

Remove the strings from the celery and cut into thin diagonal slices. Reserve a few of the leaves. Cut the Parmesan into paper-thin slivers. Cut the walnut halves into thin slices.

Right before serving, core and thinly slice the pears. If necessary, the pears can be sliced a little in advance of using them. Toss in lemon juice to prevent them from discoloring. Place the prepared ingredients on a serving dish. Drizzle with a little olive oil and lemon juice to taste, adjusting the amount of lemon juice if used previously on pears. Season with salt and pepper. Toss very gently and serve, garnished with the reserved celery leaves.

MOZZARELLA, ROASTED YELLOW PEPPERS, AND TOMATO

Mozzarella del Sud

SERVES 6

This Neapolitan version of caprese salad is a brilliant pinwheel of color, with roasted yellow pepper strips alternating with slices of tomato and mozzarella. Sprinkled with piquant capers and strong, aromatic dried oregano, this dish is unmistakably and irresistibly southern Italian.

Serve it in the fall when peppers are at their most abundant and least expensive. If possible, select a yellow pepper streaked with green. It will have a touch of tart flavor to temper its sweetness.

2 *yellow peppers*
1 *pound fresh mozzarella*
2 *large crisp tomatoes*
Salt and freshly ground black pepper to taste
2 *teaspoons dried Mediterranean oregano*
2 *tablespoons capers*
6 *tablespoons extra-virgin olive oil*

Roast the peppers over a gas flame or under the broiler until lightly charred on all sides. Yellow peppers do not require as much roasting as red peppers, so hold back a bit. After roasting, place the peppers in a paper bag and let cool. Rub off the skin with your fingers or with a paper towel. Or remove the skin under cold running water, a less messy alternative. Cut the peppers in half and pop out the core. Trim away the white membranes and remove any stray seeds. Cut the peppers into thick strips.

If the mozzarella is packed in water, drain it on paper towels. Slice the mozzarella about ¼ inch thick. Core the tomatoes and slice them.

On a serving platter alternate slices of mozzarella, strips of pepper, and tomato. Season with salt and pepper to taste. Sprinkle with oregano and capers and drizzle with olive oil.

BITE-SIZED MOZZARELLA AND CHERRY TOMATOES

Bocconcini di Mozzarella e Pomodorini

SERVES 6

This summery dish of miniature balls of moist, fresh mozzarella and cherry tomatoes tossed with red chile pepper, fresh herbs, and extra-virgin olive oil makes a good addition to an antipasto buffet. It is a visual change of pace from caprese salad, which alternates slices of mozzarella and tomato. For gardeners, this is a good way to put an abundant crop of cherry tomatoes to use.

1 *pound miniature mozzarella balls (bocconcini), drained*
1 *basket of cherry tomatoes, either red or yellow, or a mix of both*
Salt to taste
½ *teaspoon dried red chile pepper flakes*
2 *tablespoons coarsely chopped Italian parsley leaves*
12 *basil leaves, torn into fragments*
Extra-virgin olive oil

Cut the mozzarella balls in half and place them in a shallow serving bowl. Cut the cherry tomatoes in half and scatter them over the mozzarella. Season the cheese and tomatoes with salt to taste. Sprinkle the red chile pepper flakes, parsley, and basil over the top. Drizzle enough extra-virgin olive oil to lightly moisten the ingredients. Toss very gently.

Marinated Vegetables

MUSHROOMS WITH THYME AND CINNAMON

Funghi al Timo e alla Cannella

SERVES 4 TO 6

stick of cinnamon gives these marinated mushrooms an elusive spiced sweetness. Serve them as part of an offering of assorted antipasti.

1   *pound medium mushrooms of approximately equal size*
5   *tablespoons extra-virgin olive oil*
3   *garlic cloves, peeled and chopped*
3   *sprigs thyme, leaves chopped*
3   *tablespoons chopped Italian parsley*
1   *stick cinnamon, broken in half*
Salt and freshly ground black pepper to taste
Juice of 1 lemon

Clean the mushrooms carefully by wiping them with damp paper towels. Trim the stem ends.

In a large sauté pan, combine the olive oil, garlic, thyme, parsley, and cinnamon stick. Warm the ingredients over low heat for 2 to 3 minutes. Add the mushrooms, raise the heat to medium, and sauté for about 5 minutes, stirring frequently. Lower the heat, and add salt and pepper to taste and the lemon juice. Stir the mushrooms, cover the pan, and cook another 2 to 3 minutes, or until the mushrooms are tender but firm.

Transfer the mushrooms to a dish and let cool. Cover and marinate for at least 1 hour, stirring occasionally. These mushrooms can also be made several days in advance; they improve in flavor as they marinate.

BABY ARTICHOKES MARINATED IN LEMON AND HERBS

Carciofini al Limone e alle Erbe

SERVES 6

*I*f you like the market variety of marinated artichoke hearts sold in small jars, this recipe will be a revelation. When made with tender little artichokes, fresh herbs, and good extra-virgin olive oil, marinated artichokes are one of the finest antipasti you can serve. Not only do the baby artichokes look beautiful—perfectly formed, a muted gray-green in color—but each tender bud carries the special flavor of the heart.

Accompany with crusty bread and black olives or paper-thin slices of imported prosciutto.

3 *pounds fresh baby artichokes*
1 *lemon, cut in half, for trimming raw artichokes*
Salt
Juice of 3 lemons
3 *cups water*
½ *cup extra-virgin olive oil, plus extra for drizzling*
3 *sprigs thyme*
5 *sprigs Italian parsley*
4 *bay leaves*
1 *celery stalk, cut into short lengths*
10 *black peppercorns*

To trim the baby artichokes, fill a big bowl with water. Squeeze the juice of half a lemon into the bowl of water. Use the other lemon half to rub the cut portions of the artichokes as you work. Snap back the dark green outer leaves. Trim away the green portions at the base and trim the stalk. Cut about ½ inch off the tops of the leaves. Place the artichokes in the acidulated water to prevent darkening.

Bring a large pot of water to a boil. Add salt and when the water returns to a boil, add all the artichokes. Cook until the artichokes are just tender. Test them with a wooden skewer. They are ready when the skewer pierces the heart with just a slight bit of resistance. Drain them well and place in a large glass jar or deep bowl. *(continued)*

Make the marinade by combining in a saucepan the lemon juice, 3 cups water, salt, olive oil, herbs, celery, and peppercorns. Simmer for about 20 minutes uncovered. Pour the hot marinade over the artichokes and let cool. Cover and refrigerate for at least 3 days and for as long as a week.

To serve, use a slotted spoon or Chinese strainer to lift the artichokes out of the marinade. Sprinkle a little salt on the artichokes, if needed, and add a drizzle of extra-virgin olive oil.

MARINATED RAW EGGPLANT DA GEMMA STYLE

Melanzane Crude Marinate

I tasted this dish for the first time at Da Gemma, a restaurant in Amalfi. In the kitchen, I glimpsed silver-bladed knives and worn pots, the flickering flames of the grill, and a tiny, ancient woman, Gemma, dressed in black and busily tending to her cooking.

The eggplant was served as part of a mixed antipasto. Its texture was so unusual that I asked how it was prepared and was amazed to learn that the eggplant was marinated raw. The eggplant strips, with beautiful amber flesh, look like wild mushrooms, but their texture is chewy and satisfying.

I always think of Gemma when I prepare eggplant in this way.

6–8 *Japanese eggplants*
Coarse salt
4 *tablespoons red wine vinegar*
8 *fresh basil leaves*
3 *garlic cloves, peeled and sliced*
1 *teaspoon crushed red chile peppers*
Extra-virgin olive oil

Trim the stems from the eggplants and peel them. Cut the eggplants in half crosswise, then into slices no thicker than ¼ inch. Cut each slice into 1-inch-wide strips. Place the strips in a bowl and sprinkle with coarse salt. Toss and let drain for 24 hours at room temperature. Remove excess moisture by gently pressing the eggplant between the palms of your hands.

Place the eggplant strips in a bowl and add the vinegar. Toss thoroughly and let rest for 1 hour. Select a Mason jar large enough to contain the eggplant strips. Layer the eggplant in the jar, evenly distributing the basil leaves, garlic slices, and red chile pepper. Press down on the eggplant gently with the back of a wooden spoon. Pour enough olive oil over the eggplant to cover it generously. Close the lid and refrigerate. Check after several hours to see if more olive oil is needed, as the eggplant will absorb some of the oil. Although the eggplant can be eaten right away, the flavors improve after several days, and it keeps for months.

EGGPLANT PRESERVED IN OLIVE OIL

Melanzane sott'Olio

This recipe does not require canning, so you can have delicious, creamy slices of eggplant on hand for months. Perfect for impromptu eating, the eggplant can be served as part of an antipasto or tuck a few slices into a roll for a tangy sandwich.

6–8 *Japanese eggplants*
Coarse salt
Imported red wine vinegar and water in equal amounts
4 *sprigs rosemary*
4 *garlic cloves, peeled and sliced*
10 *black peppercorns*
Extra-virgin olive oil

Trim the eggplant and slice it lengthwise ¼ inch thick. Layer the eggplant slices in a colander, generously salting each layer. Let drain for 2 to 3 hours.

In a large saucepan, bring to a boil equal parts red wine vinegar and water, enough to cover the eggplant later. Add the eggplant slices and let boil for 4 minutes or until tender. Drain the eggplant and when cool enough to handle, gently squeeze out excess moisture between the palms of your hands. Arrange the eggplant slices on paper towels and let dry for 24 hours.

In a Mason jar large enough to contain the eggplant, layer the eggplant, interspersed with rosemary sprigs, garlic slices, and black peppercorns. Add enough olive oil to cover. Press down on the eggplant with the back of a wooden spoon to eliminate air bubbles. Add more olive oil if needed. Check the eggplant after several hours to see if the oil level has dropped. Since the eggplant will absorb some of the oil, it may be necessary to add more. Make sure it is generously covered in oil. Store in the refrigerator. It will be ready to eat in 2 weeks.

ANTIPASTO OF SPICY CARROTS

Antipasto di Carote Piccanti

SERVES 6

his recipe takes advantage of sweet, crisp carrots, which are abundant and inexpensive. It is a very bright and uncomplicated antipasto of carrots, herbs, and red chile pepper marinated in white wine vinegar. The freshness of the carrots and the quality of the vinegar are of equal importance. Select carrots with feathery green tops still attached, a sign that they are fresh. Taste the vinegar before committing it to the dish. It should have a mellow, not harsh taste.

For a light, simple lunch, serve the carrots with oil-cured black olives and fresh ricotta salata or tuna marinated in olive oil and lemon juice.

1 *bunch carrots, about 1 pound*
Imported white wine vinegar
2 *garlic cloves, peeled and thinly sliced*
1 *tender celery stalk, strings removed, sliced*
2–3 *branches celery leaves*
Pinch of dried Mediterranean oregano
1 *piece fresh red chile pepper or dried red chile pepper flakes*
       to taste
Salt and coarsely ground black pepper to taste
Extra-virgin olive oil

Trim and peel the carrots. Cut them into medium-thick sticks. Cook the carrots in abundant boiling salted water until barely al dente. Drain well and transfer them to a Mason jar. While the carrots are still warm, add enough white wine vinegar to completely cover them. Add the garlic, celery, celery leaves, dried oregano, red chile pepper, and enough salt and pepper to balance the flavor of the vinegar. Stir well and let cool. Cover and let marinate for 24 hours.

Lift the vegetables out of the marinade. Drizzle with extra-virgin olive oil and season with salt and pepper.

Serve as a part of an assorted antipasto platter or as an accompaniment to sandwiches.

GARDEN VEGETABLES IN WHITE WINE VINEGAR

Verdura in Marinata

MAKES APPROXIMATELY 3 CUPS

This is a very simple way to preserve vegetables when your garden has produced more than you could possibly consume or give away. You can marinate one vegetable or you can select an assortment, as in the following recipe. The vegetables can be eaten as soon as the next day, but will last for months.

The quality of the vinegar determines the success of this recipe. Select a very high-quality imported white wine vinegar. Most white wine vinegars have too sharp a taste and lack the mellow touch that is needed here.

These pickled vegetables can be used as a garnish for sandwiches, as part of an antipasto platter, or as a piquant accent to vegetable dishes such as Artichokes Braised with Thyme (see page 304).

¼ *cauliflower, flowerets separated*
¼ *pound green beans, ends trimmed*
12 *pearl onions, red or white, peeled*
½ *fennel bulb, cut into julienne*
2 *carrots, peeled, cut into julienne, or handful*
      peeled baby carrots
Handful baby zucchini, trimmed, unpeeled
Imported white wine vinegar
Salt to taste
2 *cloves garlic, peeled*
Black peppercorns
Dried red chile peppers
Extra-virgin olive oil
Freshly ground black pepper to taste

Lightly cook each vegetable separately in abundant salted boiling water. Drain well and pat dry. Arrange all the vegetables on clean dish towels and let them dry thoroughly for 24 hours. Select a Mason jar large enough to contain all the vegetables. Place the vegetables in the jar and cover with white wine vinegar. Add salt to taste, garlic, black peppercorns, and red chile peppers. Close the jar tightly and keep refrigerated. The vegetables will last for months.

To serve, use a slotted spoon to lift out as many of the mixed vegetables as you require. Place the vegetables in a small bowl and season with olive oil, salt, and pepper to taste.

PINK PICKLED PEARL ONIONS

Cipolline sott'Aceto Rosso

MAKES APPROXIMATELY 2 CUPS

These very easy, appetite-provoking and piquant pickled onions call for pearl or small boiling onions, red wine vinegar, and spices. No canning is required. They are ready in as little as a few days but acquire their deep mauve coloring after a month or so. Tart and crunchy, they make a great addition to an assorted antipasto platter or they can be served as a garnish for sandwiches. Add them to rice salads for a pretty, tangy touch.

Salt
1 *basket pearl onions*
A few black peppercorns
Bay leaves
Imported red wine vinegar

Bring a large pot of water to boil. Add salt to taste. Plunge the onions into the water and let boil for about 2 minutes. Drain the onions and peel them. Let cool.

Select a Mason jar or glass jar with a tight-fitting lid large enough to contain the onions. Place the peppercorns and bay leaves in the jar. Add the onions. Pour in enough vinegar to completely cover the onions. Tightly close the lid and set aside for at least several days before using.

Hot Antipasti

HERB FRITTERS

Erbe in Pastella

SERVES 6 TO 8

A wonderful way to spotlight the flavors of fresh herbs. Biting into these fragrant morsels transports you to the Italian countryside where herbs grow wild. Serve the fritters hot as an antipasto with a cold, crisp white wine.

You can select just one herb or an assortment of herbs. The list below contains those that are readily available in most markets. If you have an herb garden, stroll through it and pick whatever appears particularly tender and fragrant.

FRITTER BATTER

2 *eggs, separated*
2 *tablespoons olive oil*
¾ *cup beer*
1 *cup flour*
Salt and freshly ground black pepper to taste

FOR THE FRITTERS

1 *bunch basil, large leaves only*
1 *small bunch Italian parsley, coarse stems trimmed*
1 *bunch mint, leaves and tender stems only*
1 *bunch sage, large leaves only*

Olive oil for frying
Salt
Lemon wedges

Beat egg yolks, then slowly add the oil, beer, and flour. Season with salt and pepper to taste. Cover and set aside for 1 hour. Right before using, whip egg whites and fold into batter.

Place the olive oil in a skillet to a depth of 3 inches. Heat the oil until very hot but not smoking.

Dip the herbs into the batter one by one, and shake well to remove excess. Fry in oil until crisp and brown, making sure you do not crowd the pan. Drain the fritters on paper towels, sprinkle with salt, and serve hot, garnished with lemon wedges.

BAKED OLIVES

Olive al Forno

SERVES 6

A recipe from Sicily. Rich, meaty black olives are baked in the oven with white wine and whole garlic cloves until the olives plump up. They are served hot right from the oven. This dish is so simple, the wine aroma so fragrant, and the look so appealing that it can precede all manner of rustic meals or be a meal in itself.

2 *cups large, meaty oil-cured black olives*
2–3 *garlic cloves, peeled and lightly crushed*
2 *tablespoons extra-virgin olive oil*
½ *cup dry white wine*

Place olives and garlic cloves in a rustic baking dish just large enough to contain them. Add the olive oil and toss. Pour the wine over the olives and bake in a preheated 350° oven, covered, for about 20 minutes, or until the olives plump up. Serve very hot directly from the baking dish.

LEMON AND HERB-STUFFED TOMATOES

Pomodori Ripieni al Limone e Herbe

SERVES 4

Stuffed tomatoes are a classic antipasto offering, served either hot or cold and typically featuring ingredients such as capers, anchovies, and olives as piquant, lively flavor accents.

This recipe foregoes the usual complement of flavors for a more delicate stuffing that is fragrant with a generous amount of lemon zest and fresh herbs. The aromatic lemon points up the sweetness of the tomatoes in a very delightful way.

Serve these tomatoes warm or at room temperature. The flavor of the lemon becomes even more pronounced when the tomatoes are served at room temperature.

8 *Roma tomatoes*
Salt
3 *eggs*
6 *tablespoons bread crumbs*
8 *basil leaves, chopped*
3 *tablespoons Italian parsley, chopped*
Zest of 1 lemon, finely chopped
4 *tablespoons grated Parmesan cheese*
Ground nutmeg to taste
Freshly ground black pepper to taste

Cut the tomatoes in half lengthwise and scoop out the seeds. Salt the interiors and turn the tomatoes upside down on paper towels to drain for 20 minutes.

Break the eggs into a bowl and lightly beat them with a fork. Add the remaining ingredients and stir well. Arrange the tomatoes in a baking dish and divide the stuffing among them.

Bake in a 375° oven for 15 minutes or until the tomatoes are tender but still hold their shape and the stuffing is firm. Let rest 5 minutes before serving. The tomatoes can also be cooked early in the day and served that evening at room temperature.

GRILLED STUFFED RADICCHIO

Radicchio Ripieno alla Griglia

SERVES 4

his recipe features the contrasting flavors and textures of bitter, lightly crunchy radicchio and mild fresh mozzarella. The radicchio is stuffed with the fresh cheese and anchovies, then grilled until the cheese melts and the radicchio becomes tinged with gold.

4 *medium heads radicchio*
¼ *pound fresh mozzarella, cut into 4 cubes*
2–4 *anchovies*
Extra-virgin olive oil
Salt and freshly ground black pepper to taste
Lemon wedges

Bring a large pot of water to a boil. Add salt and when the water returns to the boil, plunge the radicchio into the water. Use a slotted spoon or Chinese strainer to force the heads below the surface of the water. Blanch for 2 to 3 minutes. Drain thoroughly on paper towels.

Gently open up the radicchio heads and place a cube of mozzarella at the center of each head. Place a whole anchovy or, if a less strong anchovy flavor is preferred, half an anchovy over the cheese. Carefully overlap the radicchio leaves so as to completely enclose the mozzarella filling.

Moisten the radicchio with olive oil and grill or broil the rolls for about 3 minutes on each side, or until the mozzarella melts. Season with salt and pepper to taste. Garnish with lemon wedges.

STUFFED BABY ARTICHOKES

Carciofini Ripieni

SERVES 4

V ery small artichokes, picked before the choke forms, are choice eating. Stuffed, lightly breaded, and fried in olive oil until golden, these tasty morsels make a delightful first course to nibble on while sipping cold white wine.

1 *lemon, cut in half*
8 *artichokes, each about 2 inches long*
Salt
3 *whole eggs, divided*
¾ *cup homemade bread crumbs, divided*
2 *tablespoons shredded fresh mozzarella*
2 *anchovies, chopped*
2 *tablespoons chopped Italian parsley*
2 *garlic cloves, peeled and finely chopped*
2 *tablespoons extra-virgin olive oil*
¼ *cup unbleached all-purpose flour*
Olive oil for frying
Lemon wedges

Fill a large bowl with water and squeeze in the juice of ½ lemon. As you work, rub the cut portions of the artichokes with the other lemon half to prevent the artichoke from darkening. Trim the artichokes by snapping off the dark green outer leaves. Cut away the dark green portions around the bases and stems of the artichokes. Trim the tops of the leaves. Place the trimmed artichokes in the acidulated water.

Bring a large pot of water to a boil. Add salt and when the water returns to a boil, plunge the artichokes into the water. Use a slotted spoon or Chinese strainer to force the artichokes under the water. Blanch for approximately 3 minutes. Drain on paper towels. Gently pry open the artichokes to make a cavity in the center of each one.

Break 1 egg into a small bowl and lightly beat it with a fork. Add ¼ cup bread crumbs, the mozzarella, anchovies, parsley, garlic, and extra-virgin olive oil. Mix well with a fork. Fill the center of each artichoke with some of the bread-crumb mixture, using enough so that the stuffing comes slightly over the top of the artichoke. Smooth the surface of the stuffing into a mound.

Spread the flour on one plate and remaining bread crumbs on another. Break 2 eggs into a shallow bowl and beat them lightly with a fork. Dredge the artichokes very lightly in the flour and shake off the excess. Dip each artichoke in the egg and let the excess drain back into the bowl. Roll the artichokes in the bread crumbs, patting down the crumbs to help them adhere to the artichokes.

Heat about ½ inch of olive oil in a skillet. When the oil is hot but not smoking, fry the artichokes, a few at a time, until they are golden on all sides. Use tongs to turn the artichokes to prevent piercing the bread-crumb coating, since that would allow oil to be absorbed into the artichokes.

As the artichokes turn golden brown, lift them out of the oil, letting excess oil drain back into the skillet. Place on paper towels to drain and season with salt to taste.

To serve, transfer the artichokes to a clean platter and garnish with lemon wedges.

GOLDEN FLOWER ARTICHOKES

Carciofini Fritti

SERVES 4

*L*arge, tender artichokes fried in hot olive oil are a feature of the cooking in the Jewish quarter of Rome. I was served them on the terrace of a restaurant one evening as I gazed out at a dark blue night sky and the outlines of Roman ruins illuminated by a pale golden moon.

In this dish, which is a version of the Roman recipe, baby artichokes are gently pounded until the leaves open up like flowers. They are fried in olive oil until the exterior leaves turn crunchy and golden brown, and the heart and the interior leaves become meltingly tender. A dusting of salt is the only seasoning required.

1 *lemon, cut in half*
8–12 *small artichokes, each about 2 inches in length*
Olive oil for frying
Salt to taste

Fill a big bowl with water and squeeze in the juice of ½ lemon. Use the other lemon half to rub the cut portions of the artichoke as you work. Trim the artichokes by snapping back the dark green outer leaves. Trim away the dark green portions at the base and trim the stalk. Cut about ½ inch off the tops of the leaves. Place the artichokes in the acidulated water. Then drain the artichokes and dry them well. Pound each artichoke against a hard surface, head down, until the tightly clenched leaves open up like a flower.

In a medium skillet, heat to medium hot enough olive oil to measure at least ½ inch. Fry the artichokes in the oil a few at a time, pressing them down to open up the leaves. Use tongs to turn the artichokes in the oil and brown them on all sides. Cook slowly for about 5 minutes, raising the heat toward the end of the cooking to brown the exterior of the artichokes. Lift them out of the pan and let excess oil drain back into the skillet. Drain the artichokes on paper towels and season with salt to taste.

Transfer the artichokes to a platter and serve immediately.

Salads

his chapter includes three salad categories: leafy salads, little salads, and main-dish salads. The recipes reflect a new style of eating, one that is lighter and fresher and a departure from the eating habits of the past.

The image of salads has changed and, far from being the neglected course they once were, they have taken center stage. For reasons of health, to keep trim, and because interesting ingredients are available, people are eating salads more than ever before. If I had to pick one food that I couldn't live without, it would be a salad, since it can revive, refresh, and satisfy me in a way no other food can.

Salad making offers many delights. Lettuce salads possess extraordinary beauty. The delicate leaves range in color from pale green and chartreuse to pink, red, and russet, and there is an astonishing variety of leaf formations. Vegetable salads offer bold colors and textural contrasts. Main-course salads look inviting with the muted earthy tones of beans, golden breads, rice, and cheeses. They contain the fruity bouquet of olive oil, the clean fragrance of lemon juice, the sharp-mellow tang of red wine vinegar, and the perfume of herbs.

What is most important in salad making is the freshness of ingredients. Handle fragile lettuces gently and dry all lettuces well, since water will dilute the strength of a dressing. Keep ingredients to a restrained number—too many will create a confusing jumble. With leafy greens, dress the salads just before serving them; marination improves salads made with beans, potatoes, and rice.

Salads freshen the body and the spirit, and are basic to healthy eating habits. Eating the tender, raw leaves of green plants gives us one of our closest and most profound connections to nature. And when the leaves grow in your own garden, the connection to nature is complete.

Leafy Salads

ARUGULA SALAD AS SERVED AT FIASCHETTERIA BELTRAMME

Insalata di Rucola alla Fiaschetteria Beltramme

SERVES 4

*I*t was my first meal on a recent trip to Italy at one of my favorite restaurants in Rome. It was springtime and arugula was in season. My salad arrived in a big white bowl—a handful of tender arugula dressed with good olive oil and salt, with a big chunk of lemon to squeeze over the peppery leaves. One look and I knew I was back in Italy.

> 4 *handfuls very fresh arugula*
> *Salt to taste*
> *Extra-virgin olive oil*
> 4 *thick lemon wedges*

Cut off the thick stems at the base of the arugula leaves. Gently wash and dry the leaves. Place them in a big bowl and sprinkle with salt to taste. Drizzle with olive oil to lightly coat the arugula. Toss gently.

Divide the arugula among 4 simple white bowls. In each bowl place a chunk of lemon. Each person squeezes lemon over the salad according to taste.

SALAD OF FIELD GREENS

Insalata Verde di Campo

SERVES 2 TO 4

This salad comes from the Italian tradition of gathering tender edible greens that grow wild in the countryside. It combines slightly bitter greens with a sprinkling of walnuts and garlic-rubbed dried bread. Wild greens would be ideal, but your local supermarket can yield a remarkably diverse variety of greens, such as the ones listed below, that are in keeping with the untamed spirit of the salad.

4 *big handfuls tender inner leaves of escarole, curly endive, and romaine; small spinach leaves; leaves of tender mustard greens; fresh green radish leaves; tender watercress sprigs; and arugula trimmed of tough stems*

½ *bunch chopped chives or 5 green onions, trimmed and thinly sliced*

4 *tablespoons chopped walnuts*

4 *small, thin rounds of dried bread generously rubbed with a cut clove of garlic, optional*

Salt and freshly ground black pepper to taste

Extra-virgin olive oil

Imported red wine vinegar

Combine the salad greens in a large bowl. Add the chives, walnuts, and dried bread, and toss. Season with salt and pepper to taste. Drizzle with olive oil and vinegar to taste and toss. Correct seasonings and serve immediately.

TENDER MIXED SALAD

Insalata Mista Tenera

SERVES 2 TO 4

ixed salads usually feature a mild lettuce and a few thinly sliced raw vegetables. This version is light, fresh, and springlike, and it can precede or follow a variety of dishes.

1   *head tender butter or limestone lettuce*
2   *small carrots, peeled and grated*
1   *small fennel bulb, trimmed, cut into fine julienne*
3–4   *green onions, trimmed and cut into julienne*
1   *large crisp tomato, cut into small chunks*
Salt and freshly ground black pepper to taste
Extra-virgin olive oil
Imported red wine vinegar

Detach the lettuce leaves from the core. Wash and dry well. Tear the leaves into bite-sized pieces and place in a salad bowl. Add the remaining prepared vegetables. Season with salt and pepper to taste. Drizzle with olive oil and vinegar, and toss. Correct the seasonings and serve immediately.

MIXED SALAD WITH PINE NUTS AND CAPERS

Insalata Mista ai Pignoli e Capperi

SERVES 2 AS A MAIN DISH
AND 4 AS A FIRST COURSE

A finer version of an insalata mista would be hard to find. Thinly sliced, tender raw artichoke heart, with its pleasingly bitter flavor, capers, pine nuts, Parmesan shavings, and a lemony dressing add a range of intriguing flavors—salty, tangy, piquant, and tart—to the leafy greens. I particularly enjoy this salad as a light and healthful main course for a simple supper, but you can serve it as a refreshing first course, too.

2 *small carrots*
2 *celery stalks from the heart*
1 *tender artichoke*
4 *big handfuls mixed baby lettuces*
1 *tablespoon small capers, well drained*
1 *tablespoon fresh pine nuts*
3 *anchovies, packed in olive oil*
2 *ounces imported Parmesan cheese, thinly shaved*
Salt and freshly ground black pepper to taste
4 *tablespoons extra-virgin olive oil*
4 *tablespoons lemon juice*

Peel and trim the carrots and slice thinly on the diagonal. Trim the celery, remove any tough strings, and slice thinly on the diagonal. Trim the artichoke according to the directions on page 8 and slice paper thin.

In a large shallow salad bowl, combine the raw vegetables and the mixed lettuces. Sprinkle with the capers and pine nuts. Chop the anchovies into small pieces and add to the salad. Scatter the Parmesan shavings over the top. Season with salt and pepper to taste. Drizzle with olive oil and lemon juice and toss lightly. If necessary correct the seasonings.

SALAD FROM THE GRAN RIALTO MARKET

Insalata del Gran Rialto

SERVES 4

From the Gran Rialto market in Venice comes this refreshing assortment of crisp, peppery, and tart ingredients combined with the surprising liquid sweetness of grapes.

1 *head tender romaine, bruised outer leaves removed*
1 *bunch arugula, stems trimmed*
1 *green pepper, peeled with a vegetable peeler*
1 *crisp tomato, preferably streaked with green*
6 *mushrooms, wiped clean, stems trimmed*
½ *hothouse cucumber, peeled and seeded*
½ *cup seedless red or green grapes*
¼ *cup extra-virgin olive oil*
Juice of ½ lemon
Salt and freshly ground black pepper to taste

Tear the romaine into bite-sized pieces. Cut the arugula into strips. Cut the green pepper in half and remove core, seeds, and white membranes, then cut into julienne. Slice the tomato into thin wedges. Thinly slice the mushrooms and cucumber. Cut the grapes in half.

Combine the ingredients in a shallow salad bowl. Add the olive oil, lemon juice, and salt and pepper to taste. Toss gently.

ROMAINE AND GORGONZOLA SALAD WITH WHOLE WHEAT CROSTINI

Lattuga Romana e Gorgonzola con Crostini al Pane Integrale

SERVES 4

Whole wheat bread is all the rage in Italy, where being health conscious is in fashion. There it is baked according to rustic tradition until dark brown and crusty.

In this salad small cubes of garlic-rubbed whole wheat bread and tender romaine are tossed in a dressing of dolcelatte Gorgonzola, extra-virgin olive oil, and red wine vinegar.

If you have tiny new romaine lettuces growing in your garden, use the whole heads for an especially pretty presentation.

2 *slices country whole wheat bread, cut ½ inch thick*
1 *large garlic clove, peeled and cut in half*
2 *heads romaine, or 4 large handfuls small romaine lettuces*
4 *ounces dolcelatte Gorgonzola, rind trimmed*
5 *tablespoons extra-virgin olive oil*
2 *tablespoons imported red wine vinegar*
Salt and freshly ground black pepper to taste

Lightly toast the bread and rub with the cut garlic clove. Cut the bread into ½-inch dice and place in a preheated 250° oven until the bread cubes are completely dried out.

Remove any wilted or yellow leaves from the romaine and wash and dry well. Tear the lettuce into bite-sized pieces. If using very small garden romaine, leave the heads whole but trim a little off the root ends. Wash the lettuce very well under cold running water and dry thoroughly.

In a small bowl combine the Gorgonzola, olive oil, red wine vinegar, and salt and pepper to taste. Mash the ingredients together but stop before the mixture is totally smooth. Some of the Gorgonzola should be in small chunks to give the dressing texture.

Place the bread cubes and the lettuce in a shallow salad bowl. Transfer the dressing to the salad bowl and toss well. If necessary add more olive oil, vinegar, and salt or pepper according to taste.

DOUBLE GREEN SALAD

Insalata Doppio Verde

SERVES 2

his combination of avocado and arugula with a touch of balsamic vinegar was a salad waiting to happen. The mellow, rich avocado is a perfect match for the peppery arugula.

Although avocados are available in Italy, they are still considered somewhat exotic. In southern California, avocado trees are a common sight, their branches heavy with fruit hidden in the deep shade of foliage. While I was growing up in a suburb of Los Angeles, my best friend's parents built a split-level home deep in the heart of an avocado orchard in the Covina hills. During the season, I was blessed with a steady supply, and avocados became my favorite after-school snack.

2 *bunches arugula, 4 cups loosely packed*
1 *avocado*
2 *tablespoons extra-virgin olive oil*
1 *tablespoon imported red wine vinegar*
1 *teaspoon balsamic vinegar*
Salt and freshly ground black pepper to taste

Wash the arugula well and trim the stem ends. Cut the arugula into thin strips and place in a shallow serving bowl. Peel the avocado, cut into ½-inch dice, and add to the bowl. Drizzle with the olive oil, both vinegars, and season with salt and pepper to taste. Toss gently. Serve immediately.

Spring Radish Salad

Insalatina di Rapanelli Primaverile

MAKES 4 SMALL SERVINGS

Bunches of scarlet radishes with fresh green leaves piled high in Italian market stalls are a beautiful sight in springtime. Crisp, juicy, and peppery with sparkling white flesh, radishes are much appreciated in Europe. In France radishes and sweet butter are served with bread at the beginning of the meal. In Italy they are often served raw along with other tender seasonal vegetables to dip into extra-virgin olive oil.

This salad features an entire bunch of crisp, thinly sliced radishes. Be sure to select only small, firm ones with fresh, unblemished tops.

1 *bunch fresh radishes*
2–3 *very sweet carrots*
2 *bunches arugula or watercress*
Salt and freshly ground black pepper to taste
Extra-virgin olive oil
2 *tablespoons freshly grated imported Parmesan cheese*
Lemon wedges

Trim the radishes and slice them thinly. Peel the carrots and cut them on the diagonal into very thin slices. Snap off the tough stems from the arugula or watercress. Gather the arugula into a bunch and cut it crosswise into strips.

Arrange the arugula on a platter. Scatter the sliced radishes and carrots over the arugula. Season with salt and pepper to taste. Drizzle with enough olive oil to lightly moisten the vegetables. Sprinkle the grated Parmesan cheese over the top. Serve with lemon wedges to squeeze over the salad.

BEET AND RADICCHIO SALAD

Insalata di Barbabietole e Radicchio

SERVES 4

With its scarlet-on-scarlet coloring, this exquisite salad features contrasting textures of tender beets, crisp radicchio, and rich walnuts. The beets are baked in the oven until tender—a method of cooking that concentrates their sweetness—then sliced paper thin. A spoonful of balsamic vinegar adds mellowness to the dressing and reinforces the sweetness of the beets.

This elegant and festive salad is ideal for a Christmas or Thanksgiving dinner. Serve it separate from other foods, always a good policy with beets, since everything they touch turns a deep pink.

Look for small beets with fresh leafy tops. The leaves are delicious cut into strips and sautéed in olive oil and garlic.

1   *bunch small beets, 4–5, about 1½ inches in diameter*
1   *medium head radicchio*
¼   *cup coarsely chopped fresh walnuts*
3   *tablespoons extra-virgin olive oil*
1   *tablespoon imported red wine vinegar*
1   *tablespoon balsamic vinegar*
Salt and freshly ground black pepper to taste

Trim all but about ½ inch from the tops of the beets, and if the leaves look fresh, reserve them and cook as suggested above. Wrap the beets in aluminum foil, tightly sealing the ends to form an envelope. Transfer the beets to a baking sheet and place in a preheated 450° oven. Cook until tender but slightly resistant when pierced with a skewer. Unwrap the foil and when cool enough to handle, peel and slice the beets very thinly.

Cut the radicchio in half lengthwise and wash under cold running water. Dry well. Cut out the core and cut the leaves into slivers.

Place the beets in the center of a round serving platter. Surround with the slivered radicchio. Sprinkle the walnuts over the top of the salad. Drizzle with the olive oil and the two vinegars, and season with salt and pepper to taste. Either present the salad arranged on the serving plate and toss it in front of your guests, or toss the salad before bringing it to the table. Both presentations are equally attractive.

SMASHED SALAD

Insalata Sbattuta

SERVES 4

One of the salads from *A Snob in the Kitchen*, a little cookbook written in 1967 by the legendary Italian couturière Simonetta. In her recipe cucumber, fennel, and watercress are wrapped in a clean dish towel and literally beaten against a table, then marinated, to make them "tired." To Simonetta the only good salad was a "tired" salad. If beating the salad seems too barbaric, simply omit this step. The salad is delicious eaten immediately, but it acquires its special wilted character after resting for 1 hour.

Fresh tarragon in the salad accentuates the licorice-like flavor of the fennel.

1 *hothouse cucumber*
1 *fennel bulb, trimmed*
1 *bunch watercress or 2 bunches arugula, thick stems removed*
2 *heaping tablespoons chopped tarragon leaves*
5 *tablespoons extra-virgin olive oil*
2 *tablespoons red wine vinegar*
Salt and freshly ground black pepper to taste

Peel the cucumber and cut in half lengthwise. Scoop out the seeds and cut into thin crescents. Chop the fennel into small dice. Cut the watercress or arugula into thin strips.

Wrap the cucumber, fennel, and watercress or arugula securely in a clean dish towel and beat against the table a few times. Transfer the contents to a bowl and add the tarragon, olive oil, vinegar, and salt and pepper to taste. Toss and let stand for 1 hour before serving.

SALAD OF BITTER GREENS WITH CHEESES

Insalata Piccante al Formaggio

SERVES 4 TO 6

This recipe unites thin strips of romaine, escarole, and arugula with dolcelatte Gorgonzola and Parmesan cheese for a tangy, satisfying salad with a bit of creaminess to it. Cutting the greens into thin strips softens their texture and is especially effective with sturdier greens such as escarole.

2 *slices Italian bread, cut ¾ inch thick*

1 *clove garlic, peeled and cut in half*

1 *small head escarole, coarse outer leaves removed*

1 *small head romaine, bruised outer leaves removed*

2–3 *bunches arugula, stems trimmed*

1 *ounce imported Parmesan cheese, cut into paper-thin slivers*

3 *ounces dolcelatte Gorgonzola*

6 *tablespoons extra-virgin olive oil*

3 *tablespoons imported red wine vinegar*

Salt and freshly ground black pepper to taste

Lightly toast the bread. While the bread is still warm, rub it with the cut garlic and cut it into small dice.

Cut the leaves of the escarole, romaine, and arugula into thin strips. Place the greens in a shallow serving bowl. Sprinkle with the slivers of Parmesan cheese. Crumble the Gorgonzola into the bowl and sprinkle with the cubes of toasted bread.

Drizzle the salad with olive oil and red wine vinegar, and season with salt and pepper to taste. Toss well.

Little Salads

TOMATO AND PEACH SALAD

Insalata di Pomodoro e Pesche

SERVES 4

This exquisite summer salad of scarlet tomatoes and golden peaches was inspired by a recipe in *Leaves from Our Tuscan Kitchen* written in 1899. It pairs the tart-sweet flavor and spicy scent of tomatoes with the lush sweetness of peaches.

The salad is at its best made with freshly picked tomatoes and peaches from the garden. If you have a source for fine, fresh produce, preferably organic, you can achieve wonderful results. If your produce is from the supermarket, you may wish to substitute nectarines for peaches, since market peaches are so often disappointing, mealy and barely fragrant.

4 *tomatoes, ripe but firm*
4 *peaches or nectarines*
Extra-virgin olive oil or walnut oil
Lemon juice
Salt and freshly ground black pepper
Small handful of walnut halves, thinly slivered

Core the tomatoes and cut into ¼-inch-thick slices. Cut the peaches or nectarines in half along the natural division and remove the pits. Slice to the same thickness as the tomatoes.

Arrange the slices on a serving dish in an alternating pattern. Very lightly drizzle with oil and lemon juice. Season with salt and pepper and sprinkle with the walnuts.

ORANGE AND FENNEL SALAD

Insalata di Arancia con Finocchi

SERVES 4

liced oranges seasoned with olive oil make a fine, palate-cleansing salad. The oranges can be garnished with red onion and mint leaves, or simply sprinkled with red chile pepper and garnished with olives. The following recipe is one of my favorites. It combines the brilliant juicy flesh of oranges with crisp slivers of licorice-flavored fennel.

3 *large oranges*
1 *medium fennel bulb*
A few small, tender romaine lettuce leaves
Extra-virgin olive oil
Salt and freshly ground black pepper to taste

Peel the oranges with a sharp knife, making sure you remove all the white pith. Cut the oranges into medium-sized chunks.

Trim any bruised, discolored, or tough outer leaves from the fennel, trim the root end, and cut the bulb in half lengthwise. Cut out the core at the base of the fennel bulb. Cut the fennel lengthwise into julienne strips.

Scatter the romaine leaves on a serving plate. Top with the oranges and fennel. Drizzle with olive oil and season with salt and a generous amount of coarsely ground black pepper. Toss gently.

MR. ARANCIO'S SALAD

Insalata del Signor Arancio

SERVES 4

ignor Arancio was my guide to the temples of Agrigento. We strolled through almond orchards, past blossoming acacia trees, fleshy aloes, and ancient fig trees. Along the dusty path wildflowers, brilliant blue borage and fluttery red poppies, were in bloom.

Signor Arancio, a retired teacher and expert on the ruins of Agrigento, had been conducting tours since his retirement almost twenty years earlier. Exceedingly charming, he told me about his wife, who had died the year before. The morning of the day she died, she had been working in her beloved garden by the sea. When our visit to the temples ended, he described to me his favorite salad of tomatoes, fennel, and cucumber.

I can assure you it is one of the most refreshing salads of all, like cool water on a hot day. Perfect for a torrid Sicilian summer, served in the shade of an almond tree.

1 *large crisp tomato*
½ *hothouse cucumber*
1 *small fennel bulb*
Generous salt and freshly ground black pepper to taste
4 *tablespoons extra-virgin olive oil*
Lemon juice to taste
Dried Mediterranean oregano
4 *basil leaves*
Oil-cured black olives

Core and slice the tomato. Peel the cucumber and slice in half lengthwise. Scoop out the seeds and slice. Trim the fennel bulb, removing tough outer layers and core. Slice into julienne.

Combine the vegetables on a platter and season with salt and pepper to taste. Drizzle with olive oil and lemon juice. Sprinkle with the oregano. Tear each basil leaf into 3 or 4 pieces and scatter over the top. Toss gently. Taste and correct the seasonings if necessary. Garnish the salad with oil-cured black olives.

BROCCOLI AND TOMATO SALAD

Insalata di Broccoli e Pomodoro

SERVES 4 TO 6

Broccoli, with its vivid green color and fresh, vibrant flavor, goes extremely well in salads. It is especially good when young and tender with slender, brilliant green stalks. Combined with tomatoes, fragrant basil, and black olives, broccoli creates a salad that you will enjoy over and over again. Serve this salad with a platter of fresh mozzarella for a delicious and wildly healthful lunch.

Broccoli must always be lightly cooked in boiling water to bring out the flavor and color, and to soften its texture. When I make broccoli salad in advance, I run cold water over the broccoli to set the color.

1½ *pounds tender broccoli*
2 *medium tomatoes*
⅓ *cup oil-cured black olives*
1 *garlic clove, peeled and minced*
12 *large basil leaves*
5 *tablespoons extra-virgin olive oil*
Juice of ½ lemon
Salt and freshly ground black pepper to taste

Trim a bit off the end of the broccoli stalks. Peel the stalks with a paring knife by cutting shallowly into the base of the stalk and stripping the peel upward from the base toward the flowerets. Cut the stalks in half lengthwise.

Plunge the broccoli into a generous amount of salted boiling water and cook until just tender. The cooking time will vary depending on the tenderness of the broccoli. Test frequently. Drain the broccoli into a colander. If desired, run cold water over it until it is cool to the touch. Drain on a clean dish towel to remove excess moisture. Cut the broccoli into 2-inch lengths.

Core the tomatoes and cut into medium dice.

Place the broccoli and tomatoes on a serving platter. Distribute the olives over the broccoli and tomatoes. Scatter the garlic over the top. Just before serving, tear the basil leaves into fragments and sprinkle over the salad. Drizzle with the olive oil and lemon juice, and add salt and pepper to taste. Toss and serve immediately.

CUCUMBER, BEET, AND ROASTED YELLOW PEPPER SALAD

Insalata Tricolore

SERVES 4 TO 6

This colorful salad contrasts the light green, scarlet, and gold of crisp raw cucumber, sweet baked beets, and smoky roasted yellow peppers.

5 *medium beets*
2 *yellow peppers*
½ *hothouse cucumber*
2 *heaping tablespoons capers*
Extra-virgin olive oil
Imported red wine vinegar
Salt and freshly ground black pepper to taste
8 *basil leaves, torn into fragments*

Trim the leaves from the beets, leaving about 1 inch of stem, and wrap in foil, tightly sealing the ends to form an envelope. Place on a baking sheet and bake in a preheated 450° oven until tender but slightly resistant when pierced with a skewer. When cool enough to handle, peel the beets, slice them, and cut into julienne.

Roast the peppers over a gas flame or under the broiler until lightly charred. Peel the peppers and remove the core, seeds, and white membranes. Cut the peppers into julienne.

Peel the cucumber and cut in half lengthwise. Scoop out the seeds and slice cucumber thinly.

Place each of the prepared ingredients in 3 separate small bowls. Divide the capers among the 3 bowls. Season each vegetable with olive oil, vinegar, and salt and pepper to taste.

On a platter arrange the vegetables in 3 groupings, starting with the beets, then the peppers, and finally the cucumbers. Sprinkle the basil over the top.

CAULIFLOWER SALAD WITH LEMON DRESSING

Insalata di Cavolfiore all'Agro

SERVES 4

A simple salad that allows the fresh, sweet flavor of cauliflower to emerge. A beautiful, unblemished whole cooked cauliflower, looking like a large white blossom, is placed in the center of a serving dish, drenched in a lemon dressing beaten to a creamy golden yellow, and garnished with sprigs of Italian parsley, radishes, and small black olives.

To serve the salad, break off large flowerets with a serving fork and drizzle them with generous spoonfuls of the lemon dressing. With good bread and a few slices of fresh mozzarella, this makes a simple and refreshing lunch in shades of white and gold.

1 *head cauliflower, fresh and unblemished*
Salt
¼ *cup extra-virgin olive oil*
Juice of 1 large lemon
Salt and freshly ground black pepper to taste
Sprigs of Italian parsley
1 *small bunch radishes with fresh green tops*
Handful small olives, such as Gaeta or Niçoise

Trim the cauliflower by snapping off the leaves and cutting away enough of the stalk so that the cauliflower has a flat base. Plunge the cauliflower into abundant salted boiling water. Cook until it is just tender with a touch of crispness to it. Cooking time will vary according to the size and freshness of the cauliflower. Drain completely.

In a small bowl beat together with a fork the olive oil and lemon juice, adding salt and pepper to taste.

Place the cauliflower in the center of a round serving dish. Pour the olive oil and lemon mixture over the top of the cauliflower and let the dressing pool around the edges. Grind a little black pepper over the top of the cauliflower. Garnish the platter with Italian parsley sprigs, radishes, and olives.

BEET AND BEET GREENS SALAD

Insalata di Barbabietole

SERVES 4

ake this salad with both small, sweet beets and their fresh, leafy tops. The earthy, dark red beets, cut into julienne, and the deep green leaves and their scarlet stems make a ravishing salad. If you have beets in your garden, you can use the tiny beets that you uproot when you thin out the plants. Boil the tiny beets with greens attached until just tender.

1 *bunch small beets of equal size, with fresh, leafy green tops*
Salt and freshly ground black pepper to taste
1 *garlic clove, peeled and finely chopped*
Extra-virgin olive oil
Fresh lemon juice
4 *thick lemon wedges*

Cut off the leaves of the beets, leaving a little of the stem attached. Wash the beets and greens separately. Place the beets in a large saucepan. Cover with a generous amount of water and add salt. Bring to a boil and cook until tender. Depending on the size of the beets, this will take anywhere from 15 minutes for very small beets to 40 minutes for larger beets. When the beets are tender but still slightly resistant, drain them. When cool enough to handle, slip off the dark skin and trim the area where the stems meet the root. Trim away the tails. Cut the beets into julienne strips. If using baby beets, cut into quarters lengthwise. Or you can bake the beets. Wrap them in foil and bake at 450° until tender but firm.

Meanwhile strip the leaves from the stems of the beet tops. Cut the stems into 2-inch lengths. Cook the stems and leaves in salted boiling water to cover until tender, about 5 minutes. Drain well.

Arrange the beets, stems, and greens on a serving dish. Season with salt and pepper to taste and sprinkle with the garlic. Drizzle with olive oil and lemon juice. Toss very gently. Serve while still warm, garnished with lemon wedges.

RUSSIAN SALAD

Insalata Russa

SERVES 4 TO 6

his salad of bright diced vegetables bound in homemade mayonnaise is a staple of Italian *gastronomie*, or take-out shops. A small serving of it can provide a rich counterpoint to lean foods. If you would rather do without the richness of mayonnaise, simply dress the vegetables with additional olive oil and vinegar for a tangy salad.

This very festive salad looks gorgeous mounded on a platter, with all the tiny diced vegetables forming a mosaic pattern. You can garnish it with capers, small black olives, thinly sliced lemon, or anything that strikes your fancy. Spoon it into a radicchio leaf for a pretty effect. Or use it to fill the cavity of a trimmed cooked artichoke.

3 *small golden beets, all but 1 inch of the tops trimmed*
2 *medium potatoes*
¼ *pound tender green beans*
¼ *pound tender wax beans*
2 *small carrots, trimmed and peeled*
2 *tablespoons finely chopped cornichons*
3 *tablespoons capers*
3 *tablespoons extra-virgin olive oil*
2 *tablespoons red wine vinegar*
Salt and freshly ground black pepper to taste
1 *recipe Lemon Mayonnaise (see page 53)*
3–4 *anchovies, finely chopped, optional*

Boil the beets and potatoes separately in water to cover until tender. Drain and when cool enough to handle, peel them.

Cook the green beans, wax beans, and carrots in separate pots with salted boiling water to cover. Drain when tender and refresh under cold water.

Cut all the vegetables into small dice and place in a bowl. Add the cornichons, capers, olive oil, vinegar, and salt and pepper to taste. Add enough mayonnaise to lightly bind the salad, and the anchovies, if desired.

Salads as the Main Course

RAW VEGETABLE AND MOZZARELLA SALAD

Insalata di Verdura Fresca e Mozzarella

SERVES 2 AS A MAIN-DISH SALAD
AND 4 AS AN ANTIPASTO

This mix of crisp, colorful vegetables and firm, moist mozzarella makes for a salad so light and fresh as to be habit-forming.

8 *ounces fresh mozzarella in water, drained*
1 *medium fennel bulb, stalks and feathery leaves trimmed*
6 *small carrots, trimmed and peeled*
1 *small bunch radishes, tops trimmed*
4 *tablespoons extra-virgin olive oil*
Juice of ½ lemon
Salt and coarsely ground black pepper to taste

Cut the mozzarella into thin julienne strips and place on paper towels to absorb excess moisture. If the outer layer of the fennel bulb is tough, remove it. Trim any bruised areas and remove any large, tough strings from the exterior of the bulb. Cut the fennel bulb in half lengthwise, and cut away the core, cutting deeply enough to release the layers of fennel. Cut the fennel into thin julienne slivers.

Cut the carrots diagonally into thin slices. Thinly slice the radishes.

Place the thinly sliced raw vegetables and the mozzarella strips on a serving platter. Drizzle with olive oil and lemon juice, and season with salt to taste. Toss quickly. Grind black pepper over the top and serve immediately.

POTATO SALAD WITH NASTURTIAMS

Insalata Fiorita

SERVES 4

potato salad of extraordinary flavor and color. Diced potatoes, lemony ricotta salata, and crisp onions are tossed with sweet herbs, olive oil, and red wine vinegar. The salad is served on leaves of tender bronze lettuces with orange, scarlet, and gold nasturium petals sprinkled over the top. It makes an exquisitely beautiful yet hearty salad.

1   *pound boiling potatoes, boiled, peeled, and diced*
¼   *pound fresh ricotta salata, cut into small dice*
1   *small fresh onion, peeled and sliced into rings, or 5 green
        onions, trimmed and sliced into rings*
Extra-virgin olive oil
Imported red wine vinegar
Salt and freshly ground black pepper to taste
10   *basil leaves, torn into small fragments or thinly julienned*
1   *teaspoon chopped fresh marjoram*
A few tender leaves of bronze-colored lettuces
*Handful nasturtium flowers of different colors, petals separated,
        plus a few extra blossoms for garnish*
Small black olives, such as Gaeta or Niçoise, for garnish

Combine the potatoes, ricotta salata, and onions in a bowl. Season with olive oil, vinegar, salt and pepper, and toss gently. Sprinkle with the herbs and toss again. Arrange the lettuce leaves on a platter and carefully transfer the potato salad to the serving dish. Scatter the flower petals over the salad. Garnish with nasturtium blossoms and black olives.

SALAD FROM THE VUCCIRIA MARKET

Insalata della Vucciria

SERVES 4

The Vucciria is the central marketplace of Palermo. In summer, when heat and humidity hang heavy in the air, the stoves in the house where my mother was raised were left unlighted. The young housekeeper would go to the Vucciria market to buy the ingredients for a salad: whole roasted onions dripping with caramel juices; freshly boiled green beans and potatoes; sweet roasted red and yellow peppers; tomatoes; and fragrant basil. The salad and a small platter of cheeses was dinner on nights that were too hot for cooking.

Although we may not have a market nearby where we can buy roasted onions and peppers and freshly boiled green beans, cooking everything first thing in the morning when the air is still cool allows us to enjoy the salad later on, when it's too hot to cook.

2 *onions*

3 *medium boiling potatoes*

1 *red pepper*

1 *yellow pepper*

½ *pound tender green beans*

1 *large crisp tomato*

8 *basil leaves*

5 *tablespoons extra-virgin olive oil*

¼ *cup imported red wine vinegar*

Salt and freshly ground black pepper to taste

Roast the onions in a preheated 450° oven until tender. Remove from the oven and let cool. Peel and cut into thick slices.

Meanwhile boil the potatoes until tender but firm. Drain and when cool enough to handle, peel and cut into medium dice. Roast the peppers over a gas burner or under the broiler. Peel and remove the seeds, cores, and white membranes. Cut the peppers into thick strips. Trim the ends of the green beans. Cook in salted boiling water until tender but crisp. Drain and if desired, run cold water over the green beans to set the color. Slice the tomato.

Combine the ingredients in a shallow serving bowl. Tear the basil leaves into fragments and sprinkle over the top. Drizzle with olive oil and red wine vinegar and season with salt and pepper to taste. Toss and correct the seasonings.

BREAD SALAD SIENNA STYLE

La Panzanella Senese

SERVES 4

anzanella is a peasant salad that has transcended its humble origins and become fashionable. In this version, bread is used as a base for a topping of tomato, celery, and red onion. Long ago, recipes called for dipping the bread in well water. If you have a well handy, by all means do so! Lacking that, use bottled spring water. Only the sturdiest bread works in this dish. Any other bread would become unappealingly mushy.

4 *thick slices country bread, several days old*
Imported red wine vinegar
Salt and freshly ground black pepper to taste
1 *pound tomatoes, ripe but firm, cored and sliced*
2 *tender celery stalks with leaves, thinly sliced, leaves chopped*
½ *very small red onion, thinly sliced*
Small handful basil leaves
Extra-virgin olive oil

Dip the slices of bread briefly in cool water, just long enough to barely moisten them. Press out the moisture into a clean dish towel. Place the bread slices on a platter and sprinkle with red wine vinegar and salt and pepper. Scatter the sliced vegetables over the top. Cut the basil leaves into strips and sprinkle over the top. Season the vegetables with salt and pepper. Drizzle enough olive oil over the top to moisten the salad. Chill lightly in the refrigerator before serving.

Serve 1 slice of the bread with vegetable topping per person. Place a small cruet of olive oil at the table for anyone who might like another drizzle on his or her salad.

SALAD FROM THE VEGETABLE GARDEN

Insalata dell'Orto

SERVES 4

A n unusual mix of garden vegetables—zucchini, fava beans, green beans, diced potato, and borlotti beans—goes into this salad arranged on a bed of tender lettuces. All the beautiful and subtle gradations of green look as fresh as a meadow. Potatoes and borlotti beans add heartiness and touches of contrasting color.

2 *medium boiling potatoes*
1½ *pounds fava beans, shelled and peeled*
4 *small zucchini, whole and untrimmed*
½ *pound green beans*
1 *cup cooked borlotti beans, drained*
1 *garlic clove, peeled and finely chopped*
6 *tablespoons extra-virgin olive oil*
3 *tablespoons red wine vinegar*
Salt and freshly ground black pepper to taste
2 *handfuls mixed tender lettuce leaves*

Boil the potatoes in water to cover by 2 inches until they are tender but firm. Drain and when the potatoes are cool enough to handle, peel and cut them into dice.

Cook the fava beans in a small amount of salted boiling water until tender, approximately 5 minutes. Drain and set aside.

Cook the zucchini in salted boiling water to cover until they are just tender. Rinse under cold water. Trim the ends and cut the zucchini into julienne.

Cook the green beans in salted boiling water until tender but crisp. Drain and if desired, refresh under cold running water to set the color. Drain on paper towels. Cut the beans into short lengths.

In a bowl combine the prepared vegetables, the borlotti beans, and the garlic. Drizzle with olive oil and red wine vinegar, and season with salt and pepper to taste. Toss gently. Let rest for a few minutes. Meanwhile arrange lettuce leaves on a platter. Mound the vegetables over the lettuce leaves and serve.

COOKED AND RAW SALAD

Insalata Cotta e Cruda

SERVES 4

A genre of salad that features both raw and cooked ingredients. This hearty version includes romaine lettuce, Belgian endive, and tomato and cooked artichoke hearts, fennel, diced potatoes, and carrots. A mustardy red wine vinegar dressing brings the flavors to life.

Fontina is a mountain cheese produced in the Val d'Aosta: it is cut into matchsticks and tossed into the salad mix. True Italian fontina is strong, sweet, and nutty, a perfect contrast to the vegetable flavors. If unavailable, substitute Gruyère rather than fontina produced anywhere else.

2   *artichokes, trimmed to the heart (see page 8 for directions)*
1   *small fennel bulb, stalks trimmed, quartered*
2   *carrots, peeled and trimmed*
1   *medium boiling potato*
½   *romaine lettuce*
1   *Belgian endive*
1   *large, firm tomato*
3   *ounces Italian fontina cheese, preferably from the Val
          d'Aosta, or Gruyère*
4   *tablespoons extra-virgin olive oil*
2   *tablespoons imported red wine vinegar*
1   *teaspoon good-quality mustard*
Salt and freshly ground black pepper to taste

Cook the artichoke hearts, fennel, and carrots in salted boiling water until tender but firm, about 8 minutes. Drain. When cool, cut the artichoke hearts and fennel into thin wedges. Cut the carrots on the diagonal into thin slices. Boil the potato in water to cover until tender but firm. Drain and when cool enough to handle, peel and cut into medium dice.

Cut the romaine into thin strips crosswise. Cut the Belgian endive into thin strips lengthwise. Core the tomato and cut into medium dice. Trim the rind from the fontina and cut cheese into small matchsticks.

Mound the lettuces in a shallow serving bowl and sprinkle with the tomato. Arrange the vegetables over the top and sprinkle with the fontina.

In a small bowl combine the olive oil, vinegar, mustard, and salt and pepper to taste. Beat lightly with a fork. Drizzle the dressing over the salad, bring to the table, and toss.

RADICCHIO, GRUYÈRE, AND GRILLED BREAD SALAD

Insalata di Radicchio, Groviera, e Bruschetta

SERVES 4

The colors and aromas—the deep magenta leaves of radicchio, the rich flavor of walnuts, and the golden hue and pungent fragrance of ripe cheese—make this a winter dish. The ingredients are tossed in a mustard-spiked dressing on top of large, thin slices of garlicky grilled bread, and each person is served a piece of bread with its share of salad.

4 *thin slices country bread, cut from a large, round loaf*
1 *clove garlic, peeled and cut in half crosswise*
2 *medium heads radicchio, cored and cut into thin strips*
3 *ounces Gruyère cheese, cut into paper-thin shavings*
2 *tablespoons coarsely chopped walnuts*
4 *tablespoons extra-virgin olive oil*
3 *tablespoons imported red wine vinegar*
1 *teaspoon fine-quality mustard*
Salt and freshly ground black pepper to taste

Lightly grill or toast the bread and rub one side of each slice with the cut clove of garlic.

Line a serving dish with the grilled bread and distribute the radicchio over the bread slices. Top with the Gruyère cheese shavings and sprinkle with chopped walnuts.

In a small bowl combine the olive oil, vinegar, mustard, and salt and pepper to taste. Beat with a fork until well blended. *(continued)*

Pour the dressing over the salad and carefully toss the salad on top of the bread, using it as a base. Correct the seasonings. Each person is served a piece of grilled bread topped with salad.

RUSTIC BREAD AND MUSHROOM SALAD

Insalata di Pane e Funghi

SERVES 4

This simple bread salad, true to the traditions of country cooking, features strong, sturdy bread, fresh mushrooms, and slivers of assertive Pecorino Romano cheese.

Warm-looking in shades of brown and gold, it has a special rustic appeal.

4 *slices country bread*
1 *garlic clove, peeled and cut in half*
4 *tablespoons extra-virgin olive oil, plus extra for*
     drizzling on bread
½ *pound button mushrooms*
2 *ounces shiitake mushrooms*
2 *ounces imported Pecorino Romano cheese*
Juice of ½ lemon
Salt and freshly ground black pepper to taste
1 *tablespoon chopped Italian parsley*

Toast the bread under the broiler until light golden brown. Rub the bread with the cut sides of the garlic clove. Cut the bread into cubes. Place the bread in a shallow serving platter and drizzle with olive oil.

Wipe the mushrooms clean with damp paper towels. Trim the stems. Thinly slice the mushrooms and place in a bowl. Slice the Pecorino Romano cheese into paper-thin shavings and add to the bowl. Season the mushrooms and cheese with 4 tablespoons of olive oil, lemon juice, salt and pepper to taste, and chopped parsley. Toss gently until the mushrooms soften slightly. Transfer the mushrooms to the platter and toss with the bread. Serve immediately.

WARM CANNELLINI BEAN AND HERB SALAD

Insalata Tiepida di Fagioli ed Erbe

SERVES 4

*I*n this white bean salad, herbs are warmed in extra-virgin olive oil until they turn a glowing green. Then the beans are added and gently tossed in the flavorful oil, infusing them with the fragrance of an herb garden in the hot sun. Flecked with herbs, lustrous with golden-green olive oil, and dotted with tangy oil-cured black olives, white beans are transformed into an exquisite dish.

3 *cups cooked cannellini or other white beans, drained*

½ *cup extra-virgin olive oil*

2 *garlic cloves, peeled and finely chopped*

3 *tablespoons chopped Italian parsley*

Handful basil leaves, chopped

1 *teaspoon finely chopped rosemary leaves*

4 *large sage leaves, finely chopped*

Salt and freshly ground black pepper to taste

Juice of 1 lemon

½ *cup oil-cured black olives*

Spread the drained beans on a clean dish towel to absorb excess moisture. Discard any beans that are smashed.

In a large sauté pan combine the olive oil, garlic, and herbs. Warm over very low heat for about 4 minutes, or until the garlic and herbs release their aroma. Add the beans, salt and pepper to taste, and toss very gently. Cook over low heat until the beans are warm and have absorbed the flavors of the olive oil, about 5 minutes. Off the heat add the lemon juice and toss very gently.

Place the salad on a serving platter and surround with black olives. Serve immediately.

ROMAN SUMMER BORLOTTI BEAN SALAD

Insalata di Fagioli Borlotti alla Romana

SERVES 4

Borlotti beans have a slightly chalky texture that I find irresistible, especially when combined with crisp raw yellow peppers and celery. This simple salad is a real delight and one that I serve often.

2 *cups cooked borlotti beans, drained*
2 *leafy celery stalks from the heart*
1 *ripe yellow pepper*
½ *small onion*
Extra-virgin olive oil
Red wine vinegar
Salt and freshly ground black pepper to taste
10 *basil leaves*

Place the beans in a colander and rinse under cool running water. Drain the beans on a clean dish towel. Trim the celery stalks and reserve the leaves. Cut the celery into thin slivers and coarsely chop the leaves. Cut the yellow pepper in half lengthwise. Remove the core, seeds, and white membranes. Cut the pepper into small julienne strips. Thinly slice the onion.

Place the prepared ingredients on a serving platter. Drizzle with olive oil and vinegar and season with salt and pepper to taste. Let rest for at least 15 minutes or for several hours. Correct the seasonings and sprinkle with basil leaves, torn into fragments.

COUNTRY SALAD

Insalata alla Campagnola

SERVES 4

his satisfying salad is like a tableau of Italian country life. One can imagine the ingredients casually arranged on a rough-hewn kitchen table waiting to be gathered into a salad: freshly cooked garbanzo and borlotti beans in earthenware dishes; tender green beans, luscious tomatoes, and small bouquets of parsley and basil all just picked from the garden; and potatoes from the cellar, still caked with fresh soil. Outside, the sky blazes a brilliant blue and the fields are alive with vines and orchards.

3 *medium boiling potatoes*
½ *pound tender green beans*
½ *small onion*
3 *crisp medium tomatoes*
1 *cup cooked borlotti beans, drained*
1 *cup cooked chick peas, drained*
3 *tablespoons chopped Italian parsley leaves*
2 *tablespoons chopped basil leaves*
6 *tablespoons extra-virgin olive oil*
3 *tablespoons imported red wine vinegar*
Salt and freshly ground black pepper to taste

Boil the potatoes in water to cover by 2 inches until tender but firm. Drain and when cool enough to handle, peel them. Cut into dice. Plunge the green beans into salted boiling water and cook until tender but crisp. Drain and run cold water over them to stop the cooking. This last step is optional, but it sets the color. Finely chop the onion. Core the tomatoes and cut into chunks.

Place the prepared ingredients on a large platter. Add the borlotti beans, chick peas, and herbs. Drizzle with the olive oil and vinegar, and season with salt and pepper to taste. Toss gently. Let rest for about 5 minutes before serving.

WHITE BEAN AND RADICCHIO SALAD

Insalata di Fagioli e Radicchio

SERVES 4

*T*his beautiful winter salad has at its center a mound of creamy white beans encircled by a star-burst pattern of slivered radicchio. Topped with thin slices of Parmesan cheese and black olives, the salad is tossed in a piquant caper dressing, warmed slightly to take the edge off the vinegar as well as to encourage the beans to absorb the dressing.

Serve this dish as an antipasto, a first course, or as a main dish for lunch.

2 *cups cooked white beans, drained*
1 *medium head radicchio*
2 *ounces imported Parmesan cheese, cut into paper-thin shavings*
10 *oil-cured black olives, pitted and cut in half*
1 *tablespoon coarsely chopped Italian parsley*
Freshly ground black pepper to taste
4 *tablespoons extra-virgin olive oil*
1 *garlic clove, peeled and cut into thin slivers*
4 *tablespoons imported red wine vinegar*
1 *tablespoon capers*
Salt to taste

Place the drained white beans on a clean dish towel to absorb the excess liquid.

Core the radicchio and cut into thin strips. Arrange the strips on a round serving dish. Place the beans in a mound in the center of the dish. Distribute the Parmesan cheese shavings and the black olives over the top of the salad, and sprinkle with the chopped Italian parsley and freshly ground black pepper to taste.

In a small sauté pan, combine the olive oil and the garlic, and cook over low heat until the garlic is golden. Turn off the heat and add the vinegar, capers, and salt to taste. Stir and let rest until the dressing is tepid.

Pour the dressing over the salad and bring the dish to the table. Toss the salad at the table and serve immediately.

SALAD OF GIANT WHITE BEANS

Insalata di Fagioli Spagna Bianchetti

SERVES 2 TO 4

*I*n Italy good food sometimes crops up in the most unlikely places. One day while I was waiting for a very delayed flight from Catania to Rome, a contrite Alitalia airlines treated all the stranded passengers to lunch in the airport restaurant. I loved this salad made with big, creamy white beans, redolent of olive oil and vinegar and piquant seasonings. This is my version of it.

2 *cups cooked Spagna Bianchetti or butter beans*
1 *small red pepper*
1 *small yellow pepper*
6 *green olives, cured in brine, drained*
6 *black olives, cured in brine, drained*
2 *tablespoons capers*
1 *large garlic clove, peeled, lightly crushed, impaled on a*
    toothpick
2 *teaspoons dried Mediterranean oregano*
Salt and freshly ground black pepper to taste
3 *tablespoons extra-virgin olive oil*
3 *tablespoons imported red wine vinegar*

Drain the beans of all liquid and place on paper towels to absorb excess moisture. Roast the peppers. Remove the blackened peel. Cut in half lengthwise and remove the cores, seeds, and white membranes. Cut the peppers into 1-inch-long strips. Pit the olives and cut them in halves or quarters.

Combine the beans, peppers, and olives on a serving platter along with the capers and the crushed garlic clove. Sprinkle with oregano and season with salt and pepper to taste. Drizzle with the olive oil and red wine vinegar. Toss very gently so as not to crush the beans. Let the salad marinate for at least ½ hour before serving. Toss occasionally while it marinates. Remove the garlic clove and correct the seasonings before serving.

SUMMER HOLIDAY RICE SALAD

Insalata di Riso Ferragosto

SERVES 4

When the sun beats down and something bright and refreshing to eat is needed, this is the rice salad to make. It features Arborio rice, colorful, crisp vegetables, and aromatic herbs, with black olives and capers supplying that necessary piquant touch. A high proportion of vegetables to rice makes this dish very light and healthful.

1 *cup Arborio rice (if Arborio is unavailable, substitute long-grain rice)*
1 *large crisp tomato, cored and diced*
1 *medium yellow pepper, seeded, white membranes removed, and diced*
½ *regular cucumber, or ¼ hothouse cucumber, peeled, seeded, and diced*
½ *cup finely diced mozzarella*
2 *tablespoons capers, rinsed*
12 *Kalamata olives, pitted and quartered*
10 *fresh basil leaves, chopped*
10 *fresh mint leaves, chopped*
5 *tablespoons extra-virgin olive oil*
Salt and freshly ground black pepper to taste
½ *juicy lemon, seeded, about 4 tablespoons lemon juice*

Cook the rice in a generous amount of salted boiling water until al dente. Drain in a colander and run cold water over the rice to stop the cooking. Let the rice drain thoroughly.

When the rice is dry, place it in a shallow serving bowl and add the prepared vegetables, mozzarella, capers, olives, and herbs. Drizzle the olive oil over the salad, and season with salt and freshly ground black pepper to taste. Toss well. Add the lemon juice and toss again. Correct the seasonings. Let the salad rest for at least 15 minutes before serving to let the flavors come together.

Grilled Bread and Sandwiches

*I*talians are bread eaters, so it is no wonder that many dishes have been created with bread as the focus. The traditional breads of Italy are crusty, with a firm crumb and strong flavor. Each region has its special breads, and the range of shapes and sizes is as varied and fascinating as pasta's many permutations. In Italy, a meal without bread is inconceivable, incomplete. My father, born and raised in Sicily, could not eat unless bread was on the table.

To successfully reproduce Italian-style dishes calling for bread, the bread must be honest, made with pure ingredients, and touched by the hand of the baker. It must be the kind of bread that satisfies our deepest, most primitive hungers. Supermarket loaves of French and Italian bread are sad impostors. They fall short of the mark, both nutritionally and spiritually. One of the great changes taking place in American food today is the emergence of small bakeries dedicated to preserving the old-world techniques of bread baking. The response has been tremendous, and people flock to the best of these bakeries with an almost religious zeal—to buy the golden-brown loaves, smell the sharp, warm scent of yeast in the air, and be embraced by the warmth of the ovens. The following chapter features bread used in two very basic ways—grilled and drizzled with olive oil or covered with other toppings, called bruschetta, and in panini, Italian sandwiches.

A bruschetta is a thick slice of country bread, grilled, and rubbed with a clove of cut garlic. Brushcetta is the original garlic bread. Perfect and complete in and of itself, it can also serve as the base for an endless number of toppings, everything from traditional strips of ripe, red tomato to more novel ingredients such as avocado.

Bruschette can begin a meal, be part of a buffet, or even serve as the main dish of a very simple, rustic dinner.

Panini are sandwiches Italian style. They range from the elegant to hearty, from thinly sliced bread filled with creamy, diced vegetables to a crusty roll layered with tomatoes and mozzarella. In Italy, sandwiches are traditionally served in *caffès*, and are most often eaten standing at a counter. They are considered more of a snack, a way to temper one's appetite between meals. In America, these sandwiches can assume the role they are used to playing—served as a casual, satisfying lunch, but with the surprise of a whole new range of ingredients to tuck between the slices of bread.

Grilled Bread

SIMPLE BRUSCHETTA WITH OREGANO

Bruschetta Semplice all 'Origano

SERVES 4

This is the basic recipe for bruschetta with a slight twist—a light sprinkling of oregano is added at the final moment, its pungent aroma released by contact with the hot bread. For all other recipes calling for bruschette, follow the directions below but omit the oregano.

Traditionally bruschette are grilled over a the heat of fragrant coals, but cooking the bread on a stovetop grill or even toasting it yields excellent results.

4 *slices thick country bread*
1 *large garlic clove, peeled and cut in half*
Extra-virgin olive oil
Dried Mediterranean oregano
Salt and freshly ground pepper

Grill or lightly toast the bread. Rub with the cut side of the garlic clove and drizzle generously with olive oil. Sprinkle with oregano. Season lightly with salt and a few grindings of pepper. Serve immediately.

CLASSIC BRUSCHETTA WITH ROASTED TOMATOES

Bruschetta Classica con Pomodori Arrostiti

SERVES 4

topping for bruschetta featuring strips of roasted tomatoes, anchovy, and fragrant basil. If possible, roast the tomatoes and grill the bread over aromatic charcoal to add a smoky perfume to the finished dish. Serve the bruschetta as the first course of a seafood dinner grilled out of doors.

2　*ripe tomatoes*
4　*thick slices country bread*
2　*garlic cloves, peeled and cut in half*
Extra-virgin olive oil
Salt to taste
4　*anchovy fillets, coarsely chopped*
4　*large basil leaves*

Very lightly roast the tomatoes over a gas burner or an outdoor grill until a few char marks appear. Peel and core the tomatoes. Cut them in half and gently remove the seeds. Cut the tomato halves into strips.

Grill or lightly toast the bread. Rub with the cut side of the garlic cloves and drizzle with olive oil.

Distribute the tomato strips over each slice of bread and salt very lightly. Sprinkle with the anchovies and the basil leaves, torn into fragments. Drizzle with olive oil.

BRUSCHETTA WITH BLACK OLIVE PESTO AND TOMATOES

*Bruschetta con Pesto
di Olive e Pomodoro*

SERVES 6

lices of grilled bread are served along with bowls of Black Olive Pesto and diced tomatoes. Each person spreads a small amount of the olive paste on the bread, then sprinkles tomato over it.

The Pesto can be made days, even weeks, in advance, and the diced tomatoes prepared 1 to 2 hours beforehand. Guests rave about this combination of intense olive paste and bright fresh tomato, and they enjoy assembling the bruschette themselves.

For a sophisticated version to serve with white wine before a meal, spread the Pesto on Crostini (see page 366) and top with a small sprinkling of tomato.

Make your own Black Olive Pesto or buy a high-quality imported brand.

1   *recipe Black Olive Pesto (see page 45)*
2   *medium tomatoes, cut into small dice*
8   *basil leaves, coarsely chopped*
Salt to taste
6   *thick slices country bread*
2   *large garlic cloves, peeled and cut in half*
Extra-virgin olive oil

Prepare the Black Olive Pesto and transfer it to a small ceramic bowl.

Place the tomatoes and basil in a ceramic bowl. Season with salt to taste. Mix and set side.

Grill or lightly toast the bread. Rub the bread slices with the cut side of the garlic cloves, drizzle with olive oil, and place on a platter.

To serve, place the bruschette and bowls of the olive paste and chopped tomatoes on the table. Each person spreads a thin layer of olive paste on the bruschetta and sprinkles tomatoes over the top.

BRUSCHETTA WITH AVOCADO AND GREEN ONIONS

Bruschetta con l'Avocado

SERVES 2

*I*taly and California merge seamlessly in a bruschetta topped with a rough spread of avocado. This is the grown-up version of my favorite after-school snack of mashed avocado and green onion on crackers.

Select ripe avocados with firm flesh that yields to gentle pressure.

1   *ripe avocado*
Lemon juice to taste
Salt to taste
2   *thick slices country bread*
1   *garlic clove, peeled and cut in half*
Extra-virgin olive oil
2   *green onions, tops trimmed, thinly sliced*

Peel the avocado. Place it in a bowl and mash it coarsely with a fork, adding lemon juice and salt to taste.

Grill or lightly toast the bread. Rub with the cut side of the garlic clove and drizzle with olive oil.

Mound the avocado mixture on top of the bread slices and sprinkle with green onions. Drizzle a few drops of olive oil over the top.

GRILLED BREAD WITH RAW MUSHROOM SALAD

Bruschetta con Funghi all'Insalata

SERVES 4 TO 6

A salad of thinly sliced raw mushrooms dressed with extra-virgin olive oil, lemon juice, and fresh oregano is served on warm, garlic-rubbed grilled bread. The contrast of the slightly crisp, cool mushrooms with the garlic-infused toasty bread is unusual and refreshing. This preparation brings out the best in market mushrooms, emphasizing their beguiling texture and subtle flavor.

This light and simple dish can be served as a first course during the hot summer months. The mushroom mixture is delicious on its own served as a small salad.

½ *pound firm, white mushrooms*
4 *tablespoons extra-virgin olive oil, plus extra for drizzling*
Juice of ½ lemon
1 *tablespoon chopped fresh oregano leaves*
Salt and freshly ground black pepper to taste
4–6 *thick slices country bread*
2 *garlic cloves, peeled and cut in half*

Wipe the mushrooms clean, using damp paper towels. Trim the stem ends. Slice the mushrooms thinly and place in a bowl. Add the olive oil, lemon juice, oregano, and salt and pepper to taste. Toss for 2 to 3 minutes, or until the mushrooms soften slightly but have not released their juices.

Grill or lightly toast the bread. Rub with the cut side of the garlic cloves and drizzle with extra-virgin olive oil.

Spoon the mushroom salad over the bread slices and lightly drizzle with extra-virgin olive oil.

BRUSCHETTA WITH MATCHSTICK PEPPER STRIPS

Bruschetta con Peperoni a Fiammiferi

SERVES 6

An extraordinarily pretty bruschetta. Thin strips of multicolored peppers and sliced onion are cooked in olive oil until the juices of the peppers turn rich and honeyed. Flavored with capers, anchovies, and basil, this makes a savory topping for grilled garlic-rubbed bread. The peppers can be cooked several hours or even a day in advance and then gently reheated before being spooned onto the bread.

1 *each red, yellow, and green pepper*
6 *tablespoons extra-virgin olive oil, plus extra for drizzling*
1 *small onion, thinly sliced*
Salt and freshly ground black pepper to taste
2 *tablespoons capers*
6 *thick slices country bread*
2 *large garlic cloves, peeled and cut in half*
3 *anchovies, coarsely chopped*
6 *fresh basil leaves*

Cut the peppers in half lengthwise. Remove the cores, seeds, and white membranes. Cut the peppers into thin strips.

Place the olive oil in a medium sauté pan. Add the peppers, onion, and salt and pepper to taste. Cook over low heat for 15 minutes, or until the peppers and onions are tender. Off the heat add the capers and stir.

Grill or lightly toast the bread. Rub with the cut side of the garlic cloves and drizzle with olive oil.

Spoon the peppers and the juices in the pan over the bruschette and sprinkle with the anchovies and the basil, torn into small fragments.

GRILLED BREAD WITH ROSEMARY-SCENTED WHITE BEAN PUREE

Bruschetta ai Cannellini con Rosmarino

SERVES 4

Tuscan dish of grilled bread topped with a coarse puree of white beans scented with rosemary. Whenever I prepare this dish, I remember the masses of rosemary, dark and bristling, growing wild in the Tuscan countryside, and the strong, resinous perfume that filled the air.

In summer garnish the bruschetta with finely diced tomato.

3 *tablespoons extra-virgin olive oil, plus additional*
     for drizzling
3 *garlic cloves, peeled and finely chopped*
2 *sprigs rosemary, leaves finely chopped*
2 *cups cannellini beans, cooking liquid reserved*
Salt and freshly ground black pepper to taste
4 *thick slices country bread*
2 *garlic cloves, peeled and cut in half*
1 *small tomato, finely diced, optional*

Combine the olive oil, garlic, and rosemary in a medium sauté pan and cook over very low heat for 5 minutes. The garlic should color very slightly. Add the beans, salt and pepper to taste, and stir. Cook for approximately 10 minutes, adding some of the bean liquid if the mixture begins to dry out. Mash the beans with a fork to create a rough puree.

Grill or lightly toast the bread. Rub with the cut side of the garlic cloves and drizzle lightly with olive oil.

To serve, spread the bean puree on the grilled bread and top with a drizzle of extra-virgin olive oil. Sprinkle with diced tomato, if desired.

RED ONION AND
PARMESAN CHEESE BRUSCHETTA

Bruschetta con Cipolla Rossa e Parmigiano

SERVES 4

autéed red onion and tangy slivers of Parmesan cheese top this simple bruschetta. The bruschette are placed under a hot broiler until the cheese just begins to soften, and they are served hot.

Freshly pulled red onions would be particularly sweet and succulent in this dish. If you are not a gardener, a farmers' market is your best resource; special onion varieties, such as torpedo onions, are often available.

1 *small red onion*
3 *tablespoons extra-virgin olive oil*
Salt and freshly ground black pepper to taste
1 *tablespoon chopped chives*
4 *thick slices good-quality bread*
2 *garlic cloves, peeled and cut in half*
Extra-virgin olive oil
2 *ounces imported Parmesan cheese, cut into paper-thin slices*

Peel the onion and slice it very thinly. Place the olive oil in a medium sauté pan and turn the heat to medium-low. Add the onion and sauté until it is very tender. Add the salt and pepper to taste and stir in the chives.

Grill or lightly toast the bread. Rub with the cut side of the garlic cloves and drizzle with olive oil.

Distribute the onion mixture on top of each piece of bread. Sprinkle with the slivers of Parmesan cheese. Arrange the bruschette on a baking sheet. Place under the broiler until the cheese softens. Serve immediately.

CALABRIAN BRUSCHETTA

Bruschetta Calabrese

SERVES 6

A fragrant tangle of melted cheese is the topping for creamy slices of eggplant and tart-sweet tomato. A slice of bruschetta forms the sturdy base for this dish. Serve it for a casual, tasty lunch along with a fresh, crisp salad. If caciocavallo cheese is unavailable, a mild imported provolone would be equally delicious.

4 *small Japanese eggplants*
Extra-virgin olive oil
3 *ounces caciocavallo cheese*
6 *thick slices country bread*
2 *garlic cloves, peeled and cut in half*
3 *Roma tomatoes, cored and thinly sliced*
Extra-virgin olive oil

Trim the eggplants and slice them ¼ inch thick. Arrange the eggplant slices on a lightly oiled baking sheet and brush them with olive oil. Bake the eggplant slices in a preheated 375° oven for 10 minutes. Turn the slices over, brush with oil, and cook for another 10 minutes. Remove from the oven and set aside.

Using the large side of a four-sided grater, grate the cheese into long, thin strips.

Grill or lightly toast the bread. Rub with the cut side of the garlic cloves and drizzle with olive oil.

Place a few slices of eggplant on each bruschetta, top with some sliced tomato, and sprinkle a little shredded cheese over the top.

Place the bruschette under a preheated broiler and broil until the cheese melts. Serve immediately.

BRUSCHETTA WITH SAUTÉED ESCAROLE

Bruschetta alla Scarola

MAKES 6 BRUSCHETTE

With its intriguing flavor notes, sweet, salty, resinous, and lightly bitter, this escarole topping of toasted pine nuts, plump raisins, and pungent black olives is amazingly savory served on top of grilled bread. On its own the escarole topping makes a delightful vegetable side dish.

2 *tablespoons raisins*
2 *tablespoons pine nuts*
⅓ *cup Kalamata olives*
1 *medium head escarole*
4 *tablespoons extra-virgin olive oil*
3 *garlic cloves, peeled and finely chopped*
Salt to taste
6 *thick slices country bread*
3 *garlic cloves, peeled and cut in half*
Extra-virgin olive oil

Place the raisins in a small bowl and cover with warm water for about 20 minutes, or until they plump up. Drain. In a small sauté pan, toast the pine nuts by stirring them frequently over medium-low heat. As soon as the pine nuts are light brown, transfer them to a small dish. Pit the olives and cut them into quarters.

Remove any wilted or bruised leaves from the escarole. Wash well under cold running water. Drain. Cut the escarole into strips. There will be some water clinging to the escarole strips.

Place the olive oil, garlic, and cut escarole into a large sauté pan. Season with salt to taste. Sauté over medium-low heat until the escarole is tender, about 10 to 12 minutes. A few minutes before the escarole is ready, add the raisins, pine nuts, and black olives, and toss.

Grill or lightly toast the bread. Rub with the cut side of the garlic cloves and drizzle with olive oil.

Distribute the escarole over the grilled bread and serve immediately.

GRILLED BREAD WITH SAUTÉED MUSHROOMS AND HERBS

Bruschetta ai Funghi

SERVES 4 TO 6

ﾉ, the mushrooms used in this dish should be wild. Most
mushrooms lack the intense woodsy flavor and aroma of wild
ﾉoms.

Since fresh wild mushrooms are not widely available, the recipe
calls for a mixture of cultivated mushrooms and dried porcini mushrooms,
which impart a concentrated forest essence to the dish. Strong herbs—
thyme and rosemary—and abundant garlic reinforce the rich flavors.

This dish can stand on its own as the center of a simple, cool-
weather supper. Serve with Salad of Field Greens (see page 95) and a
good red wine.

2 *ounces dried porcini mushrooms*
1 *pound fresh mushrooms*
½ *cup extra-virgin olive oil, plus additional for drizzling*
4 *garlic cloves, peeled and minced*
6 *sprigs thyme, leaves chopped*
1 *sprig rosemary, leaves finely chopped*
4–6 *thick slices country bread*
2 *garlic cloves, peeled and cut in half*
Salt and freshly ground black pepper to taste

Place the porcini mushrooms in a small bowl. Add enough hot
water to cover and soak for 20 minutes or until the porcini soften. Lift
out of the soaking liquid and rinse very thoroughly under cold running
water, checking carefully for any remaining sand or grit. Coarsely chop
the porcini. Trim a bit off the stem ends of the fresh mushrooms. Wipe
them clean with damp paper towels. Slice the fresh mushrooms.

Place the olive oil in a large sauté pan. Raise the heat to medium
and add the sliced fresh mushrooms, chopped porcini, garlic, thyme,
and rosemary. Sauté over a lively heat until the mushrooms are lightly
crusty on the surface and tender inside. Season the mushrooms with salt
and pepper to taste and remove from the heat.   *(continued)*

Grill or lightly toast the bread. Rub with the cut side of the garlic cloves and drizzle with extra-virgin olive oil.

Arrange the bread on a serving platter and top with the mushrooms and any juices that have formed. If desired, drizzle with additional extra-virgin olive oil.

BRUSCHETTA WITH WARM RICOTTA AND OREGANO

Bruschetta con Ricotta Calda all'Origano

SERVES 4

Ricotta—white, fresh, and sweet-tasting—is at its absolute best when gently warmed. Here it is piled on bruschette and sprinkled with dried oregano, which imparts its sharp, evocative perfume.

Serve this with oil-cured black olives and red wine for a first course, as a light lunch, or as part of a simple, country-style brunch.

½ *pound fresh ricotta*
4 *thick slices country bread*
1 *large garlic clove, peeled and cut in half*
Extra-virgin olive oil
Salt and freshly ground black pepper to taste
Dried Mediterranean oregano
Oil-cured black olives

Place the ricotta in a sauté pan and gently warm it over low heat.

Grill or lightly toast the bread. Rub it with the cut side of the garlic clove and drizzle with olive oil.

Spoon the ricotta over the bread and season it with salt and pepper to taste. Sprinkle with oregano and lightly drizzle with more olive oil.

Serve with black olives.

BRUSCHETTA WITH ARTICHOKES

Bruschetta al Pesto di Carciofi

SERVES 4

A rtichoke hearts braised with herbs and olive oil are transformed into a rich, coarse spread. Mixed with piquant capers, olives, and bright little squares of tomato, this makes a savory topping for grilled bread. A spoonful of the pesto is delicious on grilled fish, and it is amazingly good tossed with pasta.

4 *medium artichokes, trimmed as directed on page 8,*
    leaves completely cut away
1 *lemon, cut in half*
Water
3 *tablespoons extra-virgin olive oil*
2 *garlic cloves, peeled and finely chopped*
3 *tablespoons chopped Italian parsley leaves*
Salt to taste
2 *tablespoons capers*
10 *black oil-cured olives, pitted and coarsely chopped*
1 *small tomato, cut into small dice*
4 *thick slices country bread*
2 *garlic cloves, peeled and cut in half*
Extra-virgin olive oil

Cut the artichokes into quarters and keep in acidulated water until ready to use.

In a medium sauté pan, add the olive oil, garlic, parsley, salt to taste, and the artichokes. Add water to measure ½ inch up the side of the pan. Cover and cook artichokes over low heat until they are tender. Add a few tablespoons of water at a time if the artichokes appear to be sticking to the pan. Mash the ingredients with a fork until a coarse puree forms. Stir in the capers, black olives, and tomato.

Grill or lightly toast the bread. Rub with the cut side of the garlic cloves and drizzle with olive oil.

Top each bruschetta with some of the artichoke mixture.

BLACK TRUFFLE BRUSCHETTA

Bruschetta ai Tartufi Neri

SERVES 4

ruffles are known for their bosky, slightly decadent aroma, which can be penetrating to the point of overpowering. The haunting perfume remains in your memory—fleeting and enigmatic.

Black truffles are brown on the exterior and resemble nothing so much as a humble clod of dried earth. When the truffle is cut into, its color is dark, almost black, and the texture is fine, compact, and slightly moist.

It is said that truffles should be eaten in their place of origin to experience them fully. Umbria—mountainous and thickly wooded, with abundant streams and high-perched fortress towns disappearing into the winter mists—is indeed the perfect setting for savoring bruschetta topped with warm black truffles, anchovy, and garlic. The next best thing is to prepare this dish at home when fresh black truffles appear in specialty markets.

For an elegant presentation, serve the black truffle topping on Crostini (see page 366).

1–2 *ounces black truffles*
4 *tablespoons extra-virgin olive oil, plus additional*
   for drizzling
1 *garlic clove, peeled and finely chopped*
1 *anchovy, coarsely chopped*
Salt to taste
4 *thick slices country bread*
2 *garlic cloves, peeled and cut in half*

Clean the outside of the truffles well, using a small brush. Run the truffles briefly under cold water and wipe dry. Grate the truffles. I recommend using a one-sided, hand-held grater, but any grater with very small holes will work.

Place the olive oil and garlic in a small sauté pan and warm over low heat for 5 minutes. Add the anchovy and stir until it melts. Add the grated truffles and salt to taste. Stir. Keep warm over very low heat.

Grill or lightly toast the bread. Rub with the cut side of the garlic cloves and drizzle with olive oil.

Spread some of the truffle mixture on each slice of bruschetta and serve.

Sandwiches

ARTICHOKE AND BLACK OLIVE PESTO SANDWICH

Panino con Carciofi e Pesto di Olive

MAKES 4 SANDWICHES

A rich, tasty sandwich with glistening black olive paste and baby artichokes marinated in extra-virgin olive oil and lemon juice.

If you cannot find fresh baby artichokes, frozen ones make a satisfactory substitute. Canned or store-bought marinated artichoke hearts are best avoided.

10 *baby artichokes*
1 *lemon cut in half*
3 *tablespoons extra-virgin olive oil*
2 *garlic cloves, peeled and crushed*
Salt and freshly ground black pepper to taste
4 *round rolls, about 4 inches in diameter*
4 *tablespoons Black Olive Pesto (see page 45)*

Trim the artichokes of tough leaves, using ½ the lemon to rub the cut portions. Cook in salted boiling water until the hearts are tender but firm. Drain well. Cut the artichokes in quarters and place in a bowl. Add the olive oil, the juice from the remaining lemon half, and the garlic cloves. Season with salt and black pepper to taste. Mix well and let marinate for at least 1 hour.

Cut the rolls in half horizontally. Spread the bottom half of each roll with 1 tablespoon of Black Olive Pesto. Lift the artichokes out of the marinade and arrange them on top of the black olive paste. Place the other half of the bread over the top.

SANDWICH WITH THIN HERB FRITTATAS

Panino di Frittatine

MAKES 2 SANDWICHES

*I*n this recipe, delicate frittatas, as thin as crepes, are stacked in a sandwich. The frittatas extend beyond the edges of the bread, creating a pretty ruffled yellow border flecked with the green of marjoram, basil, and onion. This very fresh-looking sandwich is excellent to take on a picnic along with a few crisp, juicy radishes.

3   *eggs*

1   *teaspoon chopped marjoram leaves*

1   *tablespoon chopped basil leaves, plus 4 large*
      whole basil leaves

1   *green onion, trimmed of all but 3 inches of green top,*
      finely chopped

2   *tablespoons freshly grated imported Parmesan cheese*

2   *teaspoons milk*

Salt and freshly ground black pepper to taste

2   *teaspoons extra-virgin olive oil*

2   *rolls, about 4 inches in diameter*

Radishes with leafy green tops for garnish

Break the eggs into a bowl and lightly beat them with a fork. Add the chopped marjoram, chopped basil, green onion, grated Parmesan cheese, milk, and salt and pepper to taste. Lightly beat to combine the ingredients.

Heat the olive oil in a small, nonstick skillet, ideally measuring about 7½ inches. When the oil is hot, add a ladleful of the egg mixture and tilt the pan in all directions to spread the egg mixture. Turn the heat to low. When the top of the frittata is just set, carefully flip it over and cook the other side. Transfer the frittata to a plate. Continue to make the frittatas, stacking them on the plate. There should be enough egg mixture to make 6 thin frittatas.

Cut the rolls in half horizontally. Stack 3 frittatas in each roll. Arrange 2 basil leaves on top of each sandwich. Place the other half of the bread over the top. Serve with radishes as a garnish.

MOZZARELLA, TOMATO, AND ARUGULA SANDWICH

Panino con Mozzarella, Pomodoro, e Rucola

MAKES 1 SANDWICH

A bright sandwich with ribbons of pure white mozzarella, red tomato, and leafy green arugula. For extra crunch and color, add paper-thin slices of red onion, carrot, and cucumber.

1 *round roll, about 4 inches in diameter*
2 *teaspoons extra-virgin olive oil, plus extra for drizzling*
3 *ounces fresh mozzarella, sliced a little less than ½ inch thick*
1 *slice of tomato, preferably as large as the diameter of the bread*
Salt and freshly ground black pepper to taste
3–4 *arugula leaves, stems trimmed*

Cut the roll in half horizontally. Drizzle the olive oil on the bottom half of the bread. Layer the mozzarella and tomato on top and season with salt and pepper to taste. Arrange the arugula leaves over the tomato and drizzle with a few more drops of olive oil. Top with the other half of the bread.

HERBED GOAT CHEESE SANDWICH

Panino con Caprini e Erbe

MAKES 4 SANDWICHES

*T*art and lemony goat cheese mixed with chopped basil and green onions makes a delicious spread for a sandwich. Lined with a big ruffled leaf of butter lettuce, the sandwich is white and green and inviting. You can use the cheese and herb mixture right away for a fresh-tasting spread where the flavors remain distinct. Or you can make it even a day or two in advance, so the flavors have a chance to develop. You can certainly add other herbs—snipped chives, a touch of marjoram, Italian parsley, even some peppery arugula or watercress—but I find the simple pairing of sweet basil with the garden-fresh bite of green onions to be just right with the goat cheese.

Serve with Perfumed Black Olives (see page 41).

5½ *ounces fresh goat cheese, unseasoned*
1 *small, fresh garlic clove, peeled and finely chopped*
2 *green onions, trimmed of all but 3 inches of green top,*
      finely chopped
3 *tablespoons coarsely chopped basil leaves*
3 *tablespoons extra-virgin olive oil*
Salt and freshly ground black pepper to taste
4 *round rolls, about 4 inches in diameter*
4 *big, green and tender butter lettuce leaves*

Place the goat cheese in a bowl and add the garlic, green onions, basil, olive oil, and salt and pepper to taste. Mash together with a fork until well combined. If time permits, let the mixture rest for 1 hour, refrigerated, before serving, to let the flavors develop. Bring to room temperature before continuing.

Cut each roll in half horizontally and spread one fourth of the mixture on the top half of the roll. Flatten the lettuce leaf by bending back the rib until it splits in several places. Place the lettuce leaf on the bottom half of the roll so that the leaf forms a ruffled edge that extends beyond the roll. Cover with the other half of the roll. Repeat with the other 3 rolls.

RUSSIAN SALAD SANDWICH

Tramezzino all'Insalata Russa

Tramezzini are sandwiches made of thin slices of white bread with various fillings. They are usually eaten as a light afternoon snack.

In this sandwich the filling is a delicate checkerboard of finely diced vegetables bound with a touch of lemony homemade mayonnaise. Its richness would be nicely set off by a glass of cold white wine. Cut the sandwiches into small squares or diamond shapes to serve with drinks before dinner.

Find a bakery that makes high-quality fine-textured white bread. Avoid commercially produced white bread, which is too soft and spongy.

½ *recipe Russian Salad (see page 112)*
8 *slices good-quality white bread*

Divide the Russian Salad among 4 slices of bread. Spread the salad to cover the bread slices but not all the way to the edges. Top with the remaining 4 slices of bread. Cut the sandwiches in half diagonally or, if serving with drinks, in bite-sized squares.

ROMAN-STYLE GRILLED SANDWICH

Pizza alla Romana

SERVES 1

*T*his is the Italian version of the all-American grilled cheese sandwich. Mozzarella, tomato, and basil leaves are stacked in a split focaccia, a flat pizzalike bread, and grilled. When the cheese melts to a soft, fragrant tangle and the bread turns crisp and golden, the sandwich is ready to eat. I enjoyed this treat standing at the crowded counter of Bar Vanni one hot summer night in Rome. It was so good I've made it many times since. If you can't find focaccia bread, use thinly sliced, good-quality Italian bread.

> *Extra-virgin olive oil*
> 1 *5-inch square of focaccia, sliced in half horizontally*
> 3 *ounces fresh mozzarella, drained on paper towels, sliced*
> *Salt to taste*
> 2 *tomato slices, large enough to cover the mozzarella*
> 2 *basil leaves*

Very lightly moisten with olive oil both sides of each slice of focaccia. Arrange the mozzarella on one piece of the bread, leaving about a ½-inch space at the edges to prevent the mozzarella from melting onto the grill. Salt the mozzarella to taste. Arrange the tomato slices over the cheese and place 2 basil leaves on top of the tomato. Cover with the other piece of focaccia.

Lightly brush a stovetop grill with oil and bring the heat to medium high. Place the sandwich on the grill. Weigh down the sandwich with a heavy pot to flatten it. Grill the sandwich on both sides until the cheese melts and grill marks appear.

Soups for every Season

ost of the following soups are actually meals
in themselves. They call for either a single vegetable
or an assortment of vegetables and range from bright,
bracing summer soups and spring restoratives to soul-
satisfying winter soups. Small, delicate pasta shapes, creamy
potatoes, perfumed rice, and golden bread make the soups
full-bodied. Along with a leafy salad, they can be a
complete meal to serve to family and friends.

These soups are quickly assembled, and cooking times
are relatively short. Although a few require meat broth,
most are made with water. If you do not have meat broth
handy, or would rather not use it, substitute water for a
soup with a lighter character.

Many of these soups can be made ahead of time and
then reheated or frozen to provide a quick, hearty meal
when time is limited. If rice or pasta is called for in a soup
that will be eaten later, omit that ingredient. Then, when
you are ready to eat the soup, cook the rice or pasta
separately and add it to the soup in the final stages of
reheating so you can enjoy its al dente texture.

Most of these soups come to life when a final flourish
of flavor is added to each bowl just before serving. In several
of the soups a spoonful of pesto provides a burst of herbal
flavor. Or you can add a dusting of grated Parmesan or
Pecorino Romano cheese to balance and enrich the soups.
Fresh basil, mint, finely chopped fennel tops, or flowery
marjoram sprinkled over the top give the soups a perfumed
quality. The simplest and perhaps the best way to bring out
flavor is to add a few drops of extra-virgin olive oil and a
coarse grinding of black pepper.

Soups are vegetables and liquid transformed, whether the soup is a smooth and golden-colored cream or a broth brimming with glowing vegetables. Gathering the vegetables, peeling and chopping them, the aromatic vapors that fill the kitchen, the pleasant anticipation as the soup cooks—these delights can be matched only by the moment when you sit down at the table and dip your spoon into the steamy, fragrant broth.

VEGETABLE BROTH I

Brodo Vegetale I

MAKES APPROXIMATELY 1½ QUARTS

fragrant broth with a fresh, uncomplicated flavor, called for in various risotto dishes. Try adding a small piece of red chile pepper for a spicy broth, or a squeeze of lemon juice to give it a refreshing tang.

2 *tablespoons extra-virgin olive oil*
2 *onions, peeled and coarsely diced*
3 *carrots, trimmed and sliced*
2 *leeks, root ends and half of green tops trimmed, sliced*
2 *celery stalks, trimmed, stalks sliced, and leaves chopped*
4 *garlic cloves, peeled and chopped*
2 *tomatoes, diced*
3 *sprigs Italian parsley*
3 *sprigs basil*
2 *bay leaves*
12 *peppercorns*
7 *cups water*
Salt to taste

Combine the olive oil and onions in a soup pot. Sauté for several minutes. Add the carrots, leeks, and celery, and sauté briefly. Add the garlic, tomato, herbs, and peppercorns, and sauté for a couple of minutes. Add the water. Cover and bring to a boil. Lower the heat and simmer, partly covered, for about 1 hour. Add salt to taste. Strain and use immediately. Or let cool, cover, and refrigerate.

VEGETABLE BROTH II

Brodo Vegetale II

MAKES APPROXIMATELY 1½ QUARTS

A vegetable broth with a deep, mushroomy flavor, it finishes on a sweet note, due to the addition of carrot and fennel. This broth is called for in various risotto dishes. On its own it makes a delightful soup. Simply add some cooked rice or small pasta shapes and sprinkle with Parmesan cheese.

4   *tablespoons extra-virgin olive oil*
1   *medium onion, peeled and coarsely diced*
3   *garlic cloves, chopped*
2   *parsley roots, trimmed and sliced*
1   *carrot, trimmed and sliced*
1   *feathery fennel stalk, cut into short lengths*
1   *large leek, root end and half of the green top trimmed, sliced*
4   *ounces mushrooms, sliced*
½   *ounce dried porcini mushrooms*
7   *sprigs thyme*
2   *tablespoons chopped Italian parsley*
12   *black peppercorns*
7   *cups water*
Salt to taste

Combine the olive oil and onion in a soup pot. Sauté over low heat for several minutes. Add the garlic and sauté for a few more minutes. Add the parsley roots, carrot, and fennel, and sauté for several minutes. Add the leek, mushrooms, and herbs, and sauté briefly. Add the peppercorns and water, and bring to a boil. Lower the heat and simmer, partly covered, for about 1 hour. Add salt to taste. Strain and use immediately. Or let cool, cover, and refrigerate.

CHICKEN BROTH

Brodo di Pollo

MAKES APPROXIMATELY 1½ QUARTS

se this light and flavorful broth in soups and risotto dishes.

1 *medium stewing chicken*
1 *pound chicken backs and necks*
Water
2 *carrots, trimmed and coarsely chopped*
3 *celery stalks, trimmed and coarsely chopped*
3 *sprigs parsley*
2 *garlic cloves, unpeeled*
1 *small onion, unpeeled*
1 *bay leaf*
8 *peppercorns*

Wash the chicken carefully and gently pull off any extra fat. Place the whole chicken, backs, and necks in a soup pot. Cover completely with water. Bring to a boil and skim off scum that rises to the top. When there is no more scum, add the remaining ingredients and lower the heat.

Barely simmer, partly covered, for 2 hours. Strain the broth and let cool. Cover and refrigerate. When the broth is cold, carefully lift off the congealed fat and discard.

BEEF BROTH

Brodo di Manzo

MAKES APPROXIMATELY 1½ QUARTS

light beef broth for soups and risotto dishes. It is delicious served with tiny pasta shapes floating in the clear amber liquid and a sprinkling of Parmesan cheese.

6–8 *cups assorted beef bones, such as shank and flanken*
1 *small onion, unpeeled*
1 *celery stalk, trimmed and coarsely chopped*
1 *carrot, trimmed and coarsely chopped*
1 *tomato*
Handful mushrooms
5 *garlic cloves, unpeeled*
2 *sprigs Italian parsley*
2 *sprigs thyme*
1 *bay leaf*
5 *black peppercorns*
Water

Place all the ingredients in a soup pot and cover with cold water by 2 inches. Bring to a simmer with the cover partly on. Skim off any scum that appears. Simmer broth for 2 to 3 hours and do not let it come to a strong boil. Occasionally remove any additional scum that rises to the surface. Strain the broth and let cool uncovered. Cover and transfer to the refrigerator. When the broth is cold, remove the congealed fat and discard. Keep the broth refrigerated until needed.

SPRING SOUP WITH HERBS

Minestra Primaverile alle Erbe

SERVES 4 TO 6

*I*nspired by a recipe in *Leaves from Our Tuscan Kitchen*, written by Janet Ross, an Englishwoman living in Italy, this soup features tender spring greens, peas, and sweet herbs. Sometimes I put the mixture through a food mill and stir in a little cream or yogurt for a smooth and comforting soup. More often, however, I prefer to enjoy all the separate flavors. Finish the soup with a squeeze of lemon, a sprinkling of herbs, and freshly ground black pepper.

2 *tablespoons unsalted butter*
1 *small onion, peeled and finely diced*
2 *celery stalks, leaves and stalks finely chopped*
3 *medium potatoes, peeled and diced*
Salt and freshly ground black pepper to taste
3 *cups chicken broth*
3 *cups water*
1 *small head Boston lettuce, leaves cut into short strips*
Handful freshly shelled small peas or frozen peas
1 *small bunch sorrel, cut into short strips*
2–3 *tablespoons cream or plain yogurt, optional*
Lemon juice to taste
1 *tablespoon chopped chives*
1 *teaspoon chopped mint*

Place the butter in a soup pot and turn on the heat to low. Add the onion and the chopped celery stalks and leaves. Cover and cook until the vegetables soften. Add the potatoes and salt and pepper to taste. Toss in the vegetable mixture and let cook for a few minutes to allow the potatoes to absorb the flavors. Add the broth and water and bring to a boil. Cover and simmer until the potatoes are almost tender. Add the lettuce and peas, and cook until tender. At the last moment add the sorrel and stir. Season with the lemon juice, sprinkle with herbs, and grind pepper over the top.   *(continued)*

If desired, after all the vegetables are tender, the soup can be pureed in a food mill or food processor. Return the mixture to the stove and reheat. Off the heat stir in the optional cream or yogurt. Sprinkle with the herbs and grind pepper over the top.

ZUCCHINI AND BEET GREENS SOUP

Minestra Verde

SERVES 4

This soup, made from leafy green tops of freshly pulled beets and garden zucchini, is just as good when made with fresh market produce. The sweetness of the zucchini comes shining through, and the beet greens lend an earthy quality. Basil and Almond Pesto adds vibrancy to the soup; but for a gentler flavor simply sprinkle a little freshly grated cheese on top.

A summery first course of Cucumber, Beet, and Roasted Yellow Pepper Salad (see page 109) would be a good accompaniment and a way to incorporate the beets themselves into the meal.

Leafy tops of 1 bunch of beets or 1 bunch Swiss chard
Salt to taste
3   *tablespoons extra-virgin olive oil*
1   *onion, peeled and finely diced*
1   *garlic clove, peeled and finely chopped*
3   *tablespoons chopped Italian parsley leaves*
2   *tablespoons chopped basil leaves*
2   *medium zucchini, trimmed and cut into small dice*
1   *15-ounce can cannellini beans, drained*
3   *cups water*
½   *cup imported dried conchigliette*
Freshly ground black pepper to taste
1   *recipe Basil and Almond Pesto (see page 44), optional, or*
     freshly grated imported Parmesan cheese

Wash the beet greens well in several changes of water. Cut off the stems and strip the leaves from the ribs. Cook the greens until tender in the water that clings to the leaves, plus a few extra tablespoons of water and salt to taste. Drain and chop coarsely.

Place the olive oil and onion in a soup pot. Cook, partially covered, over moderate heat until the onion is tender. Add the garlic and herbs, stir, and cook for a few minutes more. Add the diced zucchini. Stir well to coat the zucchini in the oil and let cook for 5 minutes. Add the cannellini beans, water, and salt to taste. Bring to a boil and simmer for 15 minutes.

Meanwhile cook the pasta in salted boiling water until very al dente. After the soup has cooked for 15 minutes, add the pasta and the beet greens to the soup and cook for a few more minutes. Taste the broth. It should have a light, sweet flavor, but add salt if needed and a grinding of pepper.

To serve, ladle the soup into shallow bowls and add a teaspoonful of Basil and Almond Pesto or a sprinkling of Parmesan cheese and a few drops of extra-virgin olive oil.

ASPARAGUS-RICE SOUP WITH CACIOCAVALLO

Minestra di Asparagi e Riso

SERVES 4

This fresh-tasting soup is for asparagus lovers. The flavorful broth is simply the asparagus cooking water. You add chewy Arborio rice and caciocavallo cheese, which melts into the soup and enriches it with its creaminess. This soup looks like springtime with all the tender green asparagus floating in the delicate rice-flecked broth.

1   *pound asparagus*
6   *cups water*
Salt
3   *tablespoons extra-virgin olive oil*
2   *garlic cloves, peeled and finely chopped*
3   *tablespoons coarsely chopped Italian parsley*
½   *cup Arborio rice*
3   *ounces caciocavallo cheese, shredded*
Freshly ground black pepper to taste

Snap off the tough ends of the asparagus. Using a vegetable peeler, peel the asparagus about halfway up the stalk. Cook the asparagus in 6 cups of salted boiling water. When the asparagus is tender but crisp, lift it out of the water. Cut into pieces about the length of a large soup spoon. Reserve the water.

Combine in a soup pot the olive oil, garlic, and parsley. Sauté over low heat for several minutes. Add the reserved asparagus water and bring to a boil. Add the rice and cook until the rice is al dente. Add the asparagus and warm gently. Off the heat, stir in the caciocavallo cheese and grind black pepper over the top. Stir well and serve immediately.

SOUP FROM THE GARDEN

Minestra dell'Orto

SERVES 4

A simple, bright soup that features a mix of fresh, luminous vegetables, with porcini mushrooms added for depth of flavor. The vegetables cook directly in the boiling water without any preliminary sautéeing for a particularly fresh and clean taste. A spoonful of Basil and Almond Pesto, stirred in at the last moment, infuses the soup with a bright green color and an intensely aromatic perfume.

1   *ounce dried porcini mushrooms*
1½ *quarts water*
Salt to taste
½   *pound tender green beans, trimmed, cut into short lengths*
2   *boiling potatoes, peeled and diced*
2   *zucchini, trimmed and diced*
½   *pound Roma tomatoes, peeled, seeded, and chopped*
¼   *cup small fresh peas*
1   *cup cooked cannellini beans*
½   *cup dried small pasta shapes*
3   *tablespoons extra-virgin olive oil*
Salt and freshly ground black pepper
4   *teaspoons Basil and Almond Pesto (see page 44)*

Soak the porcini mushrooms in warm water to cover. After 20 minutes, lift the mushrooms out of the water, making sure there are no traces of grit left. Rinse under cold water. Drain and cut into strips.

Bring 1½ quarts water to a boil. Add salt to taste. Add the green beans and potatoes. Cook for 10 minutes. Add the zucchini, tomatoes, peas, and porcini. Simmer for 15 minutes. Add the cannellini beans, the pasta, and the olive oil. Stir. Cook until the pasta is al dente. Taste and add more salt if necessary. Grind black pepper over the top.

To serve, ladle soup in soup bowls and stir 1 teaspoon of Basil and Almond Pesto into each bowl.

AROMATIC POTATO AND ARUGULA SOUP

Minestra Aromatica

SERVES 4

This soup of potatoes, arugula, sweet herbs, and rice has a fascinating mix of textures—creamy potato and chewy rice—and flavors —sweet herbs, red chile pepper, and pungent arugula—that make it special. Part of the arugula is stirred in at the last moment to accentuate its peppery flavor. If you prefer a lighter soup, you can use water instead of broth. Just sprinkle with grated Parmesan or Pecorino Romano cheese for added zest.

3 *tablespoons butter*
2 *tablespoons extra-virgin olive oil*
½ *medium onion, peeled and finely diced*
2 *garlic cloves, peeled and finely chopped*
Red chile pepper flakes to taste
3 *potatoes, about 1 pound*
6 *cups meat broth*
2 *bunches arugula, stems trimmed, cut into strips, divided*
10 *basil leaves, cut into strips*
3 *tablespoons coarsely chopped Italian parsley*
¼ *cup Arborio rice*
Salt to taste

Place the butter and olive oil in a soup pot. Add the onion and sauté over low heat until the onion softens. Add the garlic and red chile pepper flakes during the final few minutes of cooking the onion.

Meanwhile peel the potatoes and cut into small dice. Add the potatoes to the soup pot and toss them in the olive oil. Let the potatoes cook for a few minutes so they can absorb the flavors. Cover the potatoes with the broth and bring to a boil. Simmer for 15 minutes.

Add slightly more than half the arugula, and all the basil, parsley, and rice. Continue cooking the soup until the rice is al dente. Add salt if needed. Right before serving, stir in the remaining arugula and when it softens slightly, ladle the soup into bowls and serve.

SUMMER WHITE BEAN SOUP WITH TOMATO SALAD TOPPING

Zuppa Estiva di Fagioli e Salsa Cruda

SERVES 4

A summer soup that is effortless to prepare, especially when you use canned beans. It features pasta and creamy white beans spiked with red chile pepper, topped with a bright salad of tomatoes, basil, and red onion. The contrast of hot soup and cool salad is a refreshing surprise in hot weather.

2 *Roma tomatoes, cut into small dice*

¼ *small red onion, finely diced*

10 *basil leaves, divided*

5 *tablespoons extra-virgin olive oil, divided, plus*
    extra for drizzling

Salt to taste

2 *garlic cloves, peeled and chopped*

½ *teaspoon crushed red chile pepper*

2 *cups cooked cannellini beans or white beans, with*
    about ½ cup bean broth

3 *cups water*

½ *cup imported dried mezzi tubetti, or other*
    small pasta shape

Freshly ground black pepper

Freshly grated imported Parmesan cheese, optional

Combine the tomato and red onion in a small bowl. Cut 8 basil leaves into strips and add to the bowl. Drizzle with 1 tablespoon olive oil. Toss mixture and season with salt to taste.

Combine in a soup pot 4 tablespoons olive oil, garlic, and red chile pepper. Tear the remaining 2 basil leaves into large fragments and add to the pot. Cook over low heat for 2 to 3 minutes. Add the beans and all the liquid from the can, and cook, covered, over medium-low heat. Use a wooden spoon to crush about one fourth of the beans against the side of the pot to thicken the broth. After 15 minutes, add the water and bring to a boil. Add salt to taste and stir. Add the pasta, stir well, and cook at a gentle boil until the pasta is al dente. *(continued)*

Ladle the soup into 4 shallow soup bowls. Spoon some of the topping in the center of each bowl. Grind black pepper over the top and drizzle with a fine thread of olive oil. Serve with Parmesan cheese on the side if desired.

TOMATO AND BREAD SOUP

Pane Cotto

SERVES 4

This fresh-tasting, bright, country-style tomato soup is perfumed with basil and bay leaves, and thickened with bread. It may sound stodgy, but in fact it is light and fresh, because the tomatoes give it an acidic edge. Serve it warm or, even better, at room temperature in big rustic bowls.

4 *tablespoons extra-virgin olive oil*
½ *medium onion, peeled and finely diced*
1½ *pounds tomatoes, peeled, seeded, and coarsely chopped*
6 *basil leaves, coarsely chopped*
2 *bay leaves*
Salt and freshly ground black pepper to taste
2½ *cups water*
2 *cups diced country bread*
4 *tablespoons freshly grated imported Pecorino Romano cheese*

Combine in a soup pot the olive oil and onion. Cook over low heat until the onion is golden. Add the tomatoes, basil, and bay leaves. Season with salt and pepper. Cook for 15 minutes over medium-low heat. Add 2½ cups water and bring to a boil. Add the bread cubes, stir, and turn off the heat. Cover and let rest for 10 minutes. Stir well.

To serve, ladle into soup bowls and sprinkle with grated Pecorino Romano cheese.

SUMMER MINESTRONE WITH RICE

Minestrone Estivo di Riso

SERVES 4 TO 6

inestrone is so strongly associated with winter that it may come as a surprise that it is also eaten during the summer months. In warm weather, it is served at room temperature with a generous amount of fresh basil stirred into it. A special feature of this recipe is the big spoonful of sweet, rich sun-dried tomato paste that is added as the soup cooks. This soup thickens as it cools, becoming quite dense and not a bit brothy. Get a big spoon and dig in.

3   *tablespoons extra-virgin olive oil*
1   *garlic clove, peeled and chopped*
1   *onion, peeled and finely diced*
3   *medium tomatoes, peeled, seeded, and diced*
2   *celery stalks, strings removed, diced*
2   *medium carrots, trimmed, peeled, and diced*
2   *medium zucchini, trimmed and diced*
¼   *pound green beans, ends trimmed, cut into dice*
2   *medium boiling potatoes, peeled and diced*
Salt to taste
6   *cups water*
1   *tablespoon sun-dried tomato paste*
½   *cup Arborio rice*
1   *cup cooked borlotti or cannellini beans*
¼   *cup chopped Italian parsley*
1   *bunch basil, leaves chopped, divided*
¼   *cup freshly grated imported Parmesan cheese, plus
        additional for the table*

In a soup pot, combine the olive oil, garlic, and onion. Sauté over low heat until the onion is tender. Add the tomatoes, celery, carrots, zucchini, green beans, and potatoes. Add salt to taste. Stir well and let vegetables cook for a few minutes. Add the water and tomato paste. Bring to a boil. Reduce to a slow simmer and cook covered for about 1 hour.   *(continued)*

Add the rice, beans, parsley, and half the basil. Cook, uncovered, at a simmer, stirring often, for 12 minutes, or until the rice is about three quarters done. The rice will continue to cook as the soup cools.

Off the heat, stir in the remaining basil and grated Parmesan cheese. Ladle into shallow soup bowls. Serve when the soup cools to room temperature. Have additional Parmesan cheese at the table.

YELLOW PEPPER SOUP

Zuppa di Peperoni Gialli

SERVES 4

Cibreo, a restaurant in Florence, made this soup of yellow peppers and potatoes famous. The vegetables, put through a food mill, create a golden, creamy, and lightly sweet soup. Serve it Tuscan style at room temperature to really savor the flavor of the yellow peppers.

1   *medium onion, finely chopped*
1   *small carrot, peeled and finely chopped*
1   *celery stalk, strings removed, finely chopped*
4   *tablespoons olive oil, plus additional for drizzling*
4   *yellow peppers, seeded and cut into large sections*
1   *pound boiling potatoes, peeled and cut into thin slices*
1   *cup Beef or Chicken Broth (see page 158 or page 157)*
4   *cups water*
Salt and freshly ground black pepper to taste
1   *recipe Small Crostini (see page 366)*
Freshly grated imported Parmesan cheese

Place the chopped vegetables and the olive oil in a soup pot. Cook over medium heat until the vegetables soften, about 10 minutes. Add the yellow peppers, potatoes, Beef or Chicken Broth, and water. Bring to a boil and simmer for about 30 minutes, or until the vegetables are very soft. Put the mixture through a food mill. Return the soup to a clean pot. Reheat and add salt and pepper to taste.

To serve, ladle into soup bowls. Drizzle with extra-virgin olive oil and sprinkle with Small Crostini and Parmesan cheese.

POTATO-TOMATO SOUP WITH ROSEMARY

Minestra di Pomodoro e Patate al Rosmarino

SERVES 4 TO 6

A simple amalgam of potatoes and tomatoes, perfumed with rosemary, cooked until the potatoes break down to a coarse yet creamy puree. The tomatoes provide bright color and tart-sweet flavor. For a smoother texture, put the soup through a food mill. It is quite refreshing served at room temperature with a drizzle of fine olive oil over the top and a few grindings of coarse black pepper.

4 *tablespoons extra-virgin olive oil*
1 *small onion, finely diced*
6 *Roma tomatoes, peeled, seeded, and pureed not too fine*
2 *teaspoons finely chopped fresh rosemary leaves*
Salt to taste
3 *medium russet potatoes, peeled and cut into dice*
Water
Freshly grated imported Parmesan cheese, optional

Place the olive oil and onion in a soup pot. Cook over low heat until the onion is tender and golden. Add the tomatoes, rosemary, and salt to taste, and cook at a gentle simmer for 5 minutes.

Add the potatoes and stir. Cook for 5 minutes. Add 2 cups of water. Bring to a boil and adjust to a simmer. As the potatoes become tender, break them up with the back of a wooden spoon until a coarse puree forms.

Cook the soup for about 45 minutes, or until it is thick and the flavor deepens. Ladle into soup bowls. If desired, sprinkle each serving with a little grated Parmesan cheese.

WINTER SQUASH AND LEEK SOUP

Passato di Zucca e Porri

SERVES 4

A wintry soup with the sweet flavors of winter squash, leeks, and ground cloves. Put through a food mill, it turns into a saffron-colored, fine-textured cream.

As a first course, serve Romaine and Gorgonzola Salad with Whole Wheat Crostini (see page 99).

1¼   *pounds winter squash, such as pumpkin, butternut,*
      or hubbard, peeled and diced
4   *tablespoons unsalted butter, divided*
2   *leeks, thinly sliced*
1   *celery stalk, strings removed, finely diced*
1   *clove, freshly ground, or pinch of ground cloves*
1   *cup milk*
4   *cups water*
Salt and freshly ground black pepper to taste
4   *tablespoons freshly grated imported Parmesan cheese*

Place the squash in a pan and add water to cover. Bring to a boil and simmer, covered, for 30 minutes, or until the squash is very tender.

Meanwhile in a soup pot, combine 3 tablespoons butter, leeks, and celery. Sauté over low heat until the vegetables soften. Add the ground cloves, milk, and water. Bring to a boil and add salt and pepper to taste. Cook for 10 minutes, then add the squash and squash cooking water. Cook for an additional 15 minutes. Put through a food mill or lightly puree in a food processor.

Off the heat, add the remaining butter and grated Parmesan cheese and stir.

LENTIL SOUP WITH RED SQUASH AND FENNEL

Minestra di Lenticchie con Zucca e Finocchi

SERVES 4 TO 6

This exotic soup combines earthy, aromatic lentils, saffron-colored squash, sweet fennel bulb, and fennel seeds for a tasty and nourishing dish. Since lentils do not require presoaking and take a relatively short time to cook, they are handy to have in your pantry.

Green Olive Salad (see page 66) would make a tangy antipasto to snack on while the soup is cooking.

1 *small fennel bulb*
4 *tablespoons extra-virgin olive oil*
1 *onion, cut into medium dice*
1 *cup lentils, picked over*
1 *teaspoon fennel seeds*
4 *cups water*
Salt to taste
½ *pound winter squash, such as butternut or pumpkin, peeled and cut into medium dice*
Freshly ground black pepper to taste

Cut off the stalks of the fennel bulb. Finely chop the tender feathery leaves and set aside. Discard the stalks. Cut away any bruised or blemished areas of the fennel bulb. Cut the fennel into medium dice.

Place the olive oil and onion in a soup pot. Sauté over medium heat for about 10 minutes. Add the diced fennel bulb, stir, and sauté for 5 minutes. Add the lentils, fennel seeds, water, and salt to taste. Bring to a boil, adjust to a simmer, and cook, partly covered, for 30 minutes. Add the squash and cook for 20 minutes, or until the squash and the lentils are tender. During the last few minutes of cooking, stir in the reserved chopped fennel leaves. Before serving, grind a little black pepper over the soup and stir.

PASTA AND GREENS

Minestra di Pasta e Cicoria

SERVES 4

Curly endive, like most greens, has the ability to turn the water in which it cooks into a flavorful broth. In this country-style recipe, the broth is enriched by adding small chunks of dried Pecorino Romano cheese. This is an example of Italian resourcefulness in the kitchen, a clever way to make use of cheese that has become too dry to grate; as the cheese softens in the boiling broth, it imparts its rich flavor and a subtle creaminess to this simple soup of greens and pasta.

Many other greens work well in this recipe, which is a simple, adaptable formula. A few big handfuls of garden arugula, picked late in the season when the taste is too strong for the salad bowl, would be a good choice, as would mustard greens. To sweeten the soup, you can add spinach, chard, or lettuce.

1 *large head curly endive or escarole*
3 *tablespoons extra-virgin olive oil*
3 *garlic cloves, peeled and chopped*
Pinch of dried red chile pepper flakes
4 *cups water*
Salt to taste
1 *cup imported tubetti*
2 *ounces dried ends of imported Pecorino Romano cheese,*
   cut into small chunks
Freshly grated imported Pecorino Romano cheese

Wash the endive or escarole well and chop coarsely.

Place the olive oil, garlic, and red chile pepper flakes in a soup pot. Sauté over low heat until the garlic is fragrant. Add 4 cups of water, bring to a boil, and add a little salt to taste (remember that the Pecorino Romano cheese is salty). Stir broth and then add the chopped endive or escarole. Cover and when the water returns to a boil, add the pasta and stir well. Add the pieces of cheese, and stir again. Cook until the pasta is al dente.

Ladle the soup into shallow pasta bowls. Serve with grated Pecorino Romano cheese on the side.

PASTA AND BORLOTTI BEAN SOUP

Pasta e Fagioli alla Veneta

SERVES 4 TO 6

This soup generously fulfills its mandate to soothe and comfort, of special importance in the cold and damp Veneto region of Italy. A *passato*, or puree, of potatoes is enhanced with aromatic vegetables, wintry herbs, borlotti beans, and fresh egg pasta. The result is a hearty, warming soup with a seductive, creamy background texture.

2 *medium boiling potatoes*
5 *tablespoons extra-virgin olive oil, plus additional*
    for drizzling on soup
2 *garlic cloves, peeled and finely chopped*
1 *onion, finely diced*
1 *carrot, peeled and finely chopped*
1 *celery stalk, strings removed, finely chopped*
¼ *cup chopped Italian parsley leaves*
5–6 *fresh sage leaves, finely chopped*
2 *bay leaves*
1 *cup cooked borlotti beans, plus a ladleful of reserved*
    cooking liquid
Salt to taste
6 *cups water*
6 *ounces fresh egg fettuccine, broken into short lengths*
Freshly ground black pepper to taste
Freshly grated imported Parmesan cheese, optional

Boil potatoes until tender. Drain and when cool enough to handle, peel. Put potatoes through a food mill or put them through a ricer.

Meanwhile place the olive oil in a soup pot along with the chopped vegetables, herbs, and bay leaves. Sauté over medium-low heat until the vegetables are tender, about 20 minutes. Stir occasionally and reduce the heat if the vegetables begin to stick to the bottom of the pan. Add the borlotti beans and salt to taste. Stir and cook over low heat for 5 minutes. Add the ladleful of reserved cooking liquid and the potatoes.

(continued)

Raise the heat to high and add the 6 cups of water. Bring to a boil. Add the pasta and cook the soup until the pasta is tender. Ladle into soup bowls and top each serving with a drizzle of olive oil and a grinding of black pepper. Serve with grated Parmesan cheese on the side, if desired.

SOUP OF CHICK PEAS, SWISS CHARD, AND PORCINI

Zimino di Ceci, Bietole, e Porcini

SERVES 4

The pairing of golden chick peas and dark green Swiss chard, infused with aromatic porcini mushrooms, creates a satisfying soup that is almost like a stew.

1   *ounce dried porcini mushrooms*
1   *bunch Swiss chard, about 1 pound*
Salt to taste
2   *tablespoons extra-virgin olive oil*
1   *tablespoon unsalted butter*
½   *medium onion, finely diced*
2   *garlic cloves, chopped*
1   *14-ounce can chick peas*
4   *canned imported Italian tomatoes, seeded and finely chopped*
2½   *cups water*
Freshly ground black pepper to taste
Freshly grated imported Parmesan cheese

Place the porcini mushrooms in a small bowl with enough hot water to cover. After 20 minutes, carefully lift the mushrooms out of the water and place in a fine-mesh sieve. Run cold water over the mushrooms, carefully feeling for any remaining sand. Strain the soaking liquid through several layers of paper towels or cheesecloth. Cut the mushrooms into strips.

Strip the leaves of the Swiss chard from the stalks. Reserve the stalks for another use. Put water to measure ½ inch in the bottom of a medium braising pan. Add the Swiss chard leaves and a little salt to taste. Cover and cook over high heat until the chard is tender. Drain and chop coarsely.

Place the olive oil, butter, and onion in a soup pot. Cook over low heat until the onion is tender and golden, about 10 to 12 minutes. Add the garlic during the last 2 to 3 minutes of cooking.

Add the mushrooms and sauté them for a few minutes. Add the chard, stir well, and let cook for 2 to 3 minutes. Add the chick peas and let them absorb the flavors for a few minutes. Add the tomatoes and raise the heat to high. Add the water and the porcini soaking liquid. Bring to a boil, then simmer the soup for 40 minutes with the lid partly on.

Before serving, grind black pepper over the top and stir. Serve with grated Parmesan cheese on the side.

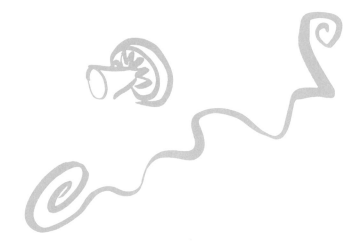

PORCINI AND RICE SOUP

Minestra con i Funghi Porcini e Riso

SERVES 4

uring cooking the juices of this risottolike soup turn a rich, dark gold, carrying the aromatic flavors of mushrooms, tomato, basil, mint, and saffron.

2 *ounces dried porcini mushrooms*
½ *pound fresh mushrooms*
3 *tablespoons extra-virgin olive oil*
2 *tablespoons unsalted butter*
2 *garlic cloves, peeled and chopped*
1 *onion, finely diced*
Small handful basil leaves, chopped
Small handful mint leaves, chopped
Salt and freshly ground black pepper to taste
1 *pound tomatoes, peeled, seeded, and chopped*
Water
½ *cup Arborio rice*
Pinch of saffron
Freshly grated imported Parmesan cheese

Place the porcini mushrooms in a small bowl and add enough hot water to cover. Let soak for at least 20 minutes. Lift the mushrooms out of the soaking liquid and reserve the liquid. Place the mushrooms in a fine sieve and run cold water over them, feeling for any traces of sand or grit. Cut the porcini into strips. Strain the soaking liquid through several layers of dampened cheesecloth.

Clean the fresh mushrooms by wiping them with damp paper towels. Trim a bit off the stem ends. Cut the mushrooms into thin slices.

Place the olive oil and butter in a soup pot and turn the heat to low. When the butter has melted, add the garlic and onion, and sauté until the onion is tender, about 10 to 12 minutes, stirring occasionally. Add the porcini, fresh mushrooms, basil, mint, and salt and pepper to taste. Turn the heat up to medium and stir the mushrooms. Cook for 5 minutes, stirring occasionally.

Add the chopped tomatoes and stir to combine the ingredients. Cover and cook for 10 minutes. Add 3 cups of water and the strained porcini soaking liquid to the pot and bring to a boil. Add the Arborio rice and saffron. Stir well. Cover and cook at a simmer until the rice is al dente, stirring often to prevent sticking.

To serve, ladle the soup into shallow soup bowls and sprinkle generously with Parmesan cheese.

SOUP OF DRIED FAVA BEANS WITH FRESH FENNEL

Maccù

SERVES 6

*M*accù can only be translated as a rough puree of sorts. It is true Sicilian soul food made from dried fava beans cooked with chopped wild fennel. The resulting soup, chalky beige flecked with green fennel and pale gold pasta, is incredibly good.

Fennel grows wild in Sicily. Its feathery leaves and tender stems are highly aromatic with a strong anise flavor and are used in cooking. Since wild fennel is not readily available here, I've substituted a combination of fennel seeds, sliced fresh fennel bulb, and the feathery tops, which carry a trace of the licorice-like flavor of the wild fennel.

In the rustic tradition, this substantial soup should be served as a main dish. Follow it with a small salad of tender bitter greens tossed with olive oil and lemon juice.

1 *pound dried fava beans, about 2 cups*
2 *teaspoons fennel seeds, divided*
1 *small fennel bulb*
3 *quarts water, divided*
Salt to taste
1 *cup imported dried ditalini*
¼ *cup extra-virgin olive oil, plus additional for drizzling*
Freshly ground black pepper to taste

Place the fava beans and 1 teaspoon fennel seeds in a large bowl. Add enough water to cover by 2 or 3 inches. Soak overnight. Drain and peel the fava beans. *(continued)*

Trim the fennel bulb and reserve the feathery tops. Remove all the thick outer layers of the bulb and reserve for another use. Cut the heart of the fennel bulb in quarters lengthwise, and cut out the core. Thinly slice the fennel bulb. Chop enough of the feathery tops to measure 4 tablespoons.

Combine in a large pot the fava beans, 1 teaspoon fennel seeds, 2 quarts water, and salt to taste. Bring to a boil and cook, uncovered, at a simmer until the beans become very tender and begin to break apart, for 1 to 2 hours or longer, depending on the age of the beans. As the beans cook, stir them to help them break down, mashing the beans against the side of the pot to form a coarse puree. At this point, the soup should resemble a thick, porridgelike mixture.

Add 1 quart water and bring to a boil. Add the ditalini, sliced fennel, and chopped fennel tops, and cook until the pasta is al dente and the fennel is tender. If the maccù becomes too thick and pastelike, add enough water to make it a coarse puree. Taste and add salt if needed. Off the heat stir in the olive oil.

To serve, ladle the soup into shallow pasta bowls. Grind black pepper over the top of each serving. If desired, drizzle each serving with a few fine threads of olive oil.

CHICK PEA AND ESCAROLE SOUP WITH GRILLED BREAD

Zuppa di Ceci e Scarola

SERVES 4

This satisfying soup boasts the warm, nutty taste of chick peas, the clean flavor of escarole, and the bright freshness of tomatoes. Served over grilled bread rubbed with garlic, this is a meal in a bowl.

3 *tablespoons extra-virgin olive oil*
½ *medium onion, peeled and finely diced*
1 *garlic clove, peeled and chopped*
3 *tablespoons chopped Italian parsley leaves*
2 *teaspoons chopped fresh marjoram leaves, divided*
½ *pound Roma tomatoes, peeled, seeded, and chopped*
2 *cups cooked chick peas with their liquid*
4 *cups water*
Salt and freshly ground black pepper to taste
½ *small head escarole, tough outer leaves removed,*
     leaves cut into strips
4 *slices country bread*
2 *garlic cloves, peeled and cut in half*
Extra-virgin olive oil
Freshly grated imported Parmesan cheese

Combine in a soup pot the olive oil and onion. Cook over low heat until the onion softens. Add the garlic, parsley, and 1 teaspoon marjoram. Cook for 2 to 3 minutes. Add the tomatoes and cook for 5 minutes.

Add the chick peas and their liquid and the water. Bring to a boil. Simmer for 30 minutes, adding salt and freshly ground black pepper to taste. Add the escarole and cook until the escarole is tender.

Grill or lightly toast the bread. Rub the slices with the cut side of the garlic clove and drizzle with extra-virgin olive oil.

To serve, arrange the bread in the bottoms of 4 shallow soup bowls. Ladle the soup over the bread. Sprinkle with the remaining marjoram and the Parmesan cheese. Serve immediately.

Pasta

asta has come so far in the last few years that we forget that not so long ago it had a bad reputation. Pasta has now become everybody's favorite food. It is easy and quick to prepare; delicious, healthful, and satisfying to eat; and inexpensive to assemble. All the authentic Italian ingredients needed to make good pasta dishes are available either in supermarkets, specialty food shops, or by mail order. Pasta has transcended its role as a first course and become a main dish.

Pasta with vegetable sauce is the dish I prepare more often than anything. Even if the refrigerator is bare, a delicious pasta dish can be made with a few zucchini, a handful of herbs from the garden, or a good can of tomatoes from the pantry. With a cupboard stocked with different shapes of pasta, a bottle of extra-virgin olive oil, and a chunk of grating cheese in the refrigerator, it is easy and fun to improvise.

The following recipes range from light raw summer sauces that use tomatoes, fresh herbs, and crunchy vegetables to earthy sauces with a wintry feel. Most of the sauces are quick-cooking and can be made in the same amount of time it takes to cook the pasta, so they can easily become part of your everyday repertoire.

Almost all the recipes specify imported dried pasta because it has a strong flavor and a chewy, al dente texture that goes well with flavorful, full-bodied sauces. The De Cecco brand is widely available and very good. The Martelli brand of dried pasta, harder to find but exceptional, is made by a small, artisan-style company. It is available in specialty food shops. There are many pasta shapes to choose from, some humorous, some reflecting nature, some superstitious or religious: for example, tiny stars, little ridged devils, apple seeds, horses' teeth, wolves' eyes, radiators, and little thimbles, to name just a few. The list reads like an odd poem or a form of Italian voodoo. The different pasta shapes bring fun and whimsy to pasta eating, and unending interest to the appearance and texture of a dish.

A few of the recipes call for fresh pasta. It should be light and tender, not sticky and stodgy like so many of the kinds sold in markets. Set aside a little extra time to make fresh pasta yourself. Or buy the De Cecco brand of dried fettuccine, a remarkably good product that I often turn to. If you are interested in learning more about making your own pasta, detailed directions are given in *Pasta Fresca*.

Raw Sauces

PASTA WITH RAW SAUCES

Pasta all'Insalata

On the tiny island of Ustica, off the coast of Palermo, summer days are made for swimming. The sea that surrounds this bare, rocky land is alive with schools of little iridescent fish that dart in all directions when you glide through the clear, blue water.

As the sun goes down, the heat of the day gives way to cooling sea breezes, and there rise from the warm earth the lingering smells of wild herbs, of smoldering wood, and the soft, sweet fragrance of oleander blossoms. Night slowly descends on the island filling the sky with the powdery crush of a million stars.

One evening at a small trattoria, after a day of intense heat that had traveled across the sea from nearby North Africa, I was served a pasta topped with a raw chopped tomato and herb sauce. It was the perfect restorative—bright, fresh-tasting, and cooling. Since then, Pasta all'Insalata, or pasta with raw sauce, has become one of my summer favorites.

The following pasta sauces feature raw ingredients—diced tomatoes, chopped vegetables, herbs, and cheeses—and imported dried pasta. Fresh pasta is not firm or chewy enough to stand up to the textures of raw ingredients, nor does the flavor of the egg in fresh pasta complement them. Fruity olive oil moistens the pastas, and occasionally lemon juice is added for its tart perfume. What characterizes these dishes is the play of cool sauce against hot pasta and the sparkle of the ingredients.

PASTA WITH FENNEL, TOMATO, AND RED ONION

Pasta a Crudo

SERVES 4 TO 6

What could be more refreshing than pasta tossed with finely diced raw fennel, tomato, and red onion? For a first course, serve fresh goat cheese sprinkled with red chile pepper flakes and drizzled with olive oil, and accompany the cheese with crusty bread.

1 *fennel bulb, trimmed and cut into small dice*
1½ *pounds tomatoes, cut into small dice*
¼ *small red onion, peeled and finely diced*
1 *garlic clove, finely chopped*
Small handful basil leaves, coarsely chopped
Small handful mint leaves, coarsely chopped
½ *cup extra-virgin olive oil, plus a small cruet for the table*
Juice of 1 lemon
Salt and freshly ground black pepper to taste
1 *pound imported dried pennette*
Freshly grated imported Parmesan cheese, optional

Combine in a bowl the fennel, tomatoes, red onion, garlic, herbs, olive oil, and lemon juice. Season with salt and pepper to taste. Set aside.

Cook the pennette in abundant salted boiling water until al dente and drain well.

Transfer the pasta to a serving dish and top with the chopped vegetable mixture. Toss well and adjust the seasonings.

Have a cruet of olive oil at the table for those who wish to drizzle a little extra oil on their pasta.

SPAGHETTI TRAPANI STYLE

Spaghetti alla Trapanese

SERVES 4 TO 6

A pasta sauce from Trapani featuring the luscious contrasts of fresh, cool raw tomatoes, rough basil pesto, fiery red chile pepper, and hot, crisp little squares of potato, all tossed with hot spaghetti.

3 *cloves garlic, peeled*
1 *bunch basil, leaves coarsely chopped*
6 *tablespoons olive oil, divided*
4 *large ripe tomatoes, peeled and chopped*
1 *very small red chile pepper, finely chopped, or ½ teaspoon crushed dried red chile pepper*
Salt and freshly ground black pepper to taste
1 *pound imported dried spaghetti*
2 *medium potatoes, boiled until tender but firm, peeled and diced*
4 *tablespoons freshly grated imported Parmesan cheese, plus extra for the table*

Combine the garlic, basil, and 4 tablespoons of the olive oil in a blender. Process until a rough pesto forms.

Place the tomatoes, pesto, and red chile pepper in a small bowl and season with salt and pepper to taste. Lightly mash the ingredients with a fork and set aside.

Cook the spaghetti in abundant salted boiling water. While the spaghetti is cooking, toss the potatoes in the remaining olive oil and arrange on a cookie sheet. Place under a preheated broiler until the potatoes are golden and crusty. Drain on paper towels.

Drain the pasta when it is al dente and place in a shallow pasta serving dish. Add the raw tomato sauce and the hot potatoes. Toss well. Sprinkle with grated Parmesan cheese and serve with extra cheese at the table.

TINY PASTA WITH TEN HERBS

Tripolini alle Dieci Erbe

SERVES 4 TO 6

ou can hear the bees droning in the herb garden when you prepare this intensely fragrant pasta dish.

A lavish assortment of fresh herbs is warmed very gently in fine olive oil. When the herbs turn a vibrant green, a matter of a few minutes, the sauce is ready to be tossed with hot pasta.

Tripolini, pinched in the middle to form two cups, is the ideal pasta shape to use with this sauce, as it traps the herbs and olive oil in its tiny hollows.

Try adding finely chopped lemon zest to the herbs for a bright citrus note. To change the character of the sauce, use butter instead of olive oil.

3 *tablespoons chopped Italian parsley*
3 *tablespoons chopped basil*
2 *tablespoons chopped chives*
2 *tablespoons chopped chervil*
1 *tablespoon chopped tarragon*
1 *tablespoon chopped sage*
1 *tablespoon chopped oregano*
1 *teaspoon chopped marjoram*
1 *teaspoon chopped thyme*
1 *teaspoon chopped rosemary*
½–¾ *cup extra-virgin olive oil*
2 *garlic cloves, peeled and finely chopped*
½ *teaspoon dried red chile pepper flakes*
Salt and freshly ground black pepper to taste
1 *pound imported dried tripolini or other small pasta shape*
Freshly grated imported Parmesan cheese, optional

In a medium saucepan, combine the fresh herbs, olive oil, garlic, and red chile pepper flakes. Turn the heat to low and, using a wooden spoon, gently stir the ingredients until the herbs turn bright green and release their fragrance, about 2 to 3 minutes. Season with salt and pepper to taste.

Meanwhile cook the pasta in abundant salted boiling water until al dente. Drain the pasta, leaving some moisture clinging to it, and place in a warm pasta serving bowl. Transfer the herb-oil mixture to the pasta bowl and toss, adding salt if needed and several grindings of coarse black pepper. Serve immediately. Although grated Parmesan cheese is not necessary, have some at the table.

TUBETTI WITH DICED TOMATO AND AVOCADO SAUCE

Tubetti al Pomodoro e all'Avocado

SERVES 4 TO 6

Crisp tomato and lush, green avocado add up to fine, effortless summer eating when tossed with hot pasta, olive oil, and a splash of tart, fragrant lemon juice. For a piquant touch, add a sprinkling of capers.

3 *large ripe tomatoes, cut into small dice*
12 *basil leaves, torn into fragments*
1 *garlic clove, peeled and finely chopped*
½ *cup extra-virgin olive oil*
1 *lemon, cut in half*
Salt and freshly ground black pepper to taste
1 *pound imported dried tubetti*
1 *large avocado*

Combine the tomatoes, basil, and garlic in a small bowl. Add the olive oil and the juice of ½ lemon. Season with salt and pepper to taste, and let marinate for at least 1 hour.

Cook the pasta in abundant salted boiling water to taste. While the pasta is cooking, peel the avocado and cut into small dice. Place the avocado in a small bowl. Season with salt and the remaining lemon juice.

When the pasta is al dente, drain well and place in a pasta serving bowl. Toss with the tomato mixture. Gently spoon the avocado and lemon juice over the top of the pasta.

PASTA WITH CHOPPED RAW VEGETABLES

Maccheroncini al Pinzimonio

SERVES 4 TO 6

A gorgeous, healthy summer pasta of very finely chopped raw vegetables and miniature penne. Bring the hot pasta to the table un-mixed, covered completely by bright vegetable confetti and then toss in front of your guests. Serve with giant crusty breadsticks.

1   *pound imported dried pennette*
½   *cup extra-virgin olive oil, plus a cruet of oil for the table*
1   *small red and 1 small green pepper, peeled with a vegetable*
      peeler, seeded, and very finely chopped
1   *large tomato, cored and very finely diced*
1   *celery stalk, strings removed, very finely chopped*
½   *small red onion, very finely diced*
1   *small carrot, peeled and very finely chopped*
½   *hothouse cucumber, peeled, seeded, and very finely chopped*
5   *baby zucchini, trimmed and very finely chopped*
Big handful basil leaves, torn into fragments
Salt and freshly ground black pepper to taste
A pepper mill filled with black peppercorns
Freshly grated imported Parmesan cheese

Cook the pasta in abundant salted boiling water. Drain well and place in a pasta serving bowl. Add the olive oil and toss. Place all the chopped vegetables on top of the hot pasta and sprinkle with the basil. Season with salt and freshly ground black pepper to taste. Toss well and serve.

Have a cruet of extra-virgin olive oil, a pepper mill, and the Parmesan cheese at the table so that each person can season the pasta to taste.

SMALL PENNE WITH ARUGULA SALAD

Pennette alla Rucola Fresca

SERVES 4 TO 6

Arugula leaves are small, tender, and deep green, with a peppery, assertive flavor that somewhat resembles watercress.

This dish for arugula lovers features an abundance of chopped raw arugula tossed with warm, garlicky extra-virgin olive oil and hot pasta. For a summery version, sprinkle with finely diced tomato.

4 *bunches arugula, tough stems trimmed*
3–4 *garlic cloves, peeled and finely chopped*
½ *teaspoon dried red chile pepper flakes*
6 *tablespoons extra-virgin olive oil, plus extra for drizzling*
1 *pound imported dried pennette or other small short pasta*
Salt and freshly ground black pepper to taste
Freshly grated imported Parmesan cheese

Cut the arugula into strips, and then cut again crosswise several times until the arugula is in small fragments.

Place the garlic, red chile pepper, and olive oil in a small sauté pan. Sauté over low heat for 2 to 3 minutes, or until the garlic is opaque and releases its perfume.

Meanwhile cook the pasta in abundant salted boiling water. When pasta is al dente, drain and transfer to a shallow serving dish. Add the garlic and olive oil mixture, and salt and freshly ground black pepper to taste. Add the arugula and toss well. Drizzle a few drops of olive oil on each serving of pasta. Serve with grated Parmesan cheese at the table.

SUMMER MIXED PASTA

Pasta Estiva

SERVES 4 TO 6

his fragrant pasta dish combines a raw sauce of cherry tomatoes, marjoram, basil, and fresh mozzarella with hot pasta. Use a mixture of pasta shapes of the same approximate size—for example, odds and ends of penne, fusilli, conchiglie, and ditali—in a happy tumble. Cook the various shapes in separate pots of boiling salted water until al dente.

This pasta salad makes choice summer eating, especially if you have cherry tomato plants heavy with bunches of red ripening fruit growing on your balcony or in your garden.

Serve with long, crunchy breadsticks and cold white wine. For dessert, a basket of peaches and assorted biscotti would be perfect.

2 *baskets of cherry tomatoes*
1 *clove garlic, peeled and finely chopped*
1 *bunch fresh basil, leaves chopped*
2 *tablespoons chopped fresh mint leaves*
2 *teaspoons chopped fresh marjoram leaves*
3 *anchovies, finely chopped*
½ *cup extra-virgin olive oil, plus extra for drizzling*
Salt and freshly ground black pepper to taste
¾ *pound fresh mozzarella, drained on paper towels*
1 *pound assorted imported dried short pasta shapes
     (select up to 4 different shapes)*

Stem the cherry tomatoes and cut them in half or, if they are large, in quarters. Place the tomatoes in a small bowl along with the garlic, herbs, anchovies, and olive oil. Season with salt and black pepper to taste and toss. This mixture can be used right away or it can rest for several hours at room temperature.

Cut the mozzarella into small dice.

Cook the pasta shapes in as many separate pots of salted boiling water as as you have shapes.

Drain each pasta when al dente, and place in a pasta serving bowl. Drizzle a little olive oil over each shape as you add it to the bowl and toss to prevent sticking.

When all the pasta is cooked and added to the serving bowl, sprinkle the mozzarella over the top and toss quickly. Add the cherry tomato mixture and toss again until ingredients are evenly distributed. Correct the seasonings, adding more salt and pepper if needed.

PASTA ISLAND STYLE

Pasta all'Isola

SERVES 4 TO 6

Using a mortar and pestle best captures the rough, island texture of this sauce. A pesto is made with garlic, parsley, oregano, cayenne pepper, and olive oil, then combined with chopped tomatoes and red wine vinegar. The sauce is just warmed through, not cooked. Try it spooned over grilled fish or tossed with pasta, as it is here.

Since most market tomatoes are filled with water, the tomatoes are drained in a colander first to rid them of excess moisture.

2 *tablespoons extra-virgin olive oil*

2 *garlic cloves, peeled and coarsely chopped*

¼ *cup chopped Italian parsley leaves*

2 *teaspoons dried oregano*

½ *teaspoon ground cayenne pepper*

Salt to taste

2 *pounds tomatoes, peeled, seeded, finely chopped, and drained in a colander*

1 *tablespoon red wine vinegar*

1 *pound imported dried fusilli*

Freshly grated imported Parmesan cheese

With a mortar and pestle, or in a blender, work to a coarse paste the olive oil, garlic, parsley, oregano, cayenne, and salt.

Place the tomatoes and vinegar in a large sauté pan and stir to mix. Transfer the pesto mixture to the sauté pan and stir again to combine. Turn on the heat to medium and gently warm the sauce.

Meanwhile cook the pasta in salted boiling water until al dente. Drain well and toss with the sauce. Serve with grated Parmesan cheese on the side.

PERCIATELLI WITH STRONG TASTES

Perciatelli ai Sapori Forti

SERVES 4 TO 6

I feel like a kid in a candy store when I eat this pasta—so many delicious temptations—yet the flavors are all amazingly complementary. When you eat this pasta, you experience a taste explosion of sugary sweet raisins; rich, meaty olives; creamy, resinous pine nuts. A shower of coarsely chopped parsley brings a fresh herbal touch to the dish, and a topping of coarse bread crumbs makes it crunchy.

Keep all the ingredients in large pieces so the flavors stay bold. Use a sturdy pasta to match the strong flavors. Perciatelli is a long, pierced pasta, broken into shorter pieces for easier handling.

This is a great late-night pasta to throw together when you think the pantry is bare.

1 *pound imported dried perciatelli, broken into short lengths*
6 *tablespoons extra-virgin olive oil*
4 *anchovies, chopped to a paste, optional*
4 *tablespoons raisins, plumped in warm water*
6 *tablespoons lightly toasted pine nuts*
16 *pitted oil-cured black olives, cut into large pieces*
6 *tablespoons coarsely chopped Italian parsley*
Salt and freshly ground black pepper to taste
Toasted coarse bread crumbs

Cook pasta in abundant salted boiling water. Drain when al dente and reserve a little of the pasta cooking water.

Meanwhile select a sauté pan large enough to contain all the cooked pasta. Warm the olive oil and the optional anchovies. Add the drained pasta and toss. Sprinkle the remaining ingredients, except the bread crumbs, over the pasta, and toss over low heat for about 5 minutes, or until everything is hot and fragrant. Season with salt and pepper but remember that the olives are salty, as are the anchovies if you use them. Sprinkle the pasta with bread crumbs and toss again.

Serve immediately with a small bowl of bread crumbs at the table.

SPAGHETTINI WITH ITALIAN PARSLEY AND MOZZARELLA

Spaghettini con Prezzemolo e Mozzarella

SERVES 4 TO 6

This farm-fresh sauce requires no cooking. Finely diced mozzarella and abundant Italian parsley are combined with raw egg yolks. When tossed with hot pasta, the egg yolks gently cook, merging with the mozzarella, to lightly coat the strands of pasta. For a spicy carbonara-style sauce, add dried red chile peppers to the pasta cooking water.

4   *tablespoons unsalted butter, at room temperature*
3   *egg yolks*
¼   *pound fresh mozzarella, cut into very fine dice or shredded*
5   *tablespoons chopped Italian parsley leaves*
5   *tablespoons freshly grated imported Pecorino Romano cheese, plus extra for the table*
Salt and freshly ground black pepper to taste
1   *pound imported dried spaghettini*
Dried red chile peppers, optional

Combine in a shallow pasta serving bowl the butter, egg yolks, mozzarella, parsley, grated Pecorino Romano cheese, and salt and pepper to taste. Mix well. Set aside in a warm place, such as on the stove next to the pasta pot.

Cook the spaghettini in abundant salted boiling water, with dried red chile peppers if desired, until al dente. Reserve about ½ cup of the pasta cooking water. Drain the spaghettini, leaving the strands dripping wet. Transfer the pasta to the serving dish and toss with the sauce. Add the reserved pasta cooking water, a little at a time, until the sauce is creamy and moist enough to lightly coat the spaghettini. There should not be any extra, unabsorbed liquid in the bottom of the bowl. Grind black pepper over the top and toss again. Serve with extra grated Pecorino Romano cheese at the table.

Simple Sauces from the Garden

SPAGHETTINI WITH TOMATO, ZUCCHINI BLOSSOMS, AND RED CHILE PEPPER

Pasta con Pomodoro,
Fiori di Zucca, e Peperoncino

SERVES 4 TO 6

Tomatoes and zucchini are the two vegetables most likely to lure people into their backyards to garden. In their enthusiasm many find that they have planted enough of each to feed the entire neighborhood. If your garden is overflowing with juicy ripe tomatoes and golden zucchini blossoms, indulge in this wonderful summer pasta.

  4 *tablespoons extra-virgin olive oil*
  2 *garlic cloves, peeled and finely chopped*
  ½ *teaspoon dried red chile pepper flakes or cayenne pepper*
  2 *tablespoons chopped Italian parsley leaves*
  2 *pounds ripe tomatoes, peeled, seeded, and diced*
  Salt and freshly ground black pepper to taste
  12 *zucchini blossoms, pistils removed, cut into strips*
  1 *pound imported dried spaghettini*
  Freshly grated imported Parmesan cheese

Place the olive oil, garlic, and red chile pepper in a large sauté pan. Cook over gentle heat for 2 to 3 minutes, or until the aromas rise. Add the parsley and cook for a moment. Add the tomatoes, salt and pepper to taste, and cook over medium heat for 15 minutes, or until the sauce begins to thicken. Add the zucchini-blossom strips and cook over low heat until they are tender.

Meanwhile cook the spaghettini in abundant salted boiling water. Drain when al dente. Toss with the sauce and serve immediately, sprinkled with Parmesan cheese.

FETTUCCINE WITH PEAS, GREEN ONIONS, AND MINT

Fettuccine con Piselli, Cipolla, e Menta

SERVES 4

A springtime dish that features brilliant green, sugary little peas and new onions. If the fresh peas in your market are large and the sugars have turned to starch, you can substitute tiny frozen peas. The pasta is tossed in saffron-tinted butter for a brightly colored, creamy finishing touch.

> *Small pinch of saffron threads or saffron powder*
> 6 *tablespoons unsalted butter, at room temperature, divided*
> 6 *green onions, trimmed and cut into rings*
> *Salt to taste*
> 1½ *pounds fresh peas, shelled, or 1½ cups frozen peas*
> *Water*
> 3 *tablespoons chopped mint leaves*
> ¾ *pound fresh fettuccine*
> *Freshly ground black pepper*
> *Freshly grated imported Parmesan cheese*

Soak the saffron in a very small bowl with 2 tablespoons hot water while you prepare the sauce.

Combine 4 tablespoons of the butter, the green onions, and salt to taste in a medium sauté pan. Cook over low heat until the onions are tender. Add the peas and ½ cup water, and cook over low heat until the peas are tender, stirring gently from time to time. Stir in the mint and keep warm.

Combine the remaining butter and the saffron water in a warm pasta serving bowl.

Meanwhile cook the fettuccine in abundant salted boiling water. Drain when just tender, leaving water dripping from the strands. Place the pasta in the serving dish, add the sauce, and gently toss. Serve sprinkled with pepper and Parmesan cheese.

PASTA WITH GREEN TOMATO AND ALMOND SAUCE

Pasta con Pomodori Verdi e Mandorle

SERVES 4 TO 6

A sauce to make with partially ripened tomatoes or end-of-the-season tomatoes that are doomed never to fully ripen. Green tomatoes make a tart, lively sauce, with basil and almonds adding notes of sweetness. Hard, unripe tomatoes do not work here, nor do green market tomatoes that have not ripened at all.

For an interesting, decidedly nontraditional alternative to green tomatoes, try using husked tomatillos along with a few ripe tomatoes.

6 *tablespoons extra-virgin olive oil*

1 *large garlic clove, peeled and finely sliced*

3 *tablespoons chopped Italian parsley leaves*

1¾ *pounds small green tomatoes with a touch of blush, cored and thinly sliced*

Salt and freshly ground black pepper to taste

3 *tablespoons freshly peeled, slivered almonds*

1 *pound imported dried spaghettini*

1 *tablespoon unsalted butter*

5–6 *basil leaves, torn into fragments*

Combine the olive oil, garlic, and parsley in a large sauté pan. Cook over low heat until the garlic releases its perfume and becomes tender. Do not let the garlic brown. Add the tomatoes, salt and pepper to taste, and cook over medium heat for a few minutes. Lower the heat and let the tomatoes cook until they begin to fall apart. Add the almonds and stir.

Meanwhile cook the spaghettini in abundant salted boiling water. When the pasta is al dente, drain and place in a serving bowl. Add the butter and toss quickly. Add the tomato sauce, toss, and sprinkle with basil. No grated cheese is required.

WHOLE WHEAT SPAGHETTI WITH FRESH TOMATO MINT SAUCE

Spaghetti Integrali alla Menta

SERVES 4 TO 6

resh tomatoes, mint, and basil are cooked without oil until a sauce forms. Off the heat, a small amount of extra-virgin olive oil is stirred in. Raw, olive oil is at its healthiest and most full-flavored. When it is added to the finished sauce, an explosion of fresh flavor and perfume results.

Purchase imported dried whole wheat pasta for its fine quality and warm, nutty flavor.

> 2 *pounds fresh ripe tomatoes*
> 10 *basil leaves, coarsely chopped*
> 5 *sprigs mint, leaves coarsely chopped, plus 1 small*
>   *handful whole mint leaves*
> 1 *garlic clove, finely chopped*
> *Salt to taste*
> 3 *tablespoons extra-virgin olive oil*
> 1 *pound imported dried whole wheat spaghetti*

Peel, seed, and chop the tomatoes. Let drain briefly in a colander. In a medium sauté pan, combine the tomatoes, chopped basil and mint, and garlic. Cook over medium heat, adding salt to taste until the sauce thickens, about 20 minutes. Off the heat, stir in the olive oil.

Meanwhile cook the pasta in abundant salted boiling water. Drain well and place in a pasta serving bowl. Add the sauce and whole mint leaves, and toss.

PASTA WITH GREEN PEPPERS AND HERBS

Pasta ai Peperoni Verdi ed Erbe

SERVES 4 TO 6

I never used to like green peppers; their tart, unripened flavor and tough skin were unappealing. But as a recent convert, I now delight in incorporating them into recipes. When I use them raw, I remove the skins with a vegetable peeler. When cooking with green peppers, I keep the recipes simple, and I look for ways to spotlight the unusual flavor of the peppers.

Here, small squares of green pepper are quickly sautéed with herbs, then tossed with ditalini, small tubular pasta that mirrors the shapes in the sauce. A little butter stirred in at the end mellows the flavors. Try roasting the green peppers first to impart a smoky accent to the finished dish.

Select peppers with vibrant green coloring and thick flesh. If you plan to roast them, make sure the peppers are smooth and evenly formed.

4   *tablespoons extra-virgin olive oil*
1   *small onion, finely chopped*
2   *garlic cloves, peeled and finely chopped*
¼   *cup chopped Italian parsley leaves*
5   *celery leaves, finely chopped*
3   *green peppers, cored, seeded, and cut into small dice*
Salt and freshly ground black pepper to taste
1   *pound imported dried ditalini or other short pasta shape*
2   *tablespoons unsalted butter, softened*
Freshly grated imported Parmesan cheese

Combine the olive oil and onion in a medium sauté pan. Cook over low heat until the onion is tender. Add the garlic, parsley and celery leaves, green peppers, and salt and pepper to taste, and cook until the peppers are tender.

Meanwhile cook the pasta in abundant salted boiling water until tender. Drain, leaving a bit of water clinging to the pasta. Place in a shallow pasta serving dish and add the butter. Toss, add the sauce, and toss again. Grind pepper over the top and dust with grated Parmesan cheese. Serve with additional grated cheese on the side.

FUSILLI WITH SPICY TOMATO AND ROASTED PEPPER SAUCE

Fusilli con Pomodoro e Peperoni Arrostiti

SERVES 4 TO 6

spicy tomato sauce is the background for small matchstick strips of roasted red and yellow pepper. The tomatoes can be peeled by roasting them, which will reinforce the smoky flavor of the dish. You can add capers, pitted black olives, or anchovies to this sauce for tang, but I like it best without the extra seasonings so the smoky sweetness predominates.

The thin strips of peppers curl around the corkscrew spirals of fusilli, making a perfect match of sauce and pasta shape.

4   *tablespoons extra-virgin olive oil, divided*
2   *garlic cloves, peeled and chopped*
½   *teaspoon dried red chile pepper flakes*
1½ *pounds tomatoes, peeled, seeded, and coarsely chopped*
Salt and freshly ground black pepper to taste
2   *peppers, 1 red and 1 yellow, roasted, peeled, seeded,*
       and cut into small matchstick strips
1   *pound imported dried fusilli*
Handful basil leaves, torn or slivered
Freshly grated imported Parmesan cheese

Place 3 tablespoons of the olive oil, garlic, and chile pepper flakes in a medium sauté pan. Cook over low heat for 2 to 3 minutes until the aromas rise. Add the tomatoes and salt and pepper to taste. Raise the heat to medium and cook for about 15 minutes, or until the sauce thickens. Put through a food mill.

Place the remaining tablespoon of oil in a medium sauté pan. Toss peppers over medium heat for a few minutes to allow them to absorb the flavor. Combine the tomato sauce and the peppers in a sauté pan and gently warm.

Meanwhile cook the fusilli until al dente. Drain well and place in a pasta serving dish. Add the sauce and toss. Sprinkle with basil leaves and dust with Parmesan cheese.

SWEET TOMATO BASIL SAUCE

Salsina di Pomodoro con Burro

SERVES 4 TO 6

A delicate, buttery tomato sauce that complements the egg-enriched flavor of tender, fresh fettuccine. It is teamed with Spinach Gnocchi (see page 286) for a very pretty special-occasion dish.

4 *tablespoons unsalted butter*
1 *medium onion, peeled and finely chopped*
12–14 *Roma tomatoes, peeled, seeded, and chopped*
10 *basil leaves, coarsely chopped*
Salt and freshly ground black pepper to taste
1 *pound fresh fettuccine*
Freshly grated imported Parmesan cheese

Melt the butter in a medium sauté pan. Add the onion and sauté over low heat until soft. Add the tomatoes to the pan and cook until the tomatoes start to give off their juices. Add the basil and salt and pepper to taste. Cook until the tomatoes thicken into a sauce.

Meanwhile cook the fettuccine in abundant salted boiling water until al dente. Drain well and return to the pot in which it cooked. Add the tomato-basil sauce and toss over very low heat for a moment or two to let the pasta absorb the flavors of the sauce. Serve immediately and pass grated Parmesan cheese at the table.

PENNE WITH TOMATO AND MOZZARELLA SAUCE SORRENTO STYLE

Penne alla Sorrentina

SERVES 4 TO 6

This is a tart-sweet tomato sauce made creamy by adding mozzarella. It's not as caloric or cloying as a cream sauce, so you can indulge in it when in the mood for something smooth and rich-tasting.

The sauce is teamed with potato gnocchi in Potato Gnocchi Sorrento Style (see page 284).

¼ *cup extra-virgin olive oil*
2–3 *cloves garlic, peeled and finely chopped*
1 *28-ounce can imported Italian tomatoes, drained, seeded, and pureed*
1 *handful basil leaves, divided*
Salt and freshly ground black pepper to taste
4–6 *ounces fresh mozzarella in water, drained and coarsely chopped*
1 *pound imported dried penne*
Freshly grated imported Parmesan cheese

Heat the extra-virgin olive oil and garlic over low heat in a heavy medium sauté pan. Add the tomato puree and half the basil leaves, and stir. Cook until the tomatoes thicken into a sauce. Add salt and pepper to taste. Add the mozzarella and stir until it becomes creamy and melts into the tomato sauce.

Meanwhile cook the pasta in abundant boiling salted water until al dente. Drain well and transfer to the sauté pan containing the sauce. Toss over low heat until well combined. Sprinkle with the grated Parmesan cheese and scatter the remaining basil leaves over the top. Stir again and serve immediately in individual shallow pasta bowls.

FRESH PASTA WITH TOMATO, EGGPLANT, RICOTTA, AND WALNUTS

Fettuccine al Doppio Gusto

SERVES 4 TO 6

airing walnuts and eggplant sounds exotic, but combined with fresh tomato and ricotta, the flavors come together in an unmistakably Italian way. Fresh ricotta lightens the sauce and gives it a creamy quality; tomatoes provide color and acidity; eggplant lends its golden flesh; and walnuts impart a rich, mellow flavor.

1½ *pounds fresh tomatoes, peeled, seeded, and chopped*
1 *tablespoon extra-virgin olive oil*
Salt and freshly ground black pepper to taste
1 *small eggplant, trimmed, cut into small dice*
Olive oil for frying
1 *pound fresh fettuccine*
4–6 *ounces ricotta*
12 *fresh walnut halves, coarsely chopped*
Freshly grated imported Parmesan cheese
Basil leaves, torn

Place the tomatoes, extra-virgin olive oil, and salt and pepper to taste in a medium saucepan. Cook slowly for 20 minutes.

Fry the diced eggplant in at least ¼ inch olive oil. Do not crowd the pan and regulate the heat as necessary. The oil should be quite hot but not smoking. Fry eggplant until golden on all sides. Drain well on several thicknesses of paper towels. Drain again on clean paper towels and lightly salt. Alternately, oil a baking sheet. Toss the eggplant cubes in olive oil, spread on the baking sheet, and place in a preheated 450° oven. Stir occasionally until the eggplant is golden. Combine the eggplant and the tomato sauce, stir, and correct the seasonings. Keep warm.

Meanwhile cook the tagliatelle in salted boiling water until tender but firm.

Place the ricotta in a warm pasta serving bowl and add the chopped walnuts and 2 to 3 tablespoons of pasta cooking water. Stir until a cream forms.

Drain the pasta, leaving a little water clinging to the strands. Place in the serving dish and toss with the ricotta. Add the tomato-eggplant sauce and toss again. Dust with Parmesan cheese and sprinkle with basil leaves. Serve with extra Parmesan cheese on the side.

BUTTERFLY PASTA WITH FENNEL AND BALSAMIC VINEGAR

Farfalle ai Finocchi

SERVES 4 TO 6

Slivers of fennel bring an intriguing sweetness to this fresh tomato and basil sauce. A spoonful of balsamic vinegar intensifies and deepens the flavors. This is an elegant pasta to serve to guests—the flavors and the lovely butterfly shapes make it special.

6 *tablespoons extra-virgin olive oil*
3 *large garlic cloves, peeled*
2 *medium heads fennel, cored and cut into slivers*
4 *large ripe tomatoes, peeled, seeded, and coarsely chopped*
Small handful basil leaves
1 *tablespoon balsamic vinegar*
Salt and freshly ground black pepper to taste
1 *pound imported dried farfalle*
Freshly grated imported Parmesan cheese

Place the olive oil in a large sauté pan. Add the garlic cloves and sauté over medium-low heat until golden. Add the fennel slivers, toss, and cook over low heat until fennel is very tender and the garlic breaks down, about 8 minutes. Stir occasionally to prevent the garlic from sticking to the pan. Add the tomatoes, the basil, torn into fragments, balsamic vinegar, and salt and pepper to taste, and cook over medium heat until a sauce forms, about 15 minutes.

Cook the farfalle in abundant salted boiling water until al dente. Drain well and place in a pasta serving dish. Add the sauce to the pasta and toss well. Serve with grated Parmesan cheese at the table.

SPAGHETTINI WITH ZUCCHINI

Spaghettini con Zucchine

SERVES 4

One of the staples of southern Italy is a dish of golden zucchini coins tossed with strands of pasta. Since the flavor of the finished dish rests almost entirely on the freshness and tenderness of the zucchini, I like to use baby zucchini with their golden blossoms still attached, when available. If you can't find baby zucchini with blossoms at your local farmer's market or specialty produce store, use firm, small zucchini with glossy skin. The pasta will be just as delicious.

1½ *pounds baby zucchini with attached blossoms or*
    4 small firm zucchini
8 *tablespoons extra-virgin olive oil*
3 *garlic cloves, peeled and thinly sliced*
Salt and freshly ground black pepper to taste
6 *tablespoons water*
¾ *pound imported dried spaghettini*
Handful fresh basil leaves
Freshly grated imported Parmesan cheese, optional

Detach the blossoms from the zucchini and wash the zucchini well. Trim the zucchini and slice into thick coins. Remove the pistils from the blossoms and coarsely chop the petals. Place the olive oil and garlic in a large sauté pan. Turn on the heat to medium high and toss briefly. Add the zucchini and fry in the olive oil until it is lightly golden. Lower the heat, add the blossoms, and toss gently. Season with salt and pepper to taste, and add 6 tablespoons of water. Simmer very gently for a few minutes, or until the blossoms are tender.

Meanwhile cook the spaghettini in abundant salted boiling water until al dente. Reserve about ½ cup of the pasta water and drain the pasta, leaving water clinging to the strands.

Place the pasta in a serving dish. Add the zucchini mixture and all the juices to the spaghettini. Sprinkle with basil and toss gently, adding salt and a generous amount of black pepper. Add enough of the reserved pasta cooking water to moisten the spaghettini. Serve with Parmesan cheese, if desired.

TAGLIOLINI WITH MUSHROOMS AND LEMON

Tagliolini con Funghi al Limone

SERVES 2

*I*f you should find fresh porcini mushrooms in your market, use them in this very simple pasta. The exquisite flavor of the mushrooms highlights the thin fresh egg pasta, fruity olive oil, and tangy lemon juice. Since fresh porcini are rarely available, shiitake mushrooms with thick, fleshy caps make a very good substitute as do brown, or Italian field, mushrooms. Crisp white mushrooms work well also. Sauté them first in half the olive oil over very high heat until a golden crust forms on the surface of the mushrooms. This evaporates some of their water content and intensifies their flavor. Add the remaining oil, the garlic, and the herbs, and proceed as directed.

½ *pound fresh mushrooms*

6 *tablespoons extra-virgin olive oil*

2 *garlic cloves, peeled and finely chopped*

2 *tablespoons chopped Italian parsley leaves*

Salt and freshly ground black pepper to taste

Juice of ½ lemon or to taste

8 *ounces fresh tagliolini*

Wipe the mushrooms clean with damp paper towels. Trim the stems. If using shiitake mushrooms, clean them in the same way as directed above, cut off the stems and discard. Cut the mushrooms into thick strips and then cut them across again into medium-sized chunks.

In a medium sauté pan, combine the olive oil, garlic, and parsley. Sauté over low heat for 2 to 3 minutes. Add the mushrooms and cook until they soften slightly and release their juices. Season with salt and pepper to taste. Off the heat, stir in the lemon juice.

Meanwhile cook the pasta in abundant salted boiling water until tender. Reserve about 4 tablespoons of the pasta water. Drain the pasta, leaving the strands dripping with water. Toss the pasta with the sauce and grind black pepper over the top.

TUBETTI WITH SPRING VEGETABLE SAUCE

Tubetti con Salsa Primaverile

SERVES 4 TO 6

Spring brings with it an abundance of sweet vegetables. Asparagus, peas, carrots, zucchini, and fava beans—the most delicate and tender of the season's offerings—find their way into this sauce. The vegetables are diced, echoing the short shape of the tubetti, so that every mouthful is a generous mix of vegetable and pasta.

6 *tablespoons unsalted butter*

2 *tablespoons extra-virgin olive oil*

3 *garlic cloves, peeled and finely chopped*

2 *small carrots, peeled and cut into small dice*

2 *small zucchini, trimmed and cut into small dice*

½ *pound slender asparagus, tough ends trimmed, tender portion cut into short pieces*

½ *cup shelled tiny peas, fresh or frozen*

½ *cup shelled small fava beans, peeled*

Salt and freshly ground black pepper to taste

3 *medium tomatoes, peeled, seeded, and chopped*

1 *pound imported dried tubetti*

Handful basil leaves, coarsely chopped

Freshly grated imported Parmesan cheese

Combine the butter, olive oil, and garlic in a large sauté pan. Cook over low heat for 2 to 3 minutes. Add the carrots and cook for about 4 minutes. Add the remaining vegetables and season with salt and pepper to taste. Stir gently and cook, covered, over low heat for 5 minutes. Add the tomatoes and cook, uncovered, until the vegetables are tender. If the mixture appears to be drying out, add a few tablespoons of water.

Meanwhile cook the pasta in abundant salted boiling water until al dente. Drain the pasta, leaving a little water clinging to it. Transfer the pasta to the sauté pan and, over very low heat, gently toss with the sauce. Sprinkle with the basil and grind a generous amount of black pepper over the top and toss again. Serve with grated Parmesan cheese at the table.

PENNE WITH GOLDEN GARLIC

Penne all'Aglio Dorato

SERVES 4

*T*welve cloves of garlic are sautéed in olive oil until golden brown, then cooked with tomatoes. The garlic melts into the tomato sauce, giving it a sweet, nutty flavor and sublimely creamy texture.

Italians have a passion for bouillon cubes and use them often. If you like, you can crush half a bouillon cube into the sauce as it cooks for extra depth of flavor.

> 4 *tablespoons extra-virgin olive oil*
> 12 *garlic cloves, peeled and lightly crushed*
> 1 *28-ounce can imported Italian tomatoes, seeded and*
>   *coarsely chopped, juice reserved*
> *Salt and freshly ground black pepper to taste*
> ½ *bouillon cube, optional*
> 1 *pound imported dried penne*
> *Freshly grated imported Parmesan cheese*

Place the olive oil and the garlic cloves in a medium sauté pan. Cook over medium-low heat until the garlic is soft and a light golden-brown. Stir frequently to prevent sticking. Add the tomatoes and their juices, salt and pepper, and the bouillon cube, if desired. Cook until a sauce forms.

Meanwhile cook the pasta in abundant salted boiling water. Drain well and place in a pasta serving bowl. Add the sauce and toss well. Serve with grated Parmesan cheese on the side.

LASAGNETTE WITH TOMATO AND MIXED MUSHROOM SAUCE

Lasagnette ai Funghi Misti

SERVES 4 TO 6

Narrow ribbons of ruffled lasagna look lovely tossed with a sauce of mushrooms, tomatoes, and basil. Dried porcini mushrooms, plumped in water, infuse the sauce with their forest essence. Unsalted butter, tossed with the hot pasta just before the sauce is added, lends a sweet, creamy note to the finished dish.

2 *ounces dried porcini mushrooms*

1 *pound assorted fresh mushrooms*

4 *tablespoons extra-virgin olive oil*

2 *tablespoons unsalted butter, divided*

½ *medium onion, finely diced*

3 *garlic cloves, chopped*

3 *tablespoons chopped Italian parsley*

Salt and freshly ground black pepper to taste

1 *28-ounce can imported Italian tomatoes, drained, seeded, and chopped*

5 *basil leaves, torn into large fragments*

1 *pound lasagnette, about ⅜ inch wide*

4 *tablespoons freshly grated imported Parmesan cheese, plus extra for the table*

Soak the porcini mushrooms in hot water to cover for 20 minutes, or until soft and moist. Lift the mushrooms out of the soaking liquid and place in a fine-mesh sieve. Rinse them under cold water, using your fingers to feel for any trapped particles of sand. Make sure the mushrooms are completely free of grit. Coarsely chop them.

Use damp paper towels to wipe clean the fresh mushrooms. Trim the stems and if using shiitake mushrooms, cut off the entire stem and discard. Slice the mushrooms.

Place the olive oil and 1 tablespoon of butter in a large sauté pan. Add the onion and cook gently over low heat until the onion is tender. During the last few minutes of cooking, add the garlic and parsley. Add the sliced mushrooms, raise the heat to medium, and sauté until the mushrooms begin to soften. Season with salt and pepper to taste. Continue cooking until the mushrooms are tender and any excess moisture has evaporated. Add the porcini mushrooms and stir once or twice.

Add the tomatoes, basil, and salt to taste. Cover and cook for 15 minutes, or until the tomatoes thicken into a sauce.

Cook the pasta in abundant salted boiling water until al dente. Drain well and place in a pasta serving dish. Add the remaining 1 tablespoon of butter and toss until the butter melts. Add the sauce, toss, and sprinkle with 4 tablespoons of grated Parmesan cheese. Toss again and serve with additional grated cheese at the table.

PASTA WITH CAULIFLOWER AND SUN-DRIED TOMATO PASTE

Pasta al Cavolfiore ed Estratto

SERVES 4 TO 6

This is a rich-tasting, slightly sweet Sicilian pasta dish in which cauliflower is braised with onion, raisins, and pine nuts until it turns into a coarse puree. In Italy a touch of tomato would be added in the form of extract (*estratto*) made from pureed tomatoes dried in the sun, unavailable in this country. Sun-dried tomato paste, either homemade or the kind sold in tubes, makes an excellent substitute. Or use imported tomato paste.

This copper-colored sauce evokes the exoticism of Sicily: the brightly painted and tasseled horse-drawn carts decorated with mirrors that reflect golden sunlight, the desserts embellished with candied fruits and ribbons of citron, and the hot-pink domes of the church of San Giovanni degli Eremiti in Palermo.

1 *head cauliflower, leaves trimmed, cut lengthwise into quarters*
4 *tablespoons extra-virgin olive oil, plus extra for drizzling on pasta*
1 *large onion, diced*
4 *tablespoons sun-dried tomato paste or imported tomato paste*
3 *tablespoons raisins*
2 *tablespoons pine nuts*
Salt and freshly ground black pepper to taste
1 *pound imported dried bucatini or mezzanelli*

Cook the cauliflower in abundant salted boiling water until tender but crisp. Lift the cauliflower out of the water, drain, and reserve the water. Cut away the base of the stalk, and cut the cauliflower into small flowerets.

In a medium braising pan, combine the olive oil and diced onion. Cook over low heat for about 5 minutes. Add a few tablespoons of the reserved cooking water and continue cooking the onion until it is light gold and meltingly tender. Add the tomato paste and 1 cup of the reserved water and stir well. Bring to a gentle simmer and cook covered for about 10 minutes. Add the cauliflower pieces, raisins, pine nuts, and salt and pepper to taste. Cook, covered, over low heat for about 30 minutes, using a fork to break down the cauliflower pieces. Add additional water as needed, up to 1 cup, until the cauliflower becomes a coarse puree and a thick sauce forms. Toward the end of the cooking, season the sauce with a generous grinding of black pepper.

Meanwhile place the remaining reserved cauliflower water in a large pasta cooking pot and add as much fresh water as needed to cook the pasta. Bring the water to a boil and add salt. Add the pasta and cook until al dente. Drain, leaving a little water clinging to the strands of pasta.

Place the pasta in a shallow serving bowl. Drizzle with about 1 tablespoon of olive oil and toss. Add the sauce to the pasta bowl and toss. Let the pasta rest for a few moments before serving, tossing it once or twice. Cheese is not served with this dish as it would conflict with the sweetness of the sauce.

FETTUCCINE WITH SWISS CHARD AND MUSHROOMS

Fettuccine con Bietole e Funghi

SERVES 4

Swiss chard and mushrooms produce a simple yet amazingly savory pasta sauce. Tender, egg-rich fettuccine is the perfect complement to the buttery vegetables.

1–2 *ounces dried porcini mushrooms*
1 *pound fresh mushrooms*
1 *bunch Swiss chard, about 1 pound*
Salt
6 *tablespoons unsalted butter*
2 *tablespoons extra-virgin olive oil*
Salt and freshly ground black pepper to taste
1 *pound fresh fettuccine*
5 *tablespoons freshly grated imported Parmesan cheese,*
     plus extra for the table

Soak the porcini mushrooms in hot water to cover for 20 minutes, or until soft. Lift the mushrooms out of the water and place in a fine-mesh sieve. Run cold water over the mushrooms and feel for any traces of sand or grit. Keep rinsing until the mushrooms are completely clean. Chop them coarsely.

Use damp paper towels to wipe clean the fresh mushrooms. Trim the stems. Slice the mushrooms.

Strip the leaves from the stalks of the Swiss chard and reserve. Bring a generous amount of water to a boil and add salt. Plunge the stalks into the water, then after a minute, add the leaves. Cook the Swiss chard until the stalks are tender. Drain in a colander and chop coarsely.

Place the butter and olive oil in a large sauté pan. Turn the heat to high. When the butter melts, add the fresh mushrooms and toss until the mushrooms become crusty and golden brown. Lower the heat to medium and add the porcini mushrooms. Toss, then cook for a few minutes. Add the Swiss chard and season with salt and pepper to taste. Stir the ingredients together and cook for about 4 minutes, or until the chard and mushrooms have absorbed the flavors of the butter and olive oil.

Meanwhile cook the fettuccine in abundant salted boiling water. When the pasta is tender, reserve ½ cup of the cooking water and drain the pasta, but leave the strands dripping wet.

Transfer the pasta to the sauté pan with the vegetables. Sprinkle with 5 tablespoons of grated Parmesan cheese. Toss and add enough of the reserved pasta cooking water to keep the sauce moist. Serve with extra Parmesan cheese at the table.

PASTA WITH GREENS, RICOTTA, AND PINE NUTS

Pasta con Verdura, Ricotta, e Pignoli

SERVES 4 TO 6

If you like the bite of mustard greens, you will want to use two bunches of the leaves in this dish. Mild ricotta and creamy, resinous pine nuts are perfect complements to the sharp flavor of the greens. Use imported De Cecco whole wheat pasta. Its warm, toasty flavor is an excellent complement to this sauce.

1–2 *pounds mustard greens, stems trimmed, washed*
     but not dried
Salt to taste
3   *tablespoons extra-virgin olive oil*
3   *garlic cloves, peeled and finely chopped*
1   *pound imported dried penne or other short pasta shape*
6   *ounces ricotta*
¼   *cup fresh pine nuts, lightly toasted*
Freshly ground black pepper to taste
Freshly grated imported Parmesan cheese

Cook the mustard greens in the water that clings to them, adding salt to taste. When the greens are tender, drain them and coarsely chop.

Place the olive oil and garlic in a medium sauté pan. Cook over low heat for a few minutes. Add the greens and sauté for 5 minutes to blend the flavors.

Meanwhile cook the pasta in salted boiling water.   *(continued)*

Place the ricotta and pine nuts in a shallow pasta serving dish. Add a few tablespoons of the pasta cooking water to the bowl and stir until a cream forms. Add salt and pepper to taste.

Drain the pasta when it is al dente, leaving a little water clinging to it. Place the pasta in the serving dish. Toss with the ricotta mixture. Add the chopped greens and toss again. Serve dusted with Parmesan cheese.

FRESH PASTA WITH SPICY ARTICHOKE SAUCE

Pasta Fresca con Crema di Carciofi

SERVES 4

This sauce contrasts the heat of red chile pepper with the mellowness of artichokes and cream. Really fresh artichokes have an incredibly rich, meaty flavor, only a hint of which remains in artichokes that have been picked long before they are cooked. Braising the artichokes slowly with herbs and other seasonings helps bring back their flavor.

Toss the sauce with fresh egg pasta and dust it with a fistful of golden Parmesan cheese before serving. Remember to be generous with the red chile pepper; the sauce should be quite spicy.

3 *tablespoons extra-virgin olive oil*
½ *teaspoon dried red chile pepper flakes, or to taste*
1 *garlic clove, peeled and chopped*
1 *bay leaf*
2 *tablespoons chopped Italian parsley*
4 *large artichokes, leaves completely cut away, hearts*
    scrupulously trimmed according to directions
    on page 8, and quartered
Salt and freshly ground black pepper to taste
½ *cup fresh cream*
1 *pound fresh fettuccine, cut into 2-inch strips*
Freshly grated imported Parmesan cheese

Place the olive oil, red chile pepper, garlic, bay leaf, and parsley in a medium sauté pan. Warm over low heat for several minutes. Add the quartered artichokes and toss in the oil briefly. Add water to cover and salt and pepper to taste. Bring to a boil and simmer, covered, until the artichokes are extremely tender, for 30 to 45 minutes. If the water evaporates before the artichokes are cooked, add a few tablespoons of water as needed. Mash the artichokes with a fork to a coarse puree. Some fibers may remain. If you wish, you can put the mixture through a fine-mesh strainer, but if the artichokes were trimmed carefully, the few remaining fibers should not cause a problem. Add the cream to the sauté pan and stir. Keep the sauce warm.

Meanwhile cook the fettuccine in abundant salted boiling water. Reserve a cup of the pasta water. Drain the fettuccine when slightly undercooked, leaving water clinging to the strands. Place the pasta in the sauté pan with the sauce and toss over low heat, adding a little of the reserved water to thin the sauce. Sprinkle with Parmesan cheese and a grinding of pepper. Toss and serve with additional cheese on the side.

PENNETTE WITH PINK CREAM SAUCE AND ZUCCHINI

Pennette con Salsa Rosa e Zucchine Dorate

MAKES 4 SMALL
FIRST-COURSE SERVINGS

A sauce made with tomato, cream, zucchini, and fresh whole basil leaves. Tossed with pennette, it makes an elegant first course.

The key to the success of this recipe lies in slicing the zucchini thinly and cooking it over high heat until golden brown. The flavor of the zucchini changes dramatically; it becomes deep and burnished, providing a rich counterpoint to the light, sweet flavors of tomato, cream, and basil.

2 *tablespoons unsalted butter*

2 *tablespoons extra-virgin olive oil*

2 *small zucchini, trimmed and thinly sliced*

1 *garlic clove, finely chopped*

2 *medium tomatoes, peeled, seeded, and finely chopped*

1 *cup fresh cream*

About 12 very small basil leaves

Salt and freshly ground black pepper to taste

½ *pound imported dried pennette*

2 *tablespoons freshly grated imported Parmesan cheese, plus extra for the table*

Place the butter and olive oil in a medium sauté pan and turn on the heat to high. Add the zucchini slices and toss until they turn dark gold. Sprinkle with the garlic and toss. Add the tomatoes, cream, basil leaves, and salt and pepper to taste. Cook over high heat for a few minutes, just until the cream sauce thickens slightly.

Meanwhile cook the pasta in abundant salted boiling water until al dente. Drain well and place in a shallow serving dish. Add the sauce and 2 tablespoons of grated Parmesan cheese. Toss and serve. Pass extra grated cheese at the table.

SPAGHETTINI WITH EGGPLANT-FLAVORED TOMATO SAUCE

Spaghettini con Pomodoro al Profumo di Melanzane

SERVES 6

A two-course meal from one recipe. Small Japanese eggplants are stuffed with caciocavallo cheese, mint, and garlic, and braised in a sauce of sweet ripe tomatoes.

When the eggplants are tender, they are lifted out of the sauce and arranged on a platter. The tomato sauce, imbued with the flavors of eggplant and fresh mint, is tossed with spaghettini and served as a first course, and the stuffed eggplants are served as a second course.

For this dish use firm, glossy, unblemished Japanese eggplants with fresh-looking stem ends. Old eggplant lacks the sweetness and creamy white tender flesh of young eggplant.

8 *Japanese eggplants, each about 5 inches long*
3 *ounces caciocavallo cheese, cut into 24 pieces*
4 *garlic cloves, sliced into 6 slices per garlic clove, plus 2 garlic cloves, finely chopped*
½ *bunch mint, leaves only*
Olive oil for frying
4 *tablespoons extra-virgin olive oil*
1 *onion, finely chopped*
2½ *pounds tomatoes, peeled, seeded, and coarsely pureed*
Salt and freshly ground black pepper to taste
1 *pound imported dried spaghettini*
Freshly grated imported Pecorino Romano cheese

Using a sharp knife, make 6 incisions in the widest part of each eggplant. Working carefully, gently insert a piece of cheese into 3 of the cuts. Place a slice of garlic and a mint leaf in each of the other 3 incisions.

Place enough olive oil to measure ¼ inch in a medium sauté pan. Brown the eggplants, a few at a time, over medium heat until they soften slightly, about 5 minutes.

(continued)

In a large saucepan, combine the extra-virgin olive oil, onion, and chopped garlic. Cook over low heat until the onion softens. Add the tomato puree and salt and pepper to taste. Raise the heat to high, and when the tomato sauce comes to a boil, reduce the heat to medium and add the eggplants and mint leaves, reserving a few leaves for garnishing. Simmer, partly covered, until the eggplants are tender and the sauce has thickened. Use a slotted spoon to transfer the eggplants to a serving dish. Sprinkle with the reserved mint leaves.

Meanwhile cook the spaghettini in abundant boiling salted water until al dente. Drain and place the pasta in a serving bowl. Add the sauce to the bowl and toss.

Serve the pasta as a first course, sprinkled with grated Pecorino Romano cheese, and have extra cheese available at the table. Serve the stuffed eggplants as the main course.

Rice and Polenta

When I feel the need for comforting food, I turn to rice. It has a mild flavor and a satisfyingly chewy texture. As rice cooks, it fills the kitchen with a soft, subtle perfume. Rice can be boiled like pasta and drained when al dente. Or it can be prepared as in risotto, by gradually adding liquid. When making risotto, use only Arborio rice because it can absorb a great deal of broth without breaking down. As Arborio rice cooks, it releases a creamy starch that give risotto its characteristic moist, flowing consistency. For other recipes calling for rice, use either Arborio or the long-grain variety.

Polenta is simply cornmeal and water, cooked slowly and stirred without cease until it thickens into a soft, golden mass. Polenta can be served immediately while it is hot and fluffy, topped with a simple tomato sauce or smothered with braised mushrooms. When cool, polenta can be sliced and grilled to accompany other foods, or the slices can be layered in the same manner as lasagna. It is a humble food, as basic as pasta and rice, and every bit as gratifying. Making polenta in the traditional way has its special rewards, but when time and energy are in short supply, I turn to the instant variety. It cooks in a matter of minutes and produces a light, soft dish that is remarkably good. Look for instant polenta imported from Italy, available in Italian and gourmet shops.

Rice Dishes and Risotto

COLD RICE WITH HOT BAKED TOMATOES

Riso Freddo con Pomodori al Forno

SERVES 4

A seductive pairing of hot and cold that makes for irresistible summer eating. Fat, luscious, tomatoes, bright red and juicy, are stuffed with herbs and baked, then served on a bed of cool rice. When you pierce the tomato with your fork, the hot juices merge with the rice. Each forkful contains cool, chewy rice and warm, soft tomato, fragrant with herbs and garlic.

2 *very large, ripe, but firm tomatoes*
Salt
1½ *cups Arborio, or, if unavailable, long-grain rice*
8 *tablespoons extra-virgin olive oil, divided, plus extra
      for drizzling*
Freshly ground black pepper to taste
2 *garlic cloves, finely chopped*
2 *tablespoons chopped Italian parsley leaves*
2 *tablespoons chopped mint leaves*
2 *tablespoons chopped basil leaves*
4 *anchovies, coarsely chopped*
3 *tablespoons homemade Bread Crumbs (see page 363),
      toasted in a small sauté pan*

Cut the tomatoes in half horizontally and, using your fingers, gently remove some of the seeds. Salt the tomatoes and turn them upside down on paper towels to drain for 20 minutes.

Cook the rice in abundant salted boiling water until al dente. Drain well. Transfer the rice to a bowl. Toss the rice in 4 tablespoons of olive oil and season with salt and pepper to taste. Let cool.

In a small bowl combine the garlic, herbs, and anchovies. Moisten with the remaining 4 tablespoons of olive oil. Lightly oil a baking dish large enough to contain the tomatoes without crowding them. Arrange the tomatoes in the baking dish. Stuff the herb mixture into the cavities of the tomatoes. Sprinkle the tomatoes with the Bread Crumbs and drizzle with a few drops of olive oil. Bake in a preheated 450° oven for 12 minutes, or until the tomatoes begin to soften but well before they lose their shape.

Divide the rice among 4 dinner plates, smoothing the rice so that it forms a bed for each tomato half. Remove the tomatoes from the oven and center a tomato half on each plate of rice.

RICE WITH RICOTTA

Riso con Ricotta

SERVES 2 TO 3

A light, simple mixture of rice, fresh ricotta, herbs, and lemon zest. Fresh and uncomplicated, it is a good dish for jaded palates.

½ *pound fresh ricotta, at room temperature*
4 *tablespoons chopped Italian parsley leaves*
2 *tablespoons chopped basil leaves*
2 *teaspoons chopped marjoram leaves*
Zest of ½ small lemon, finely chopped
Salt and freshly ground black pepper to taste
6 *tablespoons unsalted butter, at room temperature*
1½ *cups Arborio rice or, if unavailable, long-grain rice*
Freshly grated imported Parmesan cheese

In a bowl combine the ricotta, herbs, and lemon zest. Season with salt and pepper to taste. If possible, let the mixture rest for 30 minutes or so to allow the flavors to develop.

Place the butter in a shallow serving bowl.

Cook the rice in abundant salted boiling water until al dente. Reserve ½ cup of the rice cooking water. Drain the rice, leaving some moisture clinging to it. Transfer the hot rice to the serving bowl. Toss with the butter to coat the grains. Add the ricotta mixture and toss again. Serve with grated Parmesan cheese at the table.

SIMPLE RICE WITH PESTO

Riso Semplice al Pesto

SERVES 4 TO 6

Hot, buttery rice is placed on the table along with a bowl of freshly made Basil and Almond Pesto. Each person adds a spoonful of Pesto to the rice and stirs until the dish becomes bright green and heady with the perfume of basil and olive oil.

Since Pesto turns dark very quickly after it comes in contact with heat, this method keeps its flavor and color vibrant. And everyone can revel in the wonderful aroma as the Pesto hits the hot rice.

This simple way of serving rice has obvious advantages over risotto because it requires neither much attention nor broth. And the results are every bit as delectable.

> 2 *cups Arborio rice*
> *Salt*
> 6 *tablespoons unsalted butter, at room temperature*
> *A double recipe of Basil and Almond Pesto (see page 44)*

Boil the rice in abundant salted boiling water until al dente. Reserve 1 cup of the boiling water. Drain the rice and place in a serving dish. Add the butter and reserved water. Stir until the butter melts into the rice.

Bring the rice to the table. Pass the Basil and Almond Pesto around for each person to spoon into the rice.

ANGRY RICE

Riso all'Arrabbiata

SERVES 4

Pasta isn't the only food capable of becoming "angry." Here, rice is tossed with an "angry" tomato sauce made fiery with red chile pepper flakes and mashed garlic. Serve this dish with pitchers of cold wine or water to quell the fire.

4 *tablespoons extra-virgin olive oil*
1 *teaspoon dried red chile pepper flakes*
1 *28-ounce can imported Italian tomatoes, coarsely pureed*
3 *garlic cloves, mashed to a paste*
Salt to taste
4 *tablespoons coarsely chopped Italian parsley*
2 *cups Arborio rice or, if unavailable, long-grain rice*
Freshly grated imported Parmesan cheese

In a medium sauté pan, combine the olive oil and red chile pepper flakes. Cook over low heat for 2 to 3 minutes. Add the tomatoes and garlic and season with salt to taste. Cook over medium heat until the tomatoes thicken into a sauce. Add the parsley during the last few minutes of cooking.

Meanwhile cook the rice in abundant salted boiling water until al dente. Drain well. Place in a shallow serving bowl and toss with the sauce. Serve with grated Parmesan cheese on the side.

RICE WITH WINTER SQUASH AND SAGE BUTTER

Riso con Zucca Gialla

SERVES 4 TO 6

Chewy Arborio rice stirred into a puree of bright winter squash makes a warming dish on a cold winter day. The rich flavors of browned butter and musky sage give dimension to the sweetness of the squash.

Start with Salad of Bitter Greens with Cheeses (see page 104).

1 *pound winter squash, such as banana or butternut*
6 *tablespoons unsalted butter*
3 *garlic cloves, peeled and lightly crushed*
12 *fresh sage leaves, coarsely chopped*
Salt and freshly ground black pepper to taste
2 *cups Arborio rice*
⅓ *cup freshly grated imported Parmesan cheese, plus additional for the table*

Scrape away any seeds or stringy matter from the squash. Peel and cut into large dice. Cook the squash in a large pot of boiling salted water until the squash is very tender. Lift the squash out of the water with a slotted spoon. Reserve the cooking water. Put the squash through a food mill, a potato ricer, or puree it to a fine texture in a food processor.

Place the butter in a medium saucepan. Add the garlic and chopped sage to the pan, and sauté over low heat until the butter colors lightly and the garlic turns golden. Add the squash puree, salt and freshly ground black pepper to taste. Stir well and cook over low heat for about 10 minutes.

Bring the squash cooking water to a boil. Add the rice and stir. Cook over high heat until the rice is al dente. Reserve 1 cup of the cooking water. Drain the rice and add to the squash puree. Stir well. Add enough of the reserved water to create a moist and lightly soupy consistency. Off the heat stir in the Parmesan cheese. Serve with additional Parmesan cheese at the table.

RISOTTO WITH ROMAINE AND FENNEL

Risotto con Lattuga e Finocchi

SERVES 4

This risotto features the gentle flavors of lettuce and fennel. The delicious, edible core of the romaine is chopped and added to the risotto along with the other vegetables. As it cooks, the rice turns a beautiful pale green flecked with the deeper color of the romaine strips. This would be appropriate served as the main course of a lunch in early spring.

2 *tablespoons extra-virgin olive oil*

4 *tablespoons unsalted butter, divided*

½ *onion, finely diced*

1 *head romaine, leaves cut into strips, core chopped*

1 *small fennel bulb, trimmed and cut into small dice*

3 *tablespoons chopped Italian parsley*

Salt to taste

6 *cups Chicken Broth (see page 157) or Vegetable Broth I (see page 155)*

2 *cups Arborio rice*

5 *tablespoons freshly grated imported Parmesan cheese, plus extra for the table*

Freshly ground black pepper to taste

Place the olive oil and 3 tablespoons of the butter in a large, heavy-bottomed saucepan. Turn the heat to medium and add onion, romaine, fennel bulb, and parsley. Add salt to taste and stir well. Cook the vegetables over medium heat until tender, about 20 minutes. Keep the lid on until the vegetables are almost tender. Remove the lid in the final few minutes of cooking and allow the excess moisture to evaporate.

Meanwhile bring the Chicken Broth or Vegetable Broth to a boil in a saucepan. Turn off the heat and leave the pan, covered, on the burner.

Add the rice to the vegetable mixture and stir it well to coat the grains in the olive oil and butter. Add several ladlefuls of broth, or enough to just barely cover the rice. Cook over low heat, stirring often. As the rice absorbs the broth, add more broth to just barely cover the rice. Continue adding broth until the rice is al dente and the risotto has a runny, creamy consistency. Off the heat, stir in the remaining tablespoon of butter, the grated Parmesan cheese, and black pepper to taste.

Serve in shallow soup bowls with extra grated Parmesan cheese at the table.

RISOTTO WITH SWISS CHARD AND WINTER HERBS

Risotto con Bietole ed Erbe Invernali

SERVES 4

A risotto that combines rice with sweet, tender Swiss chard. Fresh sage and rosemary add a deep, resonant herbal finish to the dish.

Although the risotto can be served with Parmesan cheese, I prefer it without, since the gentle flavor of the Swiss chard comes through more fully. But serve grated cheese at the table for guests who like its salty tang in their risotto.

1 *bunch Swiss chard, about 1 pound*
Salt to taste
2 *tablespoons extra-virgin olive oil*
2 *tablespoons unsalted butter, divided*
1 *small onion, finely diced*
2 *garlic cloves, peeled and chopped*
1 *tablespoon chopped rosemary leaves*
1 *tablespoon chopped sage leaves*
3 *tablespoons chopped Italian parsley leaves*
6 *cups Chicken Broth (see page 157) or Vegetable Broth I*
   (see page 155)
2 *cups Arborio rice*
Freshly ground black pepper
Freshly grated imported Parmesan cheese, optional

Strip the leaves from the Swiss chard stalks and reserve the stalks for another use. Wash the chard leaves and, with some water clinging to the leaves, place them in a large sauté pan. Add salt to taste. Turn on the heat to high, cover, and cook the chard until it wilts and the leaves are tender, about 5 minutes. Drain in a colander. Cut the cooked chard across into strips and set aside.

In a deep, heavy-bottomed saucepan, combine the olive oil and 1 tablespoon of butter and turn the heat on to low. When the butter melts, add the onion, garlic, rosemary, sage, and parsley. Cook over low heat for about 10 minutes, or until the onion is tender and translucent. Meanwhile bring the Chicken Broth or Vegetable Broth to a boil in a saucepan. Turn off the heat and leave it on the burner, covered.

Add the rice to the onion mixture and stir until the rice is coated with oil, about 2 to 3 minutes. Add the cooked chard and stir. Add enough broth to just cover the rice, and let cook, stirring often, until the broth is absorbed. Add more broth, just enough to cover the rice, and stir often until the broth is absorbed. Continue adding broth and stirring until the rice is al dente and the risotto is creamy and liquid. Add salt if necessary. Off the heat, stir in the remaining tablespoon of butter and grind a little pepper over the top.

Serve the risotto in shallow pasta bowls. If desired, serve with Parmesan cheese.

PINK RISOTTO WITH CELERY

Risotto con Sedano e Pomodoro

SERVES 4

A celery risotto with a bracing, herbal flavor enhanced by using not only the stalks, but also the leaves and core of the celery. A touch of tomato turns the dish a soft peach color.

2 *celery hearts, white and pale green stalks and their leaves*
1 *tablespoon extra-virgin olive oil*
1 *small clove garlic, peeled and finely chopped*
1 *tablespoon chopped Italian parsley*
3 *canned imported Italian tomatoes, seeded and chopped*
Salt and freshly ground black pepper to taste
6 *cups Chicken Broth (see page 157) or Vegetable Broth II (see page 156)*
3 *tablespoons unsalted butter, divided*
2 *cups Arborio rice*
¼ *cup freshly grated imported Parmesan cheese, plus additional for the table*

Trim the celery hearts by cutting them across the base to release the stalks. Wash the stalks well, especially at the base. Cut off the top portions, reserving a few of the leafy tops. Reserve the central core. Remove any developed strings from the stalks. Finely dice the celery by cutting the stalks lengthwise into thin strips, then bunching the strips together and cutting them crosswise. Finely dice the celery core. Coarsely chop enough celery leaves to measure 2 tablespoons.

In a small sauté pan combine the olive oil, garlic, and parsley. Cook over low heat for 2 to 3 minutes, or until garlic is opaque. Add the tomatoes and salt and pepper to taste. Cook over medium-low heat for about 5 minutes. Set aside off the heat.

Bring the broth to a boil in a saucepan. Turn off the heat and keep on the stove with the lid on.

Melt 2 tablespoons of the butter in a medium, heavy-bottomed saucepan. Add the diced celery and celery core and toss in the butter. Cook over low heat for about 5 minutes. Add the tomato sauce and cook for another 5 minutes. Add the rice and stir to coat the grains. Let cook for 1 to 2 minutes. Add enough broth to just cover the rice and celery and bring to a simmer. Keep the lid partially on the saucepan and stir often, until the broth is absorbed. Continue adding broth, just enough to cover, and stir frequently, until the rice is al dente and the risotto is creamy and liquid. This should take approximately 18 minutes. In the final few minutes of cooking, stir in the celery leaves.

Off the heat, stir in the remaining tablespoon of butter and the grated Parmesan cheese. Taste for salt and add more if necessary. Grind a little black pepper over the top and stir again.

Serve in shallow pasta bowls with extra grated Parmesan cheese at the table.

RISOTTO WITH PORCINI MUSHROOMS

Risotto ai Funghi Porcini

SERVES 4

*P*orcini mushrooms infuse this dish with their bosky perfume—intense, aromatic, and evocative. The risotto is enriched with a small amount of fresh cream, stirred in off the heat so that the flavor stays fresh and sweet.

1–2 *ounces dried porcini mushrooms*

4 *tablespoons extra-virgin olive oil*

1 *small onion, finely diced*

1 *tablespoon finely chopped rosemary leaves*

1 *tablespoon finely chopped oregano leaves*

2 *garlic cloves, peeled and minced*

Salt and freshly ground black pepper to taste

¼ *cup dry white wine*

2 *cups Arborio rice*

6 *cups Chicken Broth (see page 157) or Vegetable Broth II*
   (see page 156)

2 *tablespoons fresh cream*

Freshly grated imported Parmesan cheese

Place the porcini mushrooms in a small bowl. Soak them in hot water to cover for about 15 minutes, or until soft. Carefully lift them out of the soaking liquid and place in a fine sieve. Run cold water over the mushrooms, gently tossing them in the cold water to release any trapped grit. Let drain. Coarsely chop the mushrooms. Strain the soaking liquid and reserve.

In a medium, heavy-bottomed saucepan, place the olive oil, onion, and herbs and cook over low heat until the onion is translucent and soft, about 10 minutes. Add the garlic a few minutes before the onion is ready. Add the mushrooms, season with salt and pepper to taste, and sauté over low heat for a few minutes. Add the wine, raise the heat, and let the wine evaporate completely. Lower the heat and add the rice. Stir to coat the grains.

Meanwhile bring to a boil in another saucepan the Chicken Broth or Vegetable Broth mixed with the reserved porcini soaking liquid. Turn off the heat and leave on the stove, covered.

Add enough broth to the rice to just cover the rice. Cook at a simmer, stirring frequently, until the broth is absorbed. Continue adding broth, always just enough to cover, until the rice is al dente and the risotto is creamy and liquid. Turn off the heat and stir in the cream. Cover and let the risotto rest for a minute. Serve in shallow pasta bowls with grated Parmesan cheese at the table.

RISOTTO WITH BABY ARTICHOKES

Risotto con i Carciofini

SERVES 4

This risotto features very small artichokes, picked before they develop inedible chokes. As the risotto cooks, the artichokes melt, turning the creamy mass a pale green and imbuing it with a rich, clean flavor. If baby artichokes are not available, substitute very fresh, medium-sized artichokes that are completely trimmed of tough leaves and fibers.

1 *small lemon, cut in half*

10 *baby artichokes*

4 *tablespoons unsalted butter, divided*

2 *tablespoons extra-virgin olive oil*

2 *garlic cloves, peeled and lightly crushed*

3 *tablespoons chopped Italian parsley*

Salt and freshly ground black pepper to taste

6 *cups Chicken Broth (see page 157) or Vegetable Broth II*
   (see page 156)

2 *cups Arborio rice*

5 *tablespoons freshly grated imported Parmesan cheese,*
   plus additional for the table

Fill a large bowl with water. Squeeze in the juice of half a lemon. Use the other lemon half to rub the cut portions of the artichokes as you work to prevent them from darkening. Snap off the tough, green leaves from the artichokes. Trim the dark green areas from the base and the stalk. Cut off the tops of the leaves and cut each artichoke into 6 pieces lengthwise. Immerse the artichokes in the acidulated water until needed.

In a large, heavy-bottomed saucepan, combine 3 tablespoons of the butter, olive oil, and crushed garlic cloves. Sauté the garlic over low heat until it turns golden brown. Discard the garlic. Drain the artichoke wedges and add them to the pan, along with any water that clings to them. Add the parsley and salt and pepper to taste. Cook the artichokes over medium heat for about 15 minutes, or until they are tender. Add a few tablespoons of water if the artichokes begin to dry out.

In a saucepan bring the Chicken Broth or Vegetable Broth to a boil. Turn off the heat and leave the pan, covered, on the burner.

Add the rice to the artichokes and stir until all the grains of rice are nicely coated with the oil and butter mixture. Begin adding the hot broth, a few ladlefuls at a time, or enough to just barely cover the rice. Cook over gentle heat, stirring often. As the rice absorbs the broth, add more broth, always just enough to barely cover the rice. Continue adding broth until the rice is al dente and the risotto is runny and creamy in texture. Turn off the heat at this stage, making sure that the risotto is quite moist. Off the heat stir in the remaining tablespoon of butter and 5 tablespoons of grated Parmesan cheese.

Serve the risotto in shallow soup bowls with extra grated Parmesan cheese on the side.

GREEN RISOTTO WITH CREAM AND HERBS

Risotto Verde alle Erbe

MAKES 6 SMALL, RICH SERVINGS

Spinach risotto is turned into a special-occasion dish by stirring an infusion of cream and fresh herbs into the finished dish. The result is a light, creamy risotto with strong, herbal overtones.

6 *tablespoons freshly grated imported Parmesan cheese, divided*

4 *tablespoons fresh cream*

2 *heaping tablespoons chopped herbs, including basil, chervil, chives, marjoram, mint, rosemary, and thyme*

5 *tablespoons unsalted butter, divided*

½ *onion, peeled and finely diced*

1 *bunch spinach, stemmed, cut into strips*

2 *cups Arborio rice*

Salt to taste

6 *cups Beef Broth (see page 158) or Vegetable Broth II (see page 156)*

Combine in a small bowl 2 tablespoons of the grated Parmesan cheese, the cream, and the herbs. Set aside while making the risotto.

In a large heavy-bottomed saucepan, combine 4 tablespoons of butter and the onion. Cook over low heat until tender. Add the spinach and sauté until tender. Add the rice and salt to taste, and mix well.

Meanwhile place the broth in a medium saucepan and bring to a boil. Turn off the heat and leave on the stove, covered.

Add enough broth to just cover the rice and stir over low heat until the broth is absorbed. Continue adding broth, a few ladlefuls at a time, until the rice is al dente and the risotto is lightly soupy. Stir in the remaining Parmesan cheese.

Off the heat add the herb mixture and the remaining butter. Mix well and cover. Let rest for a few moments before serving.

Polenta

TRADITIONAL POLENTA
Polenta Vecchio Stile
SERVES 4 TO 6

aking polenta the traditional way certainly requires a commitment of time and energy—not always available in our busy lives. On occasion it is a fun and gratifying task, especially when you've finished and you pour the creamy golden mass onto a platter and serve it forth.

1½ *quarts water*
2 *teaspoons salt*
1½ *cups imported coarse cornmeal*

Bring the water to a boil and add salt. When the water returns to a boil, start adding the polenta in a thin, steady stream, stirring it well as you add it. Reduce the heat to medium and continue stirring steadily for 30 minutes, or until the polenta is thick and soft. Serve immediately. To make slices, pour the hot polenta into a loaf pan and let cool. Unmold the polenta and slice to the desired thickness.

LIGHTNING-QUICK POLENTA

Polenta Istantanea

SERVES 4 TO 6

A very fast method for making polenta that produces amazingly good results. With instant polenta in your pantry, satisfying dishes can be prepared in as little time as it takes to whip up a pasta dish.

1½ *quarts water*
2 *teaspoons salt*
1 *13-ounce box imported instant polenta*

Bring the water to a boil. Add the salt. When the water returns to a boil, quickly add the polenta in a steady stream, stirring it with a wooden spoon all the while. Continue stirring for 5 minutes, or until it is thick and soft. Serve immediately. Or pour into a loaf pan and let cool. Unmold the polenta and slice to the desired thickness.

POLENTA WITH BROCCOLI SAUCE

Polenta con Broccoli

SERVES 4 TO 6

This recipe features a golden mound of soft polenta topped with a deep green sauce of broccoli cooked to a coarse garlicky puree. The broccoli is braised, a technique suited to vegetables in the *Brassica* family, like broccoli and cauliflower. The normally light, sweet flavor of these vegetables becomes richer and deeper.

If the stems of the broccoli are fresh and bright green, peel them and cook them along with the tops. If the broccoli has very thick, pale green stalks, discard the stalks and use only the flowerets. In the latter case, buy twice as much broccoli.

1 *bunch fresh broccoli, about 1½ pounds*
4 *cups water*
Salt
½ *cup extra-virgin olive oil, plus 1 tablespoon*
4 *garlic cloves, peeled and coarsely chopped*
Salt and freshly ground black pepper to taste
1 *recipe Traditional Polenta (see page 237) or Lightning-*
Quick Polenta (see page 238)
Freshly grated imported Pecorino Romano cheese

Discard broccoli stalks that are white or a very pale green. Trim the base of the tender stalks. Using a paring knife, strip the peel from the tender stalks. Cut the broccoli stalks into short lengths and break the flowerets into smaller clusters. In a medium saucepan bring the water to a boil. Add salt and when the water returns to a boil, add the broccoli. Cook for 20 minutes with the lid on. Lift the broccoli out of the water and place on a cutting board. Reserve the cooking water. Chop the broccoli coarsely.

In a medium sauté pan, combine the olive oil and garlic. Sauté over low heat for 2 to 3 minutes, or until the garlic is opaque. Add the broccoli and stir. Sauté the broccoli over low heat for about 5 minutes. Add 1 cup of the reserved broccoli cooking water. Bring to a boil, reduce heat, and simmer over medium-low heat for 15 minutes, adding salt and pepper to taste. Add more of the reserved water as needed, ½ cup at a time, as it evaporates. Use a wooden spoon to break down the broccoli into a coarse puree.

Meanwhile cook the polenta.

Oil a serving dish with 1 tablespoon of olive oil. Mound the polenta on the platter, smoothing it with the back of a large spoon or with a spatula and making a large shallow indentation in the center. Spoon the broccoli and the pan juices into the indentation and let some of the juices and olive oil run over the sides and pool around the edges. Grind a little black pepper over the broccoli. Serve with grated Pecorino Romano cheese on the side.

WHOLE GRILLED TOMATOES WITH POLENTA

Pomodori alla Griglia con Polenta

SERVES 4

Polenta is normally associated with winter, so it comes as something of a surprise when served in summer, as in this dish, which is suited to warm weather and outdoor grilling. Whole tomatoes filled with herbs, olive oil, and slices of polenta are grilled and served together, the tomato a bright red globe surrounded by brilliant gold rectangles of polenta. Make the polenta in the morning and let it cool. The rest of the cooking can be done out of doors. Grilled tomatoes are delicate, so handle with care.

This dish can also be prepared on a ridged stovetop grill or under a broiler.

1 *recipe Lightning-Quick Polenta (see page 238)*
4 *ripe, firm large tomatoes*
Salt and freshly ground black pepper
6 *tablespoons extra-virgin olive oil*
3 *garlic cloves, peeled and finely chopped*
1 *teaspoon dried Mediterranean oregano*
Handful basil leaves

Make the polenta and pour into a loaf pan. Let cool and cut into ½-inch slices.

Cut a generous opening at the stem ends of the tomatoes. Scoop out some of the seeds. Generously season the interiors with salt and pepper. In a small bowl combine the olive oil, garlic, and oregano, and stir. Spoon a little of the olive oil mixture into each tomato, dividing it equally among the 4 tomatoes.

Arrange the tomatoes and the slices of polenta on a lightly oiled grill, or lay them on a lightly oiled baking sheet and place under the broiler. Cook the tomatoes until they begin to soften and the polenta shows grill marks. If using the broiler, cook tomatoes and polenta until the polenta is golden and crusty.

To serve, place a grilled tomato in the center of each dinner plate. Surround with 3 or 4 slices of Polenta and garnish with basil leaves.

A Sampler of Main Dishes

Many of the recipes in this book lend
themselves to being served as the main course of a
meal. Pasta, risotto, and polenta dishes all have the
qualities we associate with food that takes center stage at
mealtime. They have a certain presence, a richness of flavor,
and an ability to satisfy our deepest hungers. When
temperatures soar and appetites flag, main-dish salads give
us the balance of freshness and substance we require.
Antipasti, in particular, fit in with the trend toward lighter
eating and less belabored cooking, and many, such as those
featuring raw vegetables and fresh cheese, make for a
simple, refreshing meal that requires no cooking.

This chapter deals with an assortment of recipes that
fulfill the role of main course easily and naturally. The
dishes range from light to hearty; from a large platter of
lightly cooked vegetables drizzled with olive oil and
garnished with lemon wedges to an elaborate torta layered
with potatoes, artichokes, and tomato sauce. Suggestions are
given for side dishes, but often crusty bread or garlicky
bruschetta, a salad or an informal antipasto, are all that are
needed to round out a meal.

The first section includes recipes for five cooking
techniques that transform vegetables into main-course
dishes, and describes the vegetables best suited for each
technique and ideas for serving them. Stew recipes are
related to soups, but are heartier and have a greater textural
interest. Pizza and tarts delineate by their shape their
completeness. Stuffed vegetables also work well as main
dishes—they make perfect containers for all kinds of
fillings. Gnocchi and fritters, often thought of as first-course
or side dishes, easily fit into lighter main-course eating.

Gnocchi are served with fresh-tasting sauces, but fritters require just a squeeze of lemon. Finally, the section on egg dishes includes a bright recipe for hard-cooked eggs served with a raw tomato sauce, and there is a selection of frittatas for every season.

Many of these dishes can be served at room temperature; and they can be included on the antipasto or buffet table, or taken along on picnics. None is terribly time-consuming, and most are as easy to make as the dishes in other chapters of this book. None are laden with the caloric baggage of pastry crusts, cream, or rich cheeses to justify their place at the center of the table, although I couldn't resist including a tomato tart with a puff-pastry lining. They are all fresh, appealing, and wholesome and have the ability to satisfy.

Vegetables Five Ways

STEAMED VEGETABLES ITALIAN STYLE

Verdure al Vapore

SERVES 1

Steamed vegetables take on a whole new meaning when prepared Italian style. In this unique method, the vegetables are arranged on a heatproof serving dish, drizzled with olive oil and sprinkled with herbs, wrapped in foil, then placed over a pot of boiling water to steam in their own juices. The vegetables cook beautifully, permeated with the taste of olive oil and herbs, and the juices become aromatic and full of flavor. This is cooking for one at its simplest and healthiest, with a minimum of fuss but with no loss of pleasure.

The following assortment of vegetables is merely a guide. Season and availability will dictate which ones you use. When making your selection, keep in mind the various cooking times. Those with a high water content—mushrooms, for example—will steam more quickly than dense vegetables such as broccoli. You can alter the cooking times of different vegetables by slicing them thinly or thickly, so that they all cook in the same amount of time. Always include fresh herbs in the mix and use your very best extra-virgin olive oil.

Handful tender fava beans
2 stalks asparagus
2 large shiitake mushrooms
3 large button mushrooms
3–4 cherry tomatoes
1 medium-small zucchini
2–3 green onions
Salt and freshly ground black pepper to taste
1 sprig basil
2 sprigs thyme
2–3 tablespoons extra-virgin olive oil

(continued)

Peel the fava beans. Break off the tough ends of the asparagus. Peel about halfway up the stalks. Cut each stalk in half lengthwise. Use damp paper towels to wipe clean the shiitake mushrooms. Completely cut off the stems. Clean the button mushrooms in the same way. Trim the ends of the stems. Carefully pluck off the stems of the cherry tomatoes, making sure not to tear the skin. Trim the zucchini and cut in half horizontally. Then cut each half into quarters lengthwise. Trim the green onions and cut into short lengths.

Select an ovenproof dinner plate. Find a saucepan that is 1 or 2 inches smaller in diameter than the plate. Fill the saucepan about three fourths of the way up with water and bring to a gentle boil. Arrange the vegetables on the dinner plate. Season with salt and pepper to taste. Arrange the herbs over the top and drizzle with olive oil. Wrap the plate tightly in foil. Carefully place the plate over the boiling water. Cook for 15 minutes, or until the vegetables are tender. Carefully lift the plate off the saucepan and let rest for a minute or two to cool the plate. Remove the foil and serve.

COLD COMPOSED VEGETABLE PLATTER

Gran Misto Freddo

SERVES 4

Freshly cooked and cooled vegetables make an inviting main dish arranged in separate groups on a big platter and garnished with lemon wedges.

This recipe calls for tender green beans, zucchini, potatoes, red Swiss chard, and Romanesco broccoli, but countless variations can be played on this theme depending on the season, your mood, or the occasion.

If necessary, you can prepare this dish several hours in advance, but it tastes best when the vegetables have a trace of warmth left in them. Accompany the meal with thinly sliced imported Italian prosciutto, a small platter of assorted cheeses, or ricotta mixed with fresh herbs.

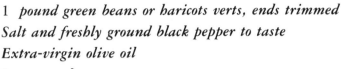

1 *large bunch red Swiss chard*
3 *medium boiling potatoes*
1 *small Romanesco broccoli*
4 *medium zucchini, untrimmed*
1 *pound green beans or haricots verts, ends trimmed*
Salt and freshly ground black pepper to taste
Extra-virgin olive oil
Lemon wedges

Strip the leaves from the stalks of the Swiss chard. Trim the ends of the stalks and cut them into matchsticks. Trim away any dark spots from the potatoes. Break the Romanesco broccoli into large flowerets.

Cook the green vegetables separately in abundant salted boiling water. Cook the red chard last, since it releases color into the water. With a large slotted spoon or a strainer, remove each vegetable when just tender, and drain well.

Meanwhile place the potatoes in a small pot and cover with water. Bring to a boil and cook until tender but firm. When the potatoes are cool enough to handle, peel them and cut into medium dice.

Cut the zucchini into strips lengthwise, then cut in half or in thirds. If the green beans are very long, cut them in half or in thirds. Cut the cauliflower into small flowerets.

Arrange the vegetables on a platter. Season with salt and pepper to taste, and drizzle generously with extra-virgin olive oil. Serve at room temperature, garnished with lemon wedges.

ROASTED VEGETABLES

Verdura al Forno

SERVES 4

oasting vegetables is an effective way to deepen and intensify their flavor. They emerge from the oven tender, fragrant, and golden brown, and require only a minimum amount of attention while cooking.

When preparing a mix of vegetables for roasting, keep their cooking times in mind, since the goal is to have them all become tender at the same time. In the following recipe, zucchini and peppers, which cook quickly, are cut into large strips. Asparagus, which is quite tender, is left uncut. Dense vegetables, such as the potatoes, must be cut into smaller chunks. Try roasting fennel, radicchio, winter squash, mushrooms, or any other vegetables whose flavor is enhanced by browning. When roasting vegetables, be sure not to crowd the pan, as this causes the vegetables to steam rather than brown.

To turn leftover roasted vegetables into a salad, toss with red wine vinegar or lemon juice and sprinkle with chopped fresh herbs. You can also cut the vegetables into thin strips and toss with hot pasta.

2 *peppers, red or yellow, cored, seeded, and cut
    into thick strips*

3–4 *Japanese eggplants, stems trimmed, cut
    into thick strips*

2 *Belgian endives, cut lengthwise into quarters*

4 *small red potatoes, cut into quarters*

3 *medium zucchini, cut lengthwise into quarters*

2 *medium onions, peeled and cut through the root
    end into eighths*

½ *pound asparagus, tough ends trimmed, peeled
    halfway up the stalks*

8 *garlic cloves, peeled*

6 *sprigs thyme*

4 *sprigs rosemary*

Salt and coarsely ground black pepper to taste

Extra-virgin olive oil

Divide the prepared vegetables between 2 large roasting pans. Scatter the garlic and herbs over the top and season with salt and pepper to taste. Drizzle with enough olive oil to coat the vegetables very lightly and toss.

Place the roasting pans side by side in a preheated 500° oven. Cook for approximately 30 minutes, or until the vegetables are tender. Stir occasionally while cooking to roast the vegetables evenly and to prevent their sticking to the pans. Grind pepper over the top before serving.

SAUTÉED GREEN VEGETABLE PLATTER

Piattone di Verdure Strascinate

SERVES 2 TO 4

Small zucchini, tiny green beans, and fresh spinach are sautéed separately in olive oil and garlic and arranged on a big platter. This brilliant dish in shades of garden green makes for a simple, fresh main course when you are in the mood for a light, restorative meal. Begin with wedges of frittata for a family supper, or serve the vegetables as a side dish with peppery grilled chicken.

> ¾ *pound tender green beans, such as haricots verts,*
>   *ends trimmed*
> 2 *bunches spinach, stems removed, or 2 bunches Swiss*
>   *chard, leaves only*
> *Salt to taste*
> 4 *tablespoons extra-virgin olive oil, divided*
> 2 *garlic cloves, peeled and lightly crushed*
> *Pinch of red chile pepper flakes to taste*
> 3 *garlic cloves, peeled and finely chopped, divided*
> ¾ *pound very small zucchini, ends trimmed*
>   *and cut into coins*

Cook the green beans in salted boiling water until tender. Drain well. Place the spinach or chard in a large braising pan. Cover and cook in just the water that clings to the leaves after washing, adding salt to taste. When the leaves are tender, drain and set aside. *(continued)*

Place 2 tablespoons of olive oil and the crushed garlic cloves in a medium sauté pan. Sauté the garlic over low heat until it is golden. Add the greens, more salt to taste, and the red chile pepper flakes to taste. Sauté over medium-low heat until the greens have absorbed the olive oil. Transfer to the center of a platter.

Place 2 tablespoons of olive oil and half the chopped garlic in a medium sauté pan. Cook over low heat for 2 to 3 minutes, then add the zucchini coins. Sauté over medium-low heat until the zucchini is tender-crisp. Season with salt to taste and place on the platter on one side of the greens. In the same pan, sauté the green beans in the remaining olive oil and garlic and season with salt as they cook. The green beans are ready when they have absorbed the flavor of the olive oil, a matter of a few minutes. Remove from the pan and place the green beans on the other side of the greens on the platter.

Serve immediately or at room temperature.

GRILLED SKEWERED VEGETABLES

Spiedini di Verdura Mista

SERVES 4

These vegetables on skewers have the glow of late summer on them. Perfumed with herbs and scented with woodsmoke, they make a great main dish served with grilled Polenta (see page 237 or page 238).

1 *red pepper*

1 *green pepper*

16 *small boiling onions*

3 *medium zucchini*

8 *plump shiitake mushrooms*

½ *pound butternut squash*

½ *cup extra-virgin olive oil*

4 *sprigs thyme, leaves chopped*

3 *sprigs rosemary, leaves chopped*

2 *large garlic cloves, peeled and sliced*

Salt and freshly ground black pepper to taste

Remove the core, seeds, and white membranes from the peppers. Cut into 1-inch dice. Blanch the onions in boiling water for 2 minutes. Drain and peel. Trim the surface of the root ends. Trim the ends of the zucchini and cut into 1-inch chunks. Cut off the stems of the shiitake mushrooms and discard. Wipe the mushroom caps with damp paper towels. Cut the mushrooms caps in half. Peel and seed the squash, and cut into 1-inch dice.

Place the vegetables in a bowl and drizzle with the olive oil. Add the herbs, garlic, and salt and pepper to taste, and toss well. Let rest for 1 hour or longer.

Thread the ingredients on 8 skewers, alternating the ingredients to create an interesting color contrast.

Heat the grill and lightly oil with an old, clean dish towel. Grill the vegetables until tender, turning them on all sides. Brush with olive oil while cooking if the vegetables appear dry.

SPRING VEGETABLE STEW

Ragù alla Primizia

SERVES 4

A colorful amalgam of tender spring vegetables in a light, buttery tomato and vegetable broth. If you prefer, the vegetables can be cooked directly in the broth. As the broth reduces, add the carrots and onions first, then the zucchini, the peas, and finally the asparagus. Time the cooking so that there is a small amount of broth in the finished dish.

Naturally, variations abound. Try adding strips of lettuce or sorrel in the final moments of cooking. Artichoke wedges, little turnips, or pearl onions would be delicious added early in the cooking.

1   *bunch slender asparagus, ends trimmed, stems peeled, cut into short lengths*
8   *green onions, roots and half of the green tops trimmed, cut into short lengths*
8   *baby zucchini, trimmed*
1   *cup fresh peas*
12 *baby carrots, trimmed and peeled*
2   *tablespoons extra-virgin olive oil*
1   *shallot, peeled and finely chopped*
3   *cups Vegetable Broth I (see page 155)*
2   *tablespoons unsalted butter*
2   *medium tomatoes, peeled, seeded, and finely diced*
Salt and freshly ground black pepper to taste
10 *basil leaves, julienned*

Cook each vegetable, except the tomatoes, separately in salted boiling water. Drain when vegetables are al dente and refresh under cold running water.

In a large sauté pan, combine the olive oil and shallot. Sauté over low heat until tender. Add the broth, bring to a boil, and reduce by half. Add the butter and diced tomatoes, and simmer for a few minutes. Add the rest of the cooked vegetables to the broth and warm over gentle heat, seasoning with salt and pepper to taste. Sprinkle with basil. Serve in shallow pasta bowls.

RUSTIC SPRING STEW

Bazzoffia

SERVES 4

This springtime stew from the Roman countryside is in subtle shades of green. Fresh fava beans, fennel, peas, lettuce, and artichokes cook slowly until the stew emerges fragrant and silvery green. After being ladled out into shallow bowls, the stew is enriched with a drizzle of olive oil and sprinkled with tangy Pecorino Romano cheese. Serve with bread to dip into the sweet, savory juices.

In rustic recipes using fresh fava beans, peeling the skin from each individual bean is not required. In fact, the slight bitterness found in the skin is desirable, especially here where it lends relief to the medley of sweet vegetable flavors.

8 *tablespoons extra-virgin olive oil, plus extra for drizzling*
1 *onion, peeled and thickly sliced*
4 *medium artichokes, trimmed (see page 8), cut into thin wedges*
1 *lemon, for trimming artichokes, cut in half*
1 *medium fennel bulb, trimmed, cut into thin wedges*
1 *pound fava beans in the pod, shelled but unpeeled*
½ *cup fresh or frozen peas*
½ *head tender romaine, ribs removed, leaves cut into strips*
Salt to taste
Freshly ground black pepper
Freshly grated imported Pecorino Romano cheese

Place the olive oil and onion in a large braising pan. Cook the onion over low heat until tender. Add the artichokes. Stir and cook for 3 minutes or so. Add the fennel. Stir and cook for 3 minutes. Add the fava beans and peas, and stir. Add the lettuce strips and sauté until the lettuce wilts slightly. Add just enough water to cover the vegetables and season with salt to taste.

Simmer gently until the vegetables are tender, stirring occasionally. If the stew begins to dry out, add water, a small amount at a time. Taste the broth and add more salt if necessary. Grind black pepper into the stew and stir.

To serve, ladle the stew into shallow pasta bowls. Drizzle a little olive oil into each bowl and top with a sprinkling of grated Pecorino Romano cheese. Have extra grated cheese at the table.

PEPERONATA WITH POTATOES AND BLACK OLIVES

Peperonata con Patate e Olive

SERVES 4 TO 6

A highly flavorful stew of red and yellow peppers, onions, potatoes, and black olives. Its rough nature is revealed not only in the choice of ingredients, but also in the style in which they are prepared. Cut the vegetables into large, coarse pieces, and do not overcook them. The separateness of each vegetable needs to be maintained to keep the character of the stew intact. Serve it with big chunks of good country bread to sop up the rich rust-colored juices.

2   *red peppers*
2   *yellow peppers*
1   *pound boiling potatoes*
1½ *pounds tomatoes*
4   *tablespoons extra-virgin olive oil*
2   *tablespoons unsalted butter*
1   *large onion, sliced*
½   *cup oil-cured black olives, pitted, cut in quarters*
10–12 *basil leaves, divided*
Salt and freshly ground black pepper to taste

Prepare the peppers by cutting them lengthwise and removing the cores, seeds, and white membranes. Cut the peppers into ½-inch strips. Peel the potatoes and cut into rough 1-inch dice. Peel, seed, and coarsely chop the tomatoes.

Place the olive oil and butter in a braising pan. Turn the heat to medium and when the butter melts, add the onion and toss quickly. Lower the heat and cook the onion until it softens and becomes light gold. Add the peppers, potatoes, tomatoes, black olives, 4 whole basil leaves, and salt and pepper to taste. Stir the mixture, cover, and cook over low heat for about 40 minutes, or until the vegetables are tender but still hold their shape. Be careful not to overcook the potatoes.

Before serving, coarsely chop the remaining basil. Transfer the stew to a shallow serving dish or to individual pasta bowls and sprinkle with the remaining basil.

BRAISED MIXED MUSHROOMS

Zimino di Funghi Misti

SERVES 4

An earthy mushroom stew seems just right on a cold rainy day, especially when surrounded by crisp, buttery Crostini or ladled over a fluffy mound of bright yellow Polenta. Choose among the variety of fresh mushrooms available, such as shiitake, Italian field mushrooms, oyster mushrooms, chanterelles, morels, and fresh porcini, and use dried porcini mushrooms to intensify the flavors.

1 *ounce dried porcini mushrooms*

2 *pounds assorted fresh mushrooms*

4 *tablespoons extra-virgin olive oil*

1 *small onion, peeled and finely diced*

2 *garlic cloves, peeled and finely chopped*

4 *sprigs thyme, leaves chopped*

Pinch of ground cloves

Salt and freshly ground black pepper to taste

1½ *pounds tomatoes, peeled, seeded, and chopped*

1 *recipe Crostini (see page 366), or 1 recipe Lightning-Quick Polenta (see page 238)*

Soak the porcini mushrooms in a small bowl of warm water. After 20 minutes, lift out the mushrooms and rinse under cold water. Strain the soaking liquid and set aside.

Meanwhile clean the fresh mushrooms with damp paper towels. Trim the stems. If using shiitake mushrooms, cut away the stems and discard. Slice the mushrooms.

Combine in a medium braising pan the olive oil and onion. Cook over low heat until the onion is tender. Add the garlic, thyme, and ground clove, and cook a few minutes more. Add all the mushrooms, raise the heat to medium, and sauté the mushrooms until they wilt, stirring often. Season with salt and pepper to taste. Add the tomatoes and the reserved porcini soaking liquid. Simmer, partly covered, over medium-low heat for about 20 minutes, or until the juices thicken.

To serve, ladle the mushrooms into individual shallow pasta bowls. Serve garnished with Crostini or ladled over Polenta.

LENTILS AND WILD GREENS

Lenticchie con Verdura Selvatica

SERVES 4

This hearty but refreshing dish combines fragrant, nut-brown lentils and tangy greens. A squeeze of lemon added at the last moment brings the flavors to life. The dish is quick and simple to prepare yet deeply satisfying to eat, especially when accompanied with bruschetta sprinkled with aromatic oregano. If mustard greens are not available, substitute a combination of spinach and radish leaves.

1 *bunch mustard greens or other tender bitter greens, stems trimmed, leaves stripped from ribs*

Salt to taste

4 *tablespoons extra-virgin olive oil, divided, plus extra for drizzling*

1 *small onion, peeled and finely diced*

2 *garlic cloves, peeled and finely chopped*

1 *celery stalk, trimmed and finely diced*

1 *small carrot, peeled and finely chopped*

1 *teaspoon chopped fresh oregano leaves*

1 *teaspoon finely chopped rosemary leaves*

2 *tablespoons chopped Italian parsley leaves*

2 *tablespoons chopped basil leaves*

2 *cups lentils, washed and picked over*

Freshly ground black pepper to taste

3 *small tomatoes, roasted, peeled, seeded, and diced*

3 *tablespoons lemon juice, plus 4 lemon wedges for garnish*

1 *recipe Simple Bruschetta with Oregano (see page 131)*

Cook the mustard greens in the water that clings to the leaves after washing. Add salt to taste. Drain in a colander. Chop very coarsely and set aside.

Select a medium braising pan and combine 3 tablespoons of the olive oil, onion, garlic, celery, and carrot. Cook, covered, over moderate heat until the vegetables are tender. Add the herbs and lentils and stir. Let the lentils absorb the flavors for a few minutes. Add 4 cups water and salt and pepper to taste. Bring to a boil, then simmer, with the cover partially on, until the lentils are just tender, approximately 35 minutes. About 10 minutes before the lentils are cooked, add the to-matoes.

Meanwhile sauté the greens very briefly in the remaining tablespoon of olive oil.

Just before serving, stir the greens and lemon juice into the lentil-tomato mixture.

Ladle the stew into shallow soup bowls. Grind a little coarse pepper over the top and add a few drops of raw olive oil. Serve with the Bruschetta sprinkled with oregano and with a wedge of lemon on the side.

COUNTRY-STYLE VEGETABLE STEW

Cianfotta

SERVES 4

Cianfotta is a golden, glowing vegetable stew. There are count-less variations on it, but they all include the classic vegetables associated with the Italian south—eggplant, tomatoes, and peppers. In this version red chile pepper spices it up, and saffron and fresh herbs perfume it. The stew can be eaten right away, but the flavors emerge more fully when the dish is served at room temperature.

Serve it in big bowls and accompany with good bread and strong red wine. Follow with a salad of leafy greens.

5 *tablespoons extra-virgin olive oil*
2 *garlic cloves, peeled and crushed*
1 *onion, peeled and cut into thick slices*
2 *celery stalks, strings removed, sliced crosswise*
1 *teaspoon finely chopped rosemary*
Small pinch of saffron

1 *small eggplant, trimmed and cut into medium dice*
2 *yellow peppers, seeded, membranes removed, cut into strips*
2 *medium boiling potatoes, peeled and cut into medium dice*
4 *ripe medium tomatoes, peeled, seeded, and cut into chunks*
1 *piece fresh red chile pepper, or dried red chile pepper*
   flakes to taste

Salt and freshly ground black pepper to taste
1½ *cups cooked white beans*
2 *tablespoons chopped Italian parsley leaves*
2 *tablespoons chopped basil leaves*

Select a wide, shallow braising pan. Place the olive oil, garlic, onion, celery, rosemary, and saffron in the pan, and sauté over medium-low heat, stirring often, until the vegetables become limp, about 5 minutes.

Add the remaining vegetables, the red chile pepper, and salt and pepper to taste. Stir well and cover tightly. Cook over low heat for about 30 minutes. Stir occasionally. If the mixture becomes dry, add water, a few tablespoons at a time. Add the beans during the last 5 minutes of cooking. At the end of the cooking time, if the juices are thin, raise the heat and cook quickly until the juices thicken. Stir in the remaining herbs and remove the pan from the heat. Serve warm or at room temperature.

Pizza and Tarts

POTATO AND ARUGULA PIZZA

Pizza di Patate e Rucola

SERVES 2 TO 4

othing is so tempting as a crispy and chewy pizza. I never tire of the classic version from Naples with its topping of bright tomatoes and fresh mozzarella, but the very nature of pizza lends itself to improvisation. A pizza without toppings is like a blank canvas. The warm, bready taste of the crust can support a whole range of flavors, from a simple sprinkling of fresh rosemary and garlic to a more elaborate *quattro stagione* featuring four different, distinct tastes. When making pizza, let simplicity be your guide. Too many toppings or too much of any one ingredient can be overwhelming.

In the following recipe, the pizza is covered with slices of mild and creamy potatoes, cooked until golden, then sprinkled with a shower of raw arugula. Other suggestions include pizza topped with paper-thin slices of eggplant and a sprinkling of provolone, or a topping of fine wedges of artichoke sprinkled with mozzarella and black olives.

1 *recipe Pizza Dough (see page 261)*
1¼ *pounds potatoes*
4 *tablespoons extra-virgin olive oil, divided*
Salt to taste
2 *garlic cloves, peeled and mashed to a paste*
Red chile pepper flakes to taste
2 *tablespoons freshly grated imported Parmesan cheese*
Handful arugula leaves, stemmed and cut into strips

Prepare the Pizza Dough and let it rest.

Meanwhile peel the potatoes. Slice thinly. Brush lightly with 2 tablespoons of the olive oil. Arrange the potato slices on a baking sheet in a single layer. Bake in a preheated oven at 350° until they begin to color lightly. Remove the potatoes from the oven and, using a spatula, carefully transfer them to a platter. Sprinkle with salt to taste.

In a small bowl combine the remaining olive oil and the crushed garlic.

Roll out the Pizza Dough as instructed in the recipe and place on a baking sheet or a well-floured pizza peel. Brush the surface of the dough with 1 tablespoon of the olive oil and garlic mixture and sprinkle with red chile pepper flakes. Arrange the potatoes over the top in an overlapping pattern. Brush the remaining oil and garlic mixture over the top and sprinkle with grated Parmesan cheese.

Place the pizza in the oven, either on the baking sheet or use the pizza peel to slide it onto the stone or tiles. Bake in a 500° oven that has been preheated for 20 minutes until the pizza is a deep golden color. Remove from the oven and sprinkle with the arugula.

PIZZA DOUGH

MAKES 1 LARGE PIZZA

This dough makes a puffy, golden pizza. For best results, invest in a pizza stone and a peel or wooden paddle. Or line your oven shelf with unglazed tiles. The direct heat will produce a wonderfully crisp, clean-tasting crust.

¾ *package dry yeast*
¼ *cup warm water*
2 *cups unbleached all-purpose flour*
½ *cup cold water*
1½ *tablespoons olive oil*
Pinch of sugar, optional
¾ *teaspoon salt*

Mix the yeast in the warm water and let rest for 10 to 15 minutes.

Place the flour in the bowl of a mixer with a dough hook. In a cup combine the cold water, olive oil, sugar, and salt. Add to flour and mix. Add yeast and stir. Mix at medium speed until a ball forms. Or combine ingredients in a bowl in the same order and mix together until a dough forms. Transfer the dough to a floured board and knead until smooth and elastic. Place in an oiled bowl. Cover with a damp towel and let rest for about 45 minutes, or until doubled in size. *(continued)*

Pound the dough down and form into a rectangle. Let rise on a floured board for about 1 hour. Form the dough into a rectangle about 6 by 18 inches. If you bake the pizza on a baking sheet, transfer it to the sheet or, if you use a pizza stone or tiles, transfer the dough to a well-floured peel. Proceed as directed in the pizza recipe on page 260.

TOMATO TART

Crostata di Pomodoro

SERVES 6

A beautiful tart of golden puff pastry topped with overlapping slices of ripe Roma tomatoes, toasted pine nuts, and basil. The ultimate picnic snack, this tart is also delicious cut into small squares and served with wine as an appetizer.

Purchase puff-pastry dough from a high-quality bakery.

4 *tablespoons extra-virgin olive oil*
1 *garlic clove, peeled and crushed to a paste*
7 *Roma tomatoes*
1 *sheet puff-pastry dough, 12 by 12 inches*
1 *egg yolk, beaten*
14 *basil leaves, julienned*
Salt and freshly ground black pepper
¼ *cup toasted pine nuts*

Combine the olive oil and garlic in a small bowl and set aside until needed.

Core, slice, and seed the tomatoes. Drain on paper towels.

Arrange the puff-pastry dough on a baking sheet. Cut ½-inch strips from all 4 sides. Brush egg yolk on the edges of the square of dough and arrange the strips along the top of the edges. Prick the bottom of the dough with a fork. Refrigerate for 1 hour.

Bake the dough in a preheated 400° oven for 10 minutes, or until it rises and turns slightly golden. Brush with 2 tablespoons of the olive oil and garlic mixture and sprinkle with half the basil. Season with salt and pepper to taste. Arrange the tomato slices over the top in an overlapping pattern and top with the remaining olive oil and garlic mixture. Bake for 10 minutes, or until the pastry is golden and the tomatoes have softened but are still intact. Let cool slightly. Sprinkle with the pine nuts and remaining basil. Serve warm or at room temperature.

RICOTTA TORTA WITH HERBS

Torta di Ricotta alle Erbe

SERVES 4

*T*his easy ricotta torta full of the perfume of fresh herbs is equally good served warm or at room temperature. If desired, pitted black or green olives or plump morsels of sun-dried tomato can be stirred into the ricotta mixture before baking to add little bursts of strong flavor. If you have extra sprigs of herbs, arrange them around the rim of the torta for a lovely garnish.

Serve the torta for brunch, cut into wedges and accompanied with Little Tomato and Basil Salad (see page 47). Or wrap it up and take it along on a picnic. Cut into small squares, it can be served as part of an assortment of antipasti.

> 2 *pounds ricotta*
> 3 *eggs, separated*
> ¼ *cup chopped Italian parsley leaves*
> ¼ *cup chopped basil leaves*
> 1 *teaspoon finely chopped rosemary leaves*
> 1 *teaspoon finely chopped thyme leaves*
> 1 *teaspoon finely chopped sage leaves*
> 5 *tablespoons freshly grated imported Pecorino Romano cheese*
> *Salt and freshly ground black pepper to taste*
> 2 *tablespoons butter*
> 3 *tablespoons bread crumbs*

Drain ricotta in several layers of cheesecloth. Place the drained ricotta in a mixing bowl and, using a wooden spoon, stir in the egg yolks. Add the herbs, grated Pecorino Romano cheese, and salt and pepper to taste. Beat the egg whites until stiff and gently fold into the mixture. *(continued)*

Select a round high-sided cake pan or a 10-inch springform pan. Generously butter the pan and sprinkle with bread crumbs. Use a spatula to carefully transfer the ricotta mixture into the prepared springform pan.

Bake the ricotta torta in a preheated 400° oven for 1 hour, or until the top of the torta is firm to the touch and golden. Remove from the oven and let rest for about 5 minutes. As it cools, it will lose volume. Unmold the torta and cut into wedges.

SWISS CHARD TORTINO

Tortino di Bietole

SERVES 4 TO 6

This golden, crusty tart lined with bread crumbs features the complementary flavors of Swiss chard and porcini mushrooms. It is good served hot or at room temperature, and is especially enjoyable as part of a picnic lunch, cut into wedges and eaten out of hand.

1–2 *ounces dried porcini mushrooms*
2 *bunches Swiss chard*
4 *tablespoons extra-virgin olive oil*
1 *medium onion, peeled and finely chopped*
2 *garlic cloves, peeled and chopped*
3 *eggs, lightly beaten*
4 *tablespoons freshly grated imported Parmesan cheese*
6 *tablespoons bread crumbs, divided*
1 *tablespoon chopped Italian parsley*
Freshly grated nutmeg to taste
Salt and freshly ground black pepper to taste
Unsalted butter

Soak the porcini mushrooms in a small bowl with enough warm water to cover. After 20 minutes, lift the mushrooms out of the liquid. Rinse the mushrooms under cool water, feeling for any hidden grit. Cut the mushrooms into strips.

Wash the Swiss chard well. Strip the leaves from the stalks. Reserve the stalks for another use. Place the chard leaves in a large braising pan and cook in the water that clings to the leaves. When the chard is tender, after about 5 minutes, drain and gently press out excess water with the back of a wooden spoon.

Place the olive oil and onion in a medium sauté pan. Cook over low heat until the onion is soft. Add the mushrooms and garlic, and cook for 3 to 4 minutes. Add the chard, stir, and cook for about 5 minutes. Let cool.

Transfer the chard mixture to a bowl. Add the eggs, grated Parmesan cheese, 2 tablespoons bread crumbs, parsley, nutmeg, salt, and pepper to taste. Mix well.

Butter a medium-sized round baking dish or a 9-inch springform pan. Sprinkle with 2 tablespoons bread crumbs. Add the chard mixture and smooth the top. Sprinkle the top with the remaining bread crumbs. Bake in a preheated 375° oven for 30 minutes, or until the tortino is golden.

POTATO AND ARTICHOKE "CAKE"

Gattò di Carciofi e Patate

SERVES 6 AS A MAIN DISH

For potato lovers there could be no greater thrill than this torta layered with creamy potatoes, tomato sauce, and artichokes. Lined with golden bread crumbs, it makes an impressive-looking main dish. Depending on the context in which it is served, it can either go country or appear rather sophisticated.

3   *artichokes, trimmed (see page 8)*
6   *tablespoons extra-virgin olive oil, divided*
Water
Salt to taste
½   *medium onion, finely diced*
1   *28-ounce can imported Italian tomatoes, drained, seeded,*
        and coarsely chopped
Salt and freshly ground black pepper to taste
6   *medium russet potatoes*
3   *eggs, lightly beaten*
6   *ounces fresh mozzarella, drained and shredded*
½   *cup freshly grated imported Pecorino Romano cheese*
¼   *cup chopped parsley*
1   *bunch basil, leaves only, coarsely chopped*
2   *tablespoons butter*
¾   *cup bread crumbs, divided*

Thinly slice the artichokes. Sauté them in 3 tablespoons of olive oil. After the artichoke slices have absorbed the flavor of the olive oil, add about ¼ cup of water and salt to taste. Cover and cook until the artichokes are tender.

Sauté the onion in the remaining 3 tablespoons of olive oil until the onion is soft. Add the tomatoes, and salt and pepper to taste. Cook over medium heat until the sauce is thick and dry.

Meanwhile boil the potatoes in salted water to cover until tender. Select 1 potato for testing. Piercing the potatoes too frequently will cause them to absorb water and make the "cake" too moist. When the potatoes are cooked, drain and peel them. Put the potatoes through a ricer into a medium bowl. Let cool and add the eggs, mozzarella, grated Pecorino Romano cheese, and chopped herbs. Mix well.

Generously butter a 9 by 2½-inch springform pan. Coat pan with the bread crumbs, reserving 2 tablespoons for the topping. Spread one third of the potato mixture in the bottom of the springform pan. Over it spread half of the tomato mixture and half of the artichoke slices. Repeat with the remaining ingredients, ending with the potato mixture. Drizzle the top with the remaining olive oil and sprinkle with the rest of the bread crumbs. Place on a baking sheet and bake in a preheated 350° oven for 1 hour, or until the surface is golden brown. Let cool for about 15 minutes, then release the springform pan. Leave the torta on the base and cool to room temperature. Serve in wedges. The torta can be made a day in advance and refrigerated. Bring to room temperature before serving.

EGGPLANT TORTA

Torta di Melanzane

SERVES 6 AS A MAIN DISH

classic dish from the repertoire of Italian eggplant dishes. This rich-tasting torta layers creamy eggplant and fresh mozzarella moistened with a tomato basil sauce. It makes a great centerpiece for a dinner or, cut into small squares, it can be served as a side dish. It is equally good eaten warm or at room temperature.

3 *medium eggplants*
Salt
3 *tablespoons extra-virgin olive oil*
3 *garlic cloves, peeled and chopped*
1 *28-ounce can imported Italian tomatoes*
Handful basil leaves, coarsely chopped
Salt and freshly ground black pepper to taste
Olive oil for frying
1 *cup unbleached, all-purpose flour*
1 *cup freshly grated imported Parmesan cheese*
½ *pound fresh mozzarella, drained and shredded*
3 *large eggs, lightly beaten*

(continued)

Trim the eggplants and slice ⅓ inch thick. Salt the slices lightly and let drain in a colander for at least 30 minutes.

Combine in a medium sauté pan the extra-virgin olive oil and garlic. Cook for 2 to 3 minutes over low heat. Add the tomatoes by lifting them out of the can and crushing them with your fingers into the pan. Add the chopped basil and salt and pepper to taste. Cook over medium heat, partly covered, until the sauce thickens.

Wipe the eggplant slices dry. Select a large skillet and pour in olive oil to a depth of ½ inch. Turn the heat to medium high and when the oil is very hot but not smoking, dredge the eggplant lightly in the flour and fry, a few slices at a time, until golden on both sides. Lift the eggplant slices out of the oil using tongs, letting the excess oil drain back into the pan. Drain the eggplant slices very well on several layers of paper towels.

In a 2-quart round baking dish, arrange enough eggplant slices to cover the bottom of the dish. Line the sides with eggplant slices placed vertically in a slightly overlapping pattern, allowing the eggplant to extend a little over the top of the dish. Cover the eggplant slices with a few tablespoons of the tomato sauce and sprinkle with a little grated Parmesan cheese and shredded mozzarella. Cover with more slices of eggplant, cutting away excess so that the slices fit neatly. Continue layering the ingredients, ending with a layer of eggplant, a little tomato sauce, and grated Parmesan and mozzarella cheese. Use a knife to pierce the layers of eggplant in 3 or 4 places. Pour the beaten eggs over the top, and let the eggs seep into the torta. Fold the overlapping edges of eggplant over the top of the torta.

Bake in a preheated 350° oven for 50 minutes, or until the eggs are set. Cool at least 15 minutes before serving.

ONION TART

Tortino di Cipolla

SERVES 6

T his dish highlights the sweet, gentle flavors of ricotta, sautéed golden onion, and basil. It makes an ideal brunch offering, especially when served with a few bright spoonfuls of fresh tomato sauce on the side.

3 *tablespoons extra-virgin olive oil*

2 *large onions, peeled and thinly sliced*

2 *pounds fresh ricotta, drained*

Small handful basil leaves, chopped

4 *eggs, lightly beaten*

½ *cup freshly grated imported Parmesan cheese*

Salt and freshly ground black pepper to taste

2 *tablespoons unsalted butter*

¼ *cup bread crumbs*

1 *recipe Sweet Tomato Basil Sauce (see page 202)*

Place the olive oil in a large sauté pan. Add the onions and cook over low heat until they become tender and golden.

Combine in a bowl the onions, ricotta, basil, eggs, grated Parmesan cheese, and salt and pepper to taste. Mix well.

Generously butter a 9-inch springform pan. Coat with the bread crumbs. Transfer the ricotta mixture to the pan and smooth the top. Bake in a preheated 375° oven for 1 hour, or until firm and lightly golden. Let rest for a few minutes before removing from the pan. Cut the tortino into wedges and pool a little of the tomato sauce to one side of each piece. Serve warm or at room temperature.

RICE AND EGGPLANT TIMBALE

Timballo di Riso e Melanzane

SERVES 4 TO 6

*I*n this bread-crumb–lined timbale, rice is tossed in tomato and basil sauce, layered with thinly sliced fried eggplant, then baked. There are a few steps involved in preparing this dish—frying the eggplant, cooking the rice, making the sauce, and grating the cheeses—but it can all be done in stages and the timbale can be assembled hours in advance. The reward is the big, generous flavor of the finished dish, full of southern exuberance. If you would rather not fry the eggplant, lightly brush the slices with olive oil and spread them on cookie sheets, then bake them in a hot oven until golden.

Delicious served hot or at room temperature, the timbale makes a delightful main course for a country-style dinner.

1   *medium eggplant*
Salt, optional
Olive oil for frying
4   *tablespoons extra-virgin olive oil, plus extra for oiling
       the pan*
3   *garlic cloves, finely chopped*
1   *28-ounce can imported Italian tomatoes, pureed with their
       juices*
8   *basil leaves, coarsely chopped*
Salt and freshly ground black pepper to taste
1½ *cups Arborio rice*
¾   *cup finely diced caciocavallo cheese or imported provolone*
4   *tablespoons freshly grated imported Pecorino Romano cheese*
½   *cup homemade bread crumbs, toasted in a small sauté pan,
       divided*

Trim the stem end of the eggplant and slice lengthwise into ¼-inch-thick pieces. If desired, salt the slices lightly and let drain for 30 minutes. Wipe them dry.

Fry the eggplant on both sides in hot olive oil measuring ¼ inch up the side of a medium sauté pan. Fry 1 layer at a time and do not crowd the pan. As the eggplant slices turn golden, remove them with tongs and let the excess oil drip back into the pan. Place the eggplant slices on several layers of paper towels and let them drain thoroughly, changing the paper towels as they absorb the excess oil until the paper is free of oil.

Meanwhile prepare the tomato sauce. Place the extra-virgin olive oil and garlic in a medium sauté pan. Cook over low heat for 2 to 3 minutes. Add the pureed tomatoes, basil, and salt and pepper to taste. Cook over medium-low heat for 15 minutes, or until the sauce thickens slightly.

Cook the rice in abundant salted boiling water until al dente. Drain in a colander.

In a bowl combine the rice, tomato sauce, the cheeses, and salt and pepper to taste.

Oil the bottom and sides of a medium baking dish and coat with half the bread crumbs.

Make layers, beginning with some of the rice mixture, spreading it evenly on the bottom of the pan. Next arrange a layer of eggplant. Continue layering rice and eggplant, ending with the rice. Sprinkle the remaining bread crumbs over the top. The dish may be refrigerated at this point if it is not to be cooked immediately. Remove the dish from the refrigerator and let it return to room temperature before proceeding with the recipe.

Cook the timbale in a preheated 450° oven for 20 minutes, or until the cheese melts and the bread crumbs are a rich golden brown. Remove from the oven and let rest for 5 minutes. Cut into wedges.

Stuffed Vegetables

SUMMERY STUFFED ZUCCHINI

Zucchine Ripiene Estive

SERVES 4 AS A MAIN DISH OR 8
AS AN ANTIPASTO

A simple cold summer main dish that epitomizes carefree, warm-weather cooking.

Begin the meal with Classic Bruschetta with Roasted Tomatoes (see page 132) and for dessert serve Fresh Figs with Anisette and Mint Leaves (see page 345). Place a pitcher of cool white wine at the table.

4 *firm medium zucchini*
Salt
½ *pound fresh ricotta salata or feta cheese*
2 *tablespoons extra-virgin olive oil plus extra for drizzling*
2 *tablespoons fresh lemon juice*
1 *large garlic clove, peeled and finely chopped*
12 *basil leaves, coarsely chopped*
Salt and freshly ground black pepper to taste
Basil leaves, optional

Wash the zucchini well. Feel the skin to make sure it is free of grit. Cook the zucchini, untrimmed, in abundant salted boiling water. Cook for about 10 minutes or until the zucchini is barely tender. Drain and let cool. Cut the zucchini in half lengthwise and carefully scoop out seeds and some of the flesh to form a shallow lengthwise cavity. Reserve the zucchini flesh that is scooped out for another use or discard. Set aside the zucchini shells.

In a bowl combine the ricotta salata, olive oil, lemon, garlic, basil, and salt and pepper to taste. Mash with a fork until the mixture is well combined.

Lightly salt the cavities of the zucchini shells and gently mound a little of the mixture into them. Grind a little black pepper over the top and drizzle with a bit of olive oil. If desired, garnish the plate with basil leaves.

RICE-STUFFED TOMATOES ON THINLY SLICED POTATOES

Pomodori Ripieni di Riso alla Romana

SERVES 6

hese big, plump baked tomatoes filled with rice are synonymous with summer in Rome, where they are a fixture of every *gastronomia*. Served at room temperature, they are excellent for reviving flagging hot-weather appetites. Savory and filling, they have a refreshing quality due to the tartness of the tomatoes. In this recipe the tomatoes bake on a bed of sliced potatoes, which absorbs all the tasty tomato juices.

6 *large tomatoes*
4 *small boiling potatoes*
⅔ *cup Arborio rice*
1 *garlic clove, peeled and finely chopped*
2 *tablespoons coarsely chopped mint leaves*
1 *tablespoons coarsely chopped Italian parsley leaves*
10 *basil leaves, cut into strips*
Salt and freshly ground black pepper to taste
Extra-virgin olive oil

Cut a slice off the stem end of the tomatoes. Reserve the tops. Very gently scoop out the seeds from the cavities and place the seeds and juices in a bowl. Strain the seeds and reserve the juices.

Cook the potatoes in salted boiling water to cover until tender but very firm. Drain well and when cool enough to handle, peel. Slice the potatoes.

Cook the rice in abundant salted boiling water until al dente. Drain well.

Transfer the rice to a bowl and add the garlic, herbs, and salt and pepper to taste. Toss well. Stuff the rice mixture into the tomatoes. Spoon a little of the reserved tomato juices into each tomato. Drizzle about a teaspoon of olive oil into each tomato.

Select a baking dish large enough to generously hold all the tomatoes. Oil the bottom of the baking dish. Arrange the potato slices on the bottom. Season with salt and pepper to taste and drizzle with olive oil. Place the tomatoes on the potato slices, and place the reserved tomato caps on top of the tomatoes.

(continued)

Bake the tomatoes and potatoes in a preheated 375° oven for 25 minutes, or until the tomatoes have softened and the potatoes are golden. Serve hot, warm, or at room temperature.

ARTICHOKES STUFFED WITH RICOTTA AND PINE NUTS

Carciofi Ripieni di Ricotta e Pignoli

SERVES 4 AS A MAIN DISH OR 8 AS A FIRST COURSE

The rich and meaty flavor of artichokes turns mellow when it is combined with the tastes of mild, sweet ricotta, butter, and toasted pine nuts. The artichokes, stuffed with ricotta and baked until golden, are delicious served warm or at room temperature. A nice beginning to the meal would be slices of rough country-style salame, raw fava beans, and spicy Italian pretzels, or a tart green salad.

4 *artichokes*
1 *lemon, cut in half*
½ *pound fresh ricotta cheese*
1 *garlic clove, peeled and finely chopped*
1 *egg, lightly beaten*
7 *tablespoons grated imported Pecorino Romano cheese, divided*
4 *tablespoons pine nuts, lightly toasted, divided*
Salt and freshly ground black pepper to taste
4 *tablespoons unsalted butter, at room temperature, divided*
2 *tablespoons bread crumbs*

Trim the artichokes according to the directions on page 8. Use the lemon to rub the cut portions as you work. Squeeze the juice of the other lemon half in a big bowl of water. Cut the artichokes in half lengthwise and cut out the chokes. Keep the trimmed artichokes in the acidulated water until needed.

Cook the artichokes in salted boiling water until tender but firm. Drain well in a colander.

Combine in a medium bowl the ricotta, garlic, egg, 6 tablespoons of the grated Pecorino Romano cheese, 2 tablespoons of the pine nuts, and salt and pepper to taste. Mix well.

Select a baking dish large enough to contain all the artichoke halves vertically. Butter the dish, using 3 tablespoons of the butter. Arrange the artichokes, cut side up, on the baking dish. Mound the ricotta mixture on the artichokes and smooth the tops. Sprinkle with the bread crumbs and the remaining grated cheese, and top with pieces of the remaining butter. Sprinkle with the remaining 2 tablespoons of pine nuts.

Bake in a preheated 350° oven for 20 minutes, or until the ricotta mixture is firm and the bread crumbs are lightly golden.

ZUCCHINI STUFFED WITH MUSHROOMS AND MARJORAM

Zucchine Ripiene

SERVES 3 AS A MAIN DISH
OR 6 AS A SIDE DISH

he concentrated woodsy flavor of dried porcini mushrooms adds depth to the gentle taste of zucchini and fresh mushrooms. Baked until golden, these stuffed zucchini make a lovely focal point for a light dinner.

1–2 *ounces dried porcini mushrooms*
6 *medium zucchini*
2 *slices of bread, crusts removed*
Milk
4 *tablespoons extra-virgin olive oil, plus extra to oil
     the baking dish*
2 *garlic cloves, peeled and finely chopped*
¼ *pound fresh mushrooms, wiped clean and thinly sliced*
1 *egg, lightly beaten*
3 *tablespoons freshly grated imported Parmesan cheese*
2 *teaspoons finely chopped fresh marjoram*
Salt and freshly ground black pepper to taste
Homemade bread crumbs

Soak the porcini mushrooms in warm water to cover for 20 minutes. Lift the mushrooms out of the soaking liquid. Run cold water over the mushrooms and feel for any grit. Cut the mushrooms into strips.

Cook the zucchini in salted boiling water for about 5 minutes or until tender but crisp. Drain and cool under running water. Trim the ends of the zucchini and cut in half lengthwise. Scoop out a small amount of the flesh along the center of the zucchini. Coarsely chop the flesh and set aside.

Soak the bread in enough milk to cover. Squeeze out the excess milk.

In a medium sauté pan, combine the olive oil, garlic, porcini mushrooms, and cultivated mushrooms. Cook over medium-low heat for about 5 minutes. Place in a bowl and add the reserved chopped zucchini, softened bread, egg, grated Parmesan cheese, marjoram, and salt and pepper to taste. Mix well. Stuff the mixture into the zucchini shells.

Generously oil a baking dish large enough to hold the zucchini in one layer. Arrange the zucchini in the dish. Sprinkle bread crumbs on the zucchini and drizzle with olive oil.

Bake in a preheated 375° oven for 30 minutes, or until the zucchini is tender.

Serve hot or at room temperature. The zucchini can be made in advance, but avoid refrigerating them since it alters their flavor.

STUFFED ZUCCHINI BLOSSOMS

Fiori di Zucca Ripieni

SERVES 4 TO 8

Bright yellow zucchini blossoms are stuffed with ricotta and herbs, and baked on a bed of onion-sweetened fresh tomato and basil sauce. The fresh flavor of the blossoms and their beautiful color shine through. If zucchini blossoms are not available, use blanched Swiss chard leaves as wrappings for the ricotta mixture.

16 *zucchini blossoms*
1 *garlic clove, peeled and finely chopped*
2 *tablespoons chopped Italian parsley*
8 *ounces fresh ricotta*
3 *tablespoons freshly grated imported Parmesan cheese*
2 *eggs, lightly beaten*
Salt and freshly ground black pepper to taste
1 *recipe Sweet Tomato Basil Sauce (see page 202)*

Gently clean the zucchini blossoms by dipping them into a bowl of cool water. Carefully remove the pistils from the flowers. Dry on a clean dish towel.

In a small bowl combine the garlic, parsley, ricotta, grated Parmesan cheese, and eggs. Season with salt and pepper to taste.

Gently open each zucchini blossom and stuff it with a little of the mixture.

Meanwhile prepare the tomato sauce. Spread the sauce in a baking dish large enough to contain the flowers in one layer. Arrange the zucchini blossoms on the sauce. Cover and bake in a preheated 350° oven for 15 minutes, or until the blossoms are tender.

GENOA-STYLE MIXED VEGETABLES

Verdure Ripiene alla Genovese

SERVES 4

platter of stuffed vegetables never fails to please, especially if it features unusually shaped and colored vegetables. Small, round summer squash, some with fluted edges, are perfect for stuffing. They come in a range of colors, and include green scaloppine, pale green pattypan, and brilliant gold sunburst. Small Japanese eggplants and red and gold tomatoes add additional interest in terms of color and shape. Use your imagination and resources, whether it be your own backyard or a farmer's market, to assemble an interesting and varied assortment.

8 *small, round summer squash, preferably several varieties*
Salt
4 *Japanese eggplants*
2 *medium red tomatoes*
2 *medium yellow tomatoes*
5 *tablespoons extra-virgin olive oil, plus extra for oiling the baking dish*
3 *garlic cloves, peeled and chopped*
1 *cup bread crumbs*
8 *basil leaves, julienned*
3 *sprigs marjoram, leaves chopped*
5 *tablespoons freshly grated imported Parmesan cheese, divided*
2 *tablespoons freshly grated imported Pecorino Romano cheese*
2 *anchovies, finely chopped*
Freshly ground black pepper to taste

Trim the stems from the summer squash. Use a small spoon to scoop out a small cavity in the center. Chop the flesh and reserve. Cook the squash shells in salted boiling water until tender-crisp. Drain and place on a clean dish towel to dry.

Trim the eggplant stems. Cut the eggplant in half lengthwise and scoop out some of the flesh to form a shallow, lengthwise cavity. Chop the flesh and reserve. Cut the tomatoes in half horizontally. Scoop out the seeds. Cut out the flesh, chop, and reserve.

Place 3 tablespoons olive oil and the garlic in a large sauté pan. Sauté for 2 to 3 minutes. Add all the reserved chopped vegetables and sauté for about 5 minutes. Transfer to a bowl. Add the bread crumbs, herbs, cheeses, anchovies, and salt and pepper to taste.

Stuff the mixture into the vegetable shells.

Lightly oil a baking dish large enough to contain the vegetables. Arrange the vegetables in the dish. Sprinkle with the remaining grated Parmesan cheese and drizzle the remaining 2 tablespoons of olive oil on top.

Place in a preheated 350° oven. When the tomatoes have softened, remove them and continue cooking the remaining vegetables. Bake until the vegetables are tender and the tops are golden.

Fritters and Gnocchi

EGGPLANT FRITTERS

Polpettine di Melanzane

SERVES 4

These aromatic eggplant fritters, with their mixture of eggplant, mint, garlic, and Pecorino Romano cheese, are a real treat—crisp and golden on the outside and creamy within. They can be served with a tomato sauce, but I prefer just a squeeze of fresh lemon juice, which sets off the rich flavors nicely and gives the dish a clean, fragrant finish.

Serve these fritters immediately after frying, since they lose their crispness quickly.

1 *large eggplant*
1 *egg, lightly beaten*
3 *garlic cloves, peeled and finely chopped*
3 *tablespoons chopped mint leaves*
¾ *cup bread crumbs, plus additional if needed*
½ *cup freshly grated imported Pecorino Romano cheese*
¼ *cup freshly grated imported Parmesan cheese*
Salt and freshly ground black pepper to taste
Unbleached all-purpose flour
Olive oil for frying
Lemon wedges

Place the eggplant on a baking sheet and bake it in a preheated 375° oven until it is very soft. Trim away the stem end. Chop the eggplant very fine and place in a medium bowl. Add the egg, garlic, mint, bread crumbs, grated cheeses, and salt and pepper to taste. Mix well. If the mixture is very soft, add additional bread crumbs.

Flour your hands and shape the eggplant mixture into small dumplings about 2 inches in diameter. As you make them, transfer them to a tray.

To cook the fritters, pour olive oil to a depth of ¼ inch in a heavy sauté pan. Heat the oil to very hot but not smoking. Roll a few of the eggplant dumplings in flour and gently lower them into the hot oil.

Cook the fritters until they are golden on all sides. Drain on paper towels. Sprinkle while hot with salt to taste.

Serve immediately with lemon wedges on the side.

GOLDEN HERBED
GOAT CHEESE ROUNDS

Formaggini Dorati

SERVES 6 ·

The contrast of the crisp, herbal, bread-crumb coating and melting, fragrant goat cheese is seductive. Served with a small leafy salad dressed with olive oil and lemon to freshen the palate, it makes a delightful main dish for a casual lunch with friends.

If you prefer, you can bake the goat cheese rounds. Place them on a cookie sheet and bake in a preheated 400° oven until the bread crumbs are golden.

18 *ounces goat cheese, log-shaped*
1 *cup bread crumbs*
1 *garlic clove, peeled and finely chopped*
1 *tablespoon finely chopped sage leaves*
1 *tablespoon finely chopped rosemary leaves*
1 *tablespoon chopped basil leaves*
Salt to taste
3 *eggs*
Olive oil for frying
Whole sage leaves for garnish
Lemon wedges

Cut the goat cheese into 18 small rounds. If the cheese crumbles, gently pat it into neat disks.

Combine the bread crumbs, garlic, herbs, and salt to taste in a bowl and stir. Spread the mixture on a dinner plate. Break the eggs into a shallow soup bowl and lightly beat them. Dip the disks in the eggs and then in the bread crumbs, patting the crumbs into the cheese to help them adhere. Repeat this step so the goat cheese has a double coating. Refrigerate them for at least 30 minutes or for several hours.

Select a heavy skillet and pour in olive oil to a depth of ¼ inch. When the oil is hot but not smoking, fry the goat cheese rounds on both sides until they are golden brown. Drain them on paper towels.

Arrange the cheese rounds on a platter and garnish with sage leaves and lemon wedges.

MIXED VEGETABLE FRITTERS

Bocconcini di Verdura

SERVES 4

Sometimes it's fun to indulge in a big platter of vegetable fritters. Fried food has an immediacy—the bubbling hot oil, watching the fritters turn to gold in the pan, popping them in your mouth while they are hot and crusty—that makes the process fun and lively. Bad fried food is abominable—a thick, spongy coating soaked in poor-quality oil in which a hapless strip of limp zucchini or tasteless shrimp is trapped. When frying is done properly, a thin, crisp coating protects the food as it cooks quickly and cleanly.

To do justice to this cooking technique, use enough fresh olive oil so that the fritters float as they cook. Make sure there is plenty of room in the pan, and keep the heat high but below the smoking point. Before serving, drain the fritters on several thicknesses of paper towels. Serve lemon wedges on the side to squeeze over the hot morsels.

The following winter fritto misto, or mixed fry, combines fennel, artichokes, zucchini, and cauliflower with cubes of mozzarella cheese and big, tart green olives. Or prepare a summer fritto misto with crisp tomato slices, zucchini blossoms, thickly sliced red onion, and small green beans.

A lettuce salad dressed lightly with olive oil and lemon juice, followed by a basket of oranges, ends the meal on a fresh, fragrant note.

1 *recipe fritter batter (see page 84)*
1 *fennel bulb, trimmed*
2 *artichokes, trimmed according to directions on page 8*
2 *small zucchini, trimmed*
Handful cauliflower flowerets
Olive oil for frying
¼ *pound fresh mozzarella, well drained, cut into 1-inch dice*
12 *large green olives, pitted*
Salt to taste
Lemon wedges
Leafy herbs for garnish, optional

Make the batter.

Cut the fennel into thin wedges. Cut the artichokes into 8 wedges. Cut the zucchini in half lengthwise, then lengthwise again into quarters.

Lightly cook separately in salted boiling water the fennel, artichokes, and cauliflower. Cook until just al dente. Drain well on clean dish towels.

Pour the olive oil into a large skillet to a depth of ½ inch, and heat until the oil is hot but not smoking. Meanwhile dip a few of the vegetables, mozzarella cubes, and green olives into the batter, letting the excess drain off. Transfer to the hot oil and fry until golden on all sides. Remove with a slotted spoon, letting the excess oil drain back into the pan. Transfer to paper towels to drain. Season with salt to taste.

Continue dipping the ingredients into the batter and frying in batches, transferring them to paper towels to drain.

Arrange the fritters on a clean platter and garnish with lemon wedges and, if desired, leafy herbs.

POTATO GNOCCHI SORRENTO STYLE

Gnocchi alla Sorrentina

SERVES 6 TO 8

Potato gnocchi are served in a luscious basil-scented sauce of tomato and mozzarella, melted to a creamy tangle. The sauce makes this dish of tender gnocchi indigenous to southern Italy and to Sorrento in particular.

2 *pounds potatoes, 1 pound each russet potatoes and
    red potatoes*
1 *egg, beaten*
1–2 *cups unbleached all-purpose flour, divided*
Salt
1 *recipe Penne with Tomato and Mozzarella Sauce Sorrento
    Style, sauce only (see page 203)*
Freshly grated imported Parmesan cheese

Cook the russet and red potatoes separately. Place the whole potatoes, unpeeled, in enough cold water to cover. Bring the water to a boil and cook until the potatoes are tender. Test only 1 potato in each pot with a wooden skewer for tenderness. Refrain from piercing the potatoes too often, since it will cause them to absorb water. When the potatoes are tender, drain and peel them.

Put all the potatoes through a ricer. Place the riced potatoes in a mixing bowl and when cool enough to handle, add the egg and 1 cup of flour. Use your hands to mix together the potatoes, egg, and flour, kneading them together as you would bread dough. Mix as little as possible, since overkneading will toughen the dough. The mixture should be soft but firm enough to hold its shape when the gnocchi are formed. Add more flour, if necessary, up to 2 cups total.

Form the gnocchi by breaking off small sections of dough. Flour your hands and roll the dough into cylinders about ¾ inch in diameter. Place the cylinders on a floured board and with a sharp knife cut the cylinders into pieces about ½ inch thick. Flour a tray and place the gnocchi on the tray, making sure they do not touch. Let dry for about 10 minutes.

Bring a big pot of water to a boil. Add salt and stir. Reduce the heat to a gentle simmer. Drop the gnocchi into the simmering water a few at a time. When they float to the surface they are done.

Meanwhile make the sauce.

Warm individual shallow pasta serving bowls. Remove the gnocchi with a slotted spoon and let the spoon rest against a clean dish towel to drain.

Place a little of the sauce in each bowl. Divide the gnocchi among the bowls and top with the remaining sauce. Sprinkle each serving with grated Parmesan cheese. Pass additional grated cheese at the table.

SPINACH GNOCCHI WITH SWEET TOMATO BASIL SAUCE

Gnocchi Verdi con Salsina di Pomodoro con Burro

SERVES 4 TO 6

Everyone loves the light, fresh flavor of spinach and ricotta gnocchi. When served with a fresh tomato and basil sauce, it makes for an elegant, impressive offering that belies its ease of preparation.

1   *recipe Sweet Tomato Basil Sauce (see page 202)*
2   *bunches spinach, washed, stems trimmed*
3   *eggs, lightly beaten*
¾   *cup freshly grated imported Parmesan cheese, plus extra to sprinkle on the gnocchi*
¾   *cup freshly grated imported Pecorino Romano cheese*
1   *pound fresh ricotta, drained in cheesecloth*
Salt and freshly ground black pepper to taste
1   *cup unbleached all-purpose flour*

Prepare the sauce and set aside.

Cook the spinach in a large braising pan with just the water that clings to its leaves after washing. When the spinach is tender, drain and cool. Squeeze the spinach, in small batches, between the palms of your hands until the spinach is dry, and chop finely. Place the spinach in a bowl and add the eggs, both grated cheeses, the ricotta, and salt and pepper to taste. Mix well.

Spread a little of the flour on a work surface. Form the ricotta mixture into balls about ¾ inch in diameter and roll lightly in the remaining flour.

Bring abundant water to a boil. Add salt and reduce heat to a simmer. Cook the gnocchi a few at a time in the simmering water. The gnocchi will rise to the surface when they are ready. Lift the gnocchi out of the water with a slotted spoon, and let the spoon rest on a clean dish towel to drain.

Meanwhile reheat the sauce.

Spoon a little of the sauce in individual warmed shallow pasta serving dishes. Distribute the gnocchi among the dishes and sprinkle with grated Parmesan cheese. Serve additional grated Parmesan cheese at the table.

Egg Dishes

HARD-COOKED EGGS WITH SUMMER RAW TOMATO SAUCE

Uova Sode con Salsa Fresca

SERVES 2

This summery dish features hard-cooked eggs served with a brilliant raw tomato sauce garnish. The tomatoes are seasoned with lemon juice, basil, and Italian parsley, then chilled in the refrigerator. The cold sauce serves as a bright foil for the richness of the eggs, and with a garnish of whole basil leaves, the dish looks fresh and cheerful.

This makes a lovely luncheon dish and can also be served as an antipasto.

5–6 *ripe but firm Roma tomatoes, peeled, seeded, and finely diced*

4 *tablespoons extra-virgin olive oil*

2 *teaspoons freshly squeezed lemon juice*

1 *garlic clove, finely diced*

1 *tablespoon coarsely chopped Italian parsley*

10 *basil leaves, torn into fragments, plus enough whole leaves for garnish*

Salt and freshly ground black pepper to taste

4 *large eggs*

Combine in a bowl the tomatoes, olive oil, lemon juice, garlic, parsley, basil, and salt and pepper to taste. Stir gently. Refrigerate for 1 hour.

Boil the eggs until they are firm but have slightly moist, golden yolks. Cool. Peel the eggs and cut in half lengthwise.

To serve, spoon the tomato mixture onto two plates. Arrange the egg halves on top and season the eggs with salt and pepper. Garnish with whole basil leaves and serve immediately.

FLOWER FRITTATA

Frittata ai Fiori

SERVES 4

elicate flowers give charm, color, and a subtle perfume to this simple frittata flavored with cinnamon, a hint of sugar, and a touch of cream. Serve this lovely frittata, dusted with powdered sugar and garnished with flowers, for a special brunch accompanied with champagne. Or cut the frittata into small diamond shapes and serve with afternoon tea in the garden.

Make sure the flowers you use are unsprayed.

6–8 *eggs*
1 *cup flowers, such as violets, rose petals, or other edible*
        flowers, plus additional flowers for garnish
2 *tablespoons cream*
Cinnamon to taste
2 *tablespoons unsalted butter*
Powdered sugar for topping

Break the eggs into a bowl. Beat them lightly with a fork. Add the flowers, cream, and cinnamon.

Place the butter in a small ovenproof sauté pan and turn the heat to medium high. Add the egg mixture and lower the heat. Cook the frittata slowly, stirring the eggs until large curds form. Stop stirring and cook until the frittata is firm except for the top. Cook the top by placing the frittata under a hot broiler or a preheated 400° oven until the top is just set. Let it cool in the pan for 1 to 2 minutes. Place a plate over the top of the pan and invert the frittata over it. Place on a serving plate. Sprinkle with powdered sugar and garnish with flowers.

MINT FRITTATA WITH TOMATO GARNISH

Frittata alla Menta

SERVES 4

Sweet, fragrant mint is a wonderful complement to the flavor of eggs and tangy Pecorino Romano cheese. I like to serve this frittata surrounded by chunks of tomato and topped with a sprinkling of mint leaves for a summery light lunch or dinner.

Spearmint is the best mint to use in cooking because it has a large tender leaf and a sweet perfume. It is the type most available in markets. Peppermint has a higher menthol content and is less desirable for cooking but wonderful in teas and iced drinks.

6–8 *eggs*

2 *tablespoons freshly grated imported Pecorino Romano cheese*

1 *tablespoon homemade bread crumbs*

3 *tablespoons chopped mint leaves, plus extra leaves for sprinkling on top of the frittata*

Salt and freshly ground black pepper

2 *tablespoons extra-virgin olive oil*

1 *large tomato, streaked with green, cut into chunks*

Crack the eggs into a bowl and beat lightly with a fork. Add the grated Pecorino Romano cheese, bread crumbs, chopped mint, and salt and pepper to taste. Beat again lightly to combine the ingredients.

Heat the olive oil in a small, nonstick ovenproof skillet, swirling the oil to coat the bottom and sides. When the oil is hot add the egg mixture. Lower the heat and cook slowly, stirring frequently until the eggs have formed small curds and the frittata is firm except for the top.

To cook the top, place the pan under a hot broiler or in a preheated 400° oven until the frittata browns lightly on top and becomes firm. Check often since overcooking will toughen the frittata. Remove the pan from the broiler or oven, and let frittata cool in the pan for 1 to 2 minutes. Place a plate over the top of the pan and invert the frittata onto it.

Let the frittata cool to room temperature. Surround the frittata with the tomato chunks and sprinkle the tomatoes with salt to taste. Sprinkle mint leaves over the frittata and the tomatoes. To serve, cut the frittata into wedges and serve with a few chunks of tomato on the side.

LETTUCE AND SORREL FRITTATA WITH HERBS

Frittata di Lattuga ed Acetosa

SERVES 4

Lettuce cooked in onions and butter and sweetened with herbs produces a delicate spring frittata. A few leaves of lemony sorrel add a tart accent to the gentle flavors. If sorrel is not available, a little grated lemon rind will do the trick.

Use tender leaves of romaine or butter lettuce, or a variety of garden lettuces. Add a handful of chives to the egg mixture for a light, perfumed onion flavor.

> 2 *tablespoons unsalted butter*
> 1 *onion, peeled and finely diced*
> 1 *head romaine lettuce or other variety of mild lettuce*
> *Small bunch sorrel*
> 6–8 *eggs*
> 3 *tablespoons chopped Italian parsley leaves*
> 2 *tablespoons chopped basil leaves*
> 2 *tablespoons freshly grated imported Parmesan cheese*
> 1 *tablespoon bread crumbs*
> *Salt and freshly ground black pepper to taste*
> 2 *tablespoons extra-virgin olive oil*

Place the butter and onion in a medium sauté pan. Cook over low heat until the onion is tender.

Meanwhile core and wash the lettuce. Cut the lettuce into strips without drying it first. Wash the sorrel and cut it into strips. Add the lettuce strips and the water that clings to them to the sauté pan and cook until lettuce is tender. In the last few moments of cooking, stir in the sorrel. There should be no water left in the pan. If any remains, bring to a boil and cook until the excess moisture evaporates. Transfer to a bowl and let cool.

Break the eggs into a bowl and beat well with a fork. Add the lettuce, parsley, basil, grated Parmesan cheese, and bread crumbs, and season with salt and pepper to taste. Stir the mixture well.

Place the olive oil in a small ovenproof skillet and turn the heat to medium high. Swirl the oil in the pan to coat the sides and bottom.

Add the egg mixture and lower the heat. Cook the frittata slowly, stirring until large curds form. Stop stirring and cook until the frittata is firm except for the top. To cook the top, place it under a hot broiler or in a preheated 400° oven. Cook until the top is firm and lightly golden. Watch it carefully, since overcooking will toughen the eggs. Remove the frittata from the oven and let it cool for a few moments in the pan. Place a plate over the top of the pan and invert the frittata onto it.

Serve the frittata warm or at room temperature.

FRITTATA WITH NEW PEAS

Frittata ai Piselli Novelli

SERVES 4

This charming frittata calls for small, sweet peas. It is especially good when made with freshly picked peas from the garden but tiny frozen ones work well, too. Mint adds its fruity bouquet, and Pecorino Romano brings all the sweetness down to earth.

4   *tablespoons extra-virgin olive oil, divided*
1   *small onion, finely diced*
1   *cup shelled small peas, fresh or frozen*
6–8 *eggs*
2   *tablespoons freshly grated imported Pecorino Romano cheese*
2   *tablespoons milk*
2   *tablespoons coarsely chopped mint leaves*
Salt and freshly ground black pepper to taste

Place 2 tablespoons of the olive oil in a medium sauté pan. Add the onion and sauté over low heat until tender and golden. Add the peas and ¼ cup water. Cook over low heat until the peas are tender and the water evaporates. Transfer the peas to a small bowl and let cool.

Break the eggs into a bowl and beat well with a fork. Add the grated Pecorino Romano cheese, milk, mint, and salt and pepper to taste. Add the peas and onion mixture. Stir with a fork to combine ingredients.

(continued)

Place a small nonstick skillet over medium heat. Add the remaining 2 tablespoons of olive oil and swirl it in the pan to coat the sides and bottom. Add the egg mixture and lower the heat. Cook the frittata slowly, stirring the eggs until small curds form. When the frittata begins to firm up, but the top is still runny, place it under the broiler or in a preheated 400° oven. Cook until the top is firm and lightly golden. Watch it carefully, since overcooking will toughen the eggs. Remove the frittata from the oven and let it cool for a few moments in the pan. Place a plate over the top of the pan and invert the frittata onto the plate.

Serve the frittata at room temperature, cut into wedges.

LEEK AND SPINACH FRITTATA

Frittata di Porri e Spinaci

SERVES 4

When you cut into this frittata you see a lovely marbled green-and-gold pattern. I enjoy the contrasts of flavors—the sweetness of the leeks and the light mineral tang of the spinach. A nice variation is to stir some shredded mozzarella into the egg and vegetable mixture before cooking.

3 *leeks*
1 *bunch spinach*
Salt
2 *tablespoons unsalted butter*
3 *tablespoons extra-virgin olive oil, divided*
6–8 *eggs, lightly beaten*
1 *garlic clove, peeled and finely chopped*
1 *tablespoon chopped mint leaves*
1 *tablespoon chopped Italian parsley*
4 *tablespoons freshly grated imported Parmesan cheese*
2 *tablespoons bread crumbs*
Freshly ground black pepper to taste

Trim the leeks at the root ends and cut off the green tops. Use only the lighter green and white portions. Cut the leeks into thin rounds and place in a colander. Separate the rings and run cold water over them to remove any dirt trapped between the layers. Trim the root ends of the spinach. Wash the spinach well in several changes of water and chop coarsely. In a large sauté pan place the spinach with water still clinging to the leaves. Add salt to taste. Cook the spinach very briefly over medium heat just until it reduces in volume and is slightly wilted. Drain in a colander and very gently press out excess water with the back of a wooden spoon.

Meanwhile place the butter and 1 tablespoon of the olive oil in a medium sauté pan. Add the leeks and cook over medium-low heat until they are tender, about 8 minutes. Add the spinach and toss for 1 minute. Transfer to a bowl and let the mixture cool.

When the vegetables are cool add the eggs, garlic, mint, parsley, grated Parmesan cheese, bread crumbs, and pepper to taste. Mix ingredients well.

Heat a small nonstick ovenproof skillet over medium heat. Add the remaining olive oil and swirl it in the pan to coat the bottom and sides. Add the egg mixture and lower the heat. Cook the frittata slowly, stirring the eggs until small curds form. Stop stirring and cook until the frittata is firm except for the top.

To cook the top, place the pan under a hot broiler or in a preheated 400° oven until the top browns lightly. Let it cool in the pan for 1 to 2 minutes. Place a plate over the top of the pan and invert the frittata onto it. Serve the frittata at room temperature, cut into wedges.

FRITTATA WITH GARLICKY RAPINI

Frittata con Rapini

SERVES 4

Eggs go well with a variety of flavors, from sweet green beans and basil to the assertive rapini and garlic called for here.

When buying rapini look for slender stalks with tightly closed clusters of blossoms.

1   *bunch rapini, about ¾ pound*
Salt
3   *tablespoons extra-virgin olive oil*
2   *garlic cloves, peeled and finely chopped*
6–8   *eggs*
3   *tablespoons freshly grated imported Pecorino Romano cheese*
Freshly ground black pepper to taste
2   *tablespoons olive oil*

Trim the rapini stalks and use a paring knife to strip the peel. Cut the stalks in half lengthwise.

Place enough water to measure ½ inch in a large sauté pan. Bring to a boil and add salt. Add the rapini and cook for 4 to 5 minutes, or until tender. Drain well and chop coarsely.

In a sauté pan combine the extra-virgin olive oil and garlic. Sauté for 2 to 3 minutes over low heat. Add the rapini and salt to taste. Sauté over low heat for about 2 to 3 minutes, or until the rapini has absorbed the flavor of the olive oil and garlic and any excess water has evaporated. Let cool.

Break the eggs into a bowl and beat lightly with a fork. Add the rapini, grated cheese, and salt and pepper to taste, and gently beat with a fork. Heat the olive oil in a medium skillet and swirl the oil in the pan to coat the bottom and sides. When the oil is hot, add the egg mixture. Lower the heat. Cook slowly, stirring frequently until the eggs have formed small curds but the top is still runny.

To cook the top, place the pan under a hot broiler or in a preheated 400° oven until the frittata browns very lightly and the top is firm. Check often, since overcooking the frittata will toughen it. Remove the pan from the broiler or oven, and let cool for 1 to 2 minutes. Place a plate over the top of the pan and invert the frittata onto it. Serve the frittata at room temperature, cut into wedges.

BAKED RED PEPPER FRITTATA

Frittata di Peperoni al Forno

SERVES 4

This simple, brightly colored frittata is baked rather than cooked on top of the stove, and emerges light and fluffy. The topping of fragrant, nutty, melted fontina and crisp bread crumbs contrasts beautifully with the sweetness of red peppers and onions.

2 *red peppers*
3 *tablespoons extra-virgin olive oil*
2 *onions, peeled and thinly sliced*
6–8 *eggs*
2 *tablespoons chopped Italian parsley leaves*
2 *tablespoons chopped basil leaves*
Salt and freshly ground black pepper to taste
Butter for the baking dish
6 *tablespoons bread crumbs, divided*
½ *cup shredded imported fontina*

Core, seed, and julienne the peppers.

Place the olive oil in a medium sauté pan. Add the peppers and onions, and sauté until the vegetables soften and are lightly golden. Let cool.

Crack the eggs into a bowl and beat them lightly with a fork. Add the pepper and onion mixture, herbs, and salt and pepper to taste.

Butter a round 10-inch baking dish and sprinkle with 4 tablespoons of bread crumbs. Pour the egg mixture into the baking dish and sprinkle with the cheese. Top with the bread crumbs. Bake in a preheated 375° oven for 20 minutes, or until the frittata is slightly puffy and firm. Serve hot or warm.

THIN PARSLEY FRITTATA STUFFED WITH RICOTTA

Frittatine Ripiene di Ricotta

SERVES 4 TO 6

*I*n this dish, lightly beaten eggs, parsley, and grated Pecorino Romano cheese are turned into large, thin frittatas, similar to crepes, and stuffed with fresh ricotta. Served with hot sautéed black olives, the rolled frittatas make a hearty farm-style breakfast on a cold morning. If olives sound too intense for such an early hour, serve this dish for brunch or for a light evening meal, accompanied with Salad of Field Greens (see page 95).

The taste of fresh ricotta is mild and light. Commercially made ricotta lacks the astonishing freshness that good ricotta captures in every spoonful. If possible, find a source for ricotta made by a small, artisan-style company that produces fresh Italian cheeses.

> 8 *eggs, lightly beaten*
> *Salt and freshly ground black pepper to taste*
> ½ *cup chopped Italian parsley leaves*
> ¼ *cup freshly grated imported Pecorino Romano cheese*
> *Olive oil*
> ¾ *pound fresh ricotta, at room temperature, drained*
> ½ *cup oil-cured black olives*

In a bowl combine the eggs, salt and pepper to taste, parsley, and cheese. Beat together with a fork.

Lightly coat with olive oil the bottom of a medium nonstick skillet and turn on the heat to medium high. When the oil is hot, add one fourth of the egg mixture or enough to produce a thin pancake. Swirl the pan to distribute the egg mixture evenly. Reduce the heat and cook until the frittata is just firm. Flip it over and lightly cook it on the other side. Quickly make the remaining frittatas.

Warm the ricotta in a sauté pan. Divide the ricotta among the frittatas, spooning it along one side of each one. Roll them up loosely and keep warm in the oven.

Meanwhile heat the olives in a small sauté pan over medium heat. Remove the frittatas from the oven and garnish with the hot olives.

THIN FRITTATA STUFFED WITH ASPARAGUS

Frittatine Ripiene di Asparagi

SERVES 4

A large, thin basil frittata serves as a wrapper for spears of asparagus. Ideally this dish should be made with wild asparagus, a long and slender variety that is dark green and violet. Wild asparagus grows here in America but is generally unavailable. In its place I suggest using very thin asparagus, sometimes referred to as spaghetti asparagus, available in markets in the spring.

This is the perfect brunch dish for Easter morning. The bright golden frittatas flecked with green, each holding its delicate bundle of asparagus, seem emblematic of spring—a time when the earth is reborn. For a special festive touch, sprinkle the rolled frittatas with toasted pine nuts.

6 *eggs*
1 *bunch basil, leaves only, coarsely chopped, a few whole leaves reserved*
2 *garlic cloves, peeled and finely chopped*
¼ *cup freshly grated imported Parmesan cheese, plus extra for sprinkling*
Salt and freshly ground black pepper to taste
½ *pound thin asparagus*
3 *tablespoons extra-virgin olive oil, plus a little extra for drizzling on the asparagus*

Break the eggs into a bowl and beat them lightly with a fork. Add the basil, garlic, grated Parmesan cheese, and salt and pepper to taste. If possible, let the mixture rest for 30 minutes to let the basil flavor permeate the eggs.

Tie the spaghetti asparagus together in a bunch using kitchen twine. Cut off the fibrous ends of the stalks. Plunge the asparagus into a pot of salted boiling water and cook until it is tender but crisp. Drain well. Season with salt and a few drops of olive oil. Keep warm.

Place the olive oil in a large sauté pan and turn on the heat to medium. Pour a ladleful of the egg mixture into the pan and swirl it around just as you would when making crepes. Lower the heat to medium low. When the frittata turns opaque, carefully flip it over and lightly cook the other side. Repeat, making 4 thin crepelike frittatas.

Divide the asparagus into 4 bunches. Place 1 bunch on the far side of a frittata. Roll it up, completely enfolding the asparagus. Repeat with the other 3 bunches. Arrange each frittata on a plate and sprinkle with torn basil leaves and grated Parmesan cheese.

Side Vegetables

The recipes in this chapter focus on and highlight the flavors and textures of individual vegetables. Other ingredients serve to bring out each vegetable's special characteristics. Since the seasonings are kept to a minimum, it is especially important to try to find the best raw ingredients you can.

These dishes can be served in the traditional way, as side dishes, but most of them can stand on their own as first-course offerings. A selection of three or four dishes adds up to one bright, varied main dish. For example, in summer you could serve the potato torta layered with tomato and mozzarella along with zucchini blossoms on a bed of fennel; lemony grilled eggplant; and red Swiss chard seasoned with cayenne. Served with a leafy salad either before or after, and you have a delightful dinner. Many of these dishes can be served at room temperature and lend themselves to the antipasto table and to picnics.

The recipes range from a sophisticated presentation of leeks in a pink mascarpone sauce to a plate of country-style greens and black olives. Every season is represented and each one is celebrated.

ASPARAGUS WITH ANCHOVY AND LEMON, WILD STYLE

Asparagi di Campo con Acciughe e Limone

SERVES 4

*I*n the outdoor markets of Italy, nothing is so thrilling as the first sight of wild asparagus, long and thin, its green blending into deep violet. Italians gather asparagus in the countryside and prize its intense flavor. In this recipe, wild asparagus would be ideal, but cultivated asparagus gains a deeper, stronger flavor when prepared in this way.

1½ *pounds asparagus*
Salt
4 *tablespoons extra-virgin olive oil*
6 *anchovies, chopped to a paste*
3 *tablespoons chopped Italian parsley*
2 *tablespoons lemon juice*

Trim the ends of the asparagus by cutting off just the part of the spear that is lighter in color and discard. Use a vegetable peeler to peel the tender spear about halfway up.

In a sauté pan large enough to contain the asparagus lengthwise, bring to a boil enough water to just cover the asparagus. Add salt and cook the asparagus until tender but crisp. Drain well in a colander.

In the same sauté pan, add the olive oil and anchovies. Turn the heat to low and gently heat until the anchovies melt into the olive oil. Add the asparagus, tips all facing in the same direction, the parsley, and salt to taste. Gently turn the spears over several times in the olive oil mixture until they are lightly coated. Add the lemon juice and turn again once or twice.

Carefully transfer the asparagus and the juices in the pan to a serving platter, making sure that the asparagus is neatly arranged.

SARDINIAN-STYLE ARTICHOKES WITH SUN-DRIED TOMATOES

Carciofi alla Sarda

SERVES 4

*I*n a landscape of scrub, wild, windswept olive trees, and strange rock formations, it isn't difficult to imagine strings of tomatoes hanging from the doorways of stone houses, drying in the heat of the fierce Sardinian sun.

The cooking of Sardinia has a primitive and earthy quality about it. With its odd juxtaposition of lonely shepherd and glittering jet-setter, Sardinia remains rooted to its past through its culinary traditions.

This recipe features artichokes sautéed with strips of sun-dried tomatoes, which impart a sweetness and golden, tomato-red tint to the finished dish.

1 *lemon, cut in half*
4 *medium artichokes*
Salt
4 *tablespoons extra-virgin olive oil*
½ *onion, cut into medium dice*
2 *garlic cloves, peeled and chopped*
¼ *cup chopped Italian parsley*
8 *sun-dried tomatoes in olive oil, cut into ¼-inch strips*
Freshly ground black pepper to taste

Squeeze the juice of half a lemon into a large bowl of cold water. Use the other lemon half to rub the cut portions of the artichokes as you work. Trim the artichokes according to the directions on page 8. Cut the artichokes into quarters and cut away the chokes. Squeeze the remaining juice of the lemon into a pot containing enough water to generously cover the artichoke quarters.

Bring the water to a boil, add salt, and when the water returns to a boil, add the artichoke quarters. Cook for about 5 to 8 minutes, or until the artichoke hearts are almost tender. Use a thin bamboo skewer to pierce the hearts. There should be some resistance. Drain the artichokes well. Wrap them in a clean dish towel and let dry.

Place the olive oil and onion in a medium sauté pan. Sauté the onion over low heat until it is pale gold and tender. Add the garlic and parsley and cook for a few minutes. Add the artichokes, sun-dried tomatoes, and salt and pepper to taste. Cook over medium-low heat for 5 minutes, or until the artichokes are completely tender. If the mixture appears dry, add a few tablespoons of water.

Transfer the artichokes to a serving dish and serve hot or at room temperature.

ARTICHOKES BRAISED WITH THYME

Carciofi al Timo

SERVES 4

Thyme lends its earthy perfume to this dish of silvery-green braised artichokes. Garnished with shiny black olives, the brilliant white and gold of freshly boiled eggs, leafy radishes, and a sprinkling of bright pickled vegetables, it makes for a very fine lunch or picnic offering.

4 *medium artichokes*
1 *lemon, cut in half*
6 *tablespoons extra-virgin olive oil*
3 *cups water*
½ *onion, thickly sliced*
1 *tablespoon chopped fresh thyme leaves*
2 *bay leaves*
2 *cloves*
½ *teaspoon whole black peppercorns*
Salt to taste
½ *cup oil-cured black olives*
6 *anchovies, cut in half*
3 *hard-cooked eggs, quartered lengthwise*
1 *small bunch radishes with leafy tops*
¼ *cup Garden Vegetables in White Wine Vinegar (see page 82) or bottled giardiniera, cut into julienne*

Trim the artichokes according to the directions on page 8. Cut the artichokes into quarters and leave as much as possible of the tender pale yellow leaves and tender portion of the stems. Use half the lemon to make the acidulated water and the other half of the lemon to rub the cut portions of the artichokes as you trim them.

Place the artichokes in a braising pan and add the olive oil, water, onion, thyme, bay leaves, cloves, peppercorns, and salt to taste. Simmer the artichokes, partly covered, for about 15 minutes, stirring occasionally. Remove the lid and cook until the artichoke hearts are tender but slightly resistant and the water has evaporated, leaving a small amount of olive oil–rich juice. Transfer to a serving platter. If the artichokes are tender but the juices are too diluted, transfer the artichokes to a serving platter and boil the juices down to a more concentrated flavor. Spoon the juices over the artichokes and let cool to room temperature.

Before serving, arrange black olives, anchovies, hard-cooked eggs, and radishes around the edges of a platter. Sprinkle the pickled vegetables over the top.

The artichokes can be made 1 to 2 days in advance. Cover with plastic wrap and refrigerate. Return the artichokes to room temperature before serving and garnish as indicated above.

GRATIN OF ARTICHOKES AND POTATOES

Tiella di Carciofi e Patate

SERVES 4

A rtichokes and potatoes, two of my favorite vegetables, have an affinity for each other. Both have an earthy flavor, the artichokes with a trace of bitterness, the potatoes, touched with sweetness. Their compact textures require similar cooking times.

Only a small amount of water is used in cooking, just enough to allow the vegetables to soften but not so much as to dilute their flavor or compromise their texture. What comes through is a rich, concentrated vegetable dish redolent of olive oil, garlic, and fresh thyme.

1   *lemon, cut in half*
3   *medium artichokes*
3   *medium potatoes, unpeeled, thinly sliced*
4   *tablespoons extra-virgin olive oil, plus extra for the baking dish and for drizzling*
3   *garlic cloves, peeled and chopped*
1   *tablespoon chopped thyme leaves*
Salt and freshly ground black pepper to taste
2   *tablespoons homemade bread crumbs*

Squeeze the juice of half a lemon into a big bowl of water. Use the other half to rub the cut portions of the artichokes as you work. Trim the artichokes according to directions on page 8, and remove the chokes. Thinly slice the artichoke hearts lengthwise and place in the acidulated water until needed. Right before using, drain and dry them in a clean dish towel.

Lightly oil a low-sided rustic baking dish large enough to contain the artichokes and potatoes to a depth of about 2 inches. Place a layer of potato slices on the bottom of the dish. Arrange a layer of artichoke slices over the potato slices, and sprinkle with garlic, thyme, and salt and pepper to taste. Drizzle with some of the olive oil. Continue layering the ingredients, ending with a top layer of potatoes drizzled with olive oil and seasoned with salt and pepper. Spoon 4 tablespoons of water into the corners of the baking dish, allowing the water to trickle to the bottom of the dish. Sprinkle bread crumbs over the top and drizzle with remaining olive oil.

Bake in a preheated 400° oven for about 1 hour, or until the artichokes and potatoes are tender but hold their shape.

BROCCOLI WITH GARLIC AND RED CHILE PEPPER

Broccoli con Aglio e Peperoncino

SERVES 4 TO 6

When slender young broccoli appears in the markets, rush to buy it. It is every bit as delectable as the first asparagus of early spring.

In this recipe the broccoli is lightly cooked, then quickly sautéed with a touch of fresh garlic and red chile pepper, and served garnished with lemon wedges.

For a delightful, healthy, light lunch, accompany the brocolli with slices of fresh mozzarella and oil-cured black olives.

1 *bunch tender broccoli, about 1½ pounds*
Salt
4 *tablespoons extra-virgin olive oil*
3–4 *garlic cloves, peeled and chopped*
Small piece of fresh red chile pepper, chopped
Thick lemon wedges

Trim the ends of the broccoli. Use a paring knife to strip the peel from the stalks. Cut the broccoli in half lengthwise, or if the stalks are thick, cut it into quarters. Cook the broccoli in abundant salted boiling water until just tender. Cooking time will depend on the freshness of the broccoli, but it can cook in as little as 4 minutes. Drain well in a colander.

Combine the olive oil, garlic, and red chile pepper in a large sauté pan. Cook over low heat for 2 to 3 minutes, or until the garlic is opaque. Add the broccoli and salt to taste. Turn the stalks over gently in the olive oil and garlic once or twice. Carefully transfer the broccoli to a platter. Serve hot or at room temperature garnished with lemon wedges.

BROCCOFLOWER WITH PROVOLONE

Cavolfiore Verde con Provolone

SERVES 4 TO 6

Broccoflower, as its name suggests, is a cross between broccoli and cauliflower. New to markets, it looks exactly like cauliflower except for one startling difference—the "flower" is jade green instead of white. In this recipe, fresh herbs and tangy provolone highlight the unique color and intriguing flavor—a flavor that lies somewhere between the two vegetables. I suggest serving the broccoflower garnished with Crostini, but it is also delicious tossed with hot pasta.

1 *head broccoflower*
5 *tablespoons extra-virgin olive oil*
3 *garlic cloves, peeled and chopped*
Salt and freshly ground black pepper to taste
3 *tablespoons chopped Italian parsley*
6 *ounces shredded imported provolone*
1 *recipe Crostini (see page 366), using 16 pieces of bread*

Remove the leaves from the broccoflower and trim the stem. Boil it whole in abundant boiling salted water until tender but firm. Drain well. When cool enough to handle, cut into flowerets.

Place the olive oil and garlic in a medium sauté pan. Cook the garlic over low heat for 2 to 3 minutes. Add the broccoflower and salt and pepper to taste. Add the herbs and stir. Raise the heat to medium low and toss until the vegetable is hot and has absorbed the flavors in the pan. Sprinkle with provolone, cover, and cook until the cheese melts.

Meanwhile prepare the Crostini.

Transfer the broccoflower to a serving dish and garnish with the Crostini. Serve immediately.

CARDOONS WITH BLACK OLIVES AND ANCHOVIES

Cardi al Forno con Olive e Acciughe

SERVES 4 TO 6

Y ou may have seen cardoons in produce markets that cater to Italians and been puzzled by their appearance. The cardoon resembles celery grown to monumental proportions. If you are not daunted by its size, you will be won over by its unique characteristics. It has a subtle artichoke-like flavor, not surprising since the two vegetables are related. Its texture is tender like that of cooked celery.

In this dish cardoons are layered over with rich black olives, anchovies, and fresh parsley. Then a topping of bread crumbs is added, and the dish is baked until the crumbs turn golden brown.

Enjoy this fascinating vegetable dish as a first course to savor its unique flavor properly.

About 3 pounds cardoons
1 *lemon, cut in half*
Salt
10 *oil-cured black olives, pitted and quartered*
4 *anchovies, very coarsely chopped*
2 *tablespoons chopped Italian parsley, divided*
Salt and freshly ground black pepper to taste
2 *tablespoons homemade bread crumbs, divided*
3 *tablespoons extra-virgin olive oil, divided, plus extra*
for the baking dish

To clean the cardoons use one half of the lemon to rub the cut portions to prevent blackening. Fill a bowl with water and squeeze the juice of the other lemon half into the bowl. Trim the ends of the cardoons and use a knife to cut away the jagged leaves that border the stalks. Remove the strings from the large stalks just as with celery, making a shallow cut at the top and pulling the strings free from the stalks in a downward motion. Cut the stalks into 2-inch pieces and place in the acidulated water.

Bring an abundant amount of water to a boil. Add to the water the juice remaining from the lemon used to rub the cut cardoons. Add salt. Add the cardoons and cook the narrow inner stalks for about 30 minutes, and the tougher outer stalks for 1 hour or longer. Check for tenderness often, using the tip of a knife, since cooking times vary greatly. Remove the pieces of cardoon as they become tender and drain them on paper towels.

Oil a shallow glass or enamel dish large enough to contain the cardoons in 2 layers. Place a layer of cardoons on the bottom of the dish. Scatter half the olives and anchovies over the top and sprinkle with 1 tablespoon of the parsley. Season with salt and pepper to taste. Top with 1 tablespoon of bread crumbs and drizzle with half the olive oil. Arrange the second layer of cardoons and add the remaining ingredients in the same order as above.

Bake in a preheated 400° oven for 15 to 20 minutes, or until the bread crumbs are lightly golden.

CANNELLINI BEANS BRAISED IN TOMATO AND HERBS

Fagioli Cannellini in Umido

SERVES 4

Creamy cannellini beans are braised in a tomato sauce seasoned with rosemary, cloves, and red chile pepper for a highly flavorful side dish. Doubling the recipe and using canned beans turns this into a quick stew to serve a hungry family. Drizzle each portion with good olive oil and grind coarse pepper over the top before serving.

4 *tablespoons extra-virgin olive oil*
2 *garlic cloves, peeled and chopped*
½ *teaspoon crushed dried red chile pepper flakes*
1 *small sprig rosemary*
3 *cloves*
6 *Roma tomatoes, peeled, seeded, and finely chopped*
Salt and freshly ground black pepper to taste
2 *cups cooked cannellini or white beans, drained*

In a medium braising pan combine the olive oil, garlic, red chile pepper flakes, rosemary, and cloves. Cook over low heat for 2 to 3 minutes.

Add the tomatoes and salt and pepper to taste. Cook for 5 minutes over medium-low heat until the tomatoes thicken slightly.

Add the beans and stir gently once or twice, being careful not to mash them. Cook briefly over low heat.

CARROTS WITH CREAM AND FRESH BASIL

Carote con Panna e Basilico

SERVES 4

seductive side dish of tender, sugary carrots, cooked briefly in cream and fresh basil, which emerges almost as sweet as a dessert. Serve with an uncomplicated, mild-tasting main dish such as crisp roasted chicken.

1 *pound carrots*
3 *tablespoons unsalted butter*
Salt and freshly ground black pepper to taste
½ *cup fresh cream*
8 *large basil leaves*

Trim the carrots and peel them. Cut the carrots on the diagonal into short 1-inch pieces.

Place the butter in a large sauté pan and turn on the heat to medium-low. Add the carrots and salt and pepper to taste. Toss the carrots in the butter until they are lightly coated. Cover the pan and cook over low heat until the carrots are tender but firm. Add the cream. Tear the basil into large fragments and sprinkle over the carrots. Turn the heat up to high and let the cream boil for 1 to 2 minutes, or until it thickens slightly.

Before serving, grind a little black pepper over the top.

CARROTS WITH PORCINI MUSHROOMS

Carote ai Funghi Porcini

SERVES 4

cool-weather vegetable dish, in which porcini mushrooms impart a deep wintry flavor to the sweetness of the carrots.

2   *ounces dried porcini mushrooms*

1½   *pounds sweet carrots*

5   *tablespoons unsalted butter*

½   *medium onion, peeled and finely diced*

2   *garlic cloves, peeled and finely chopped*

Salt and freshly ground black pepper to taste

3   *tablespoons chopped Italian parsley*

Soak the porcini mushrooms in warm water to cover. After 20 minutes lift the mushrooms out of the liquid and rinse under cold water. Carefully feel for any grit embedded in the mushroom pieces. Cut the mushrooms into strips.

Meanwhile peel the carrots and cut into julienne.

Combine in a medium sauté pan the butter and onion. Cook over low heat until the onion is golden. Add the garlic and cook for another 1 to 2 minutes. Add the julienned carrots and toss them in the butter. Add salt and pepper to taste. Cook for a few minutes over low heat. Add about 4 tablespoons of water, cover, and cook until the carrots are tender. Stir in the parsley during the final minute of cooking.

LEMONY GRILLED EGGPLANT

Melanzane alla Griglia con Limone

SERVES 6 AS A SIDE DISH OR AS
PART OF AN ANTIPASTO

Grilled eggplant looks beautiful—pale, creamy flesh with the dark imprint of the grill upon it. After grilling, it is often marinated in a splash of red wine vinegar, and it is undeniably delicious that way. In this recipe from Sicily, lemon juice takes the place of vinegar to produce a dish that is a little sweeter and more perfumed than the red wine vinegar version. The eggplant goes especially well with grilled seafood such as swordfish, tuna, or shrimp. It makes a delicious addition to a platter of assorted antipasti, or tuck a few slices in a roll for a fabulous sandwich.

Salt
1 *firm medium eggplant, sliced horizontally ¼ inch thick*
¼ *cup extra-virgin olive oil, plus extra for brushing*
     on the eggplant
Juice of 1 lemon
2–3 *garlic cloves, peeled and finely chopped*
2 *tablespoons chopped Italian parsley leaves*
2 *tablespoons chopped basil leaves*
Salt and freshly ground black pepper to taste

Lightly salt the eggplant slices and let drain for 30 minutes. Wipe dry.

Combine the olive oil, lemon juice, garlic, parsley, and basil. Season with salt and pepper to taste. Beat lightly with a fork. Set olive oil mixture aside until needed.

Heat up a grill. Lightly oil the grill with a clean old dishcloth moistened in oil. Brush a few slices of eggplant on both sides with olive oil. Grill the eggplant on both sides. As the eggplant slices become ready, arrange them on a serving platter. Season with salt and pepper. Beat the olive oil mixture until it is creamy and spoon a little over the grilled eggplant. Continue grilling the eggplant slices and arranging them on the platter in layers, spooning the mixture over each slice. Let the eggplant marinate overnight refrigerated. Bring to room temperature before serving.

CHAYOTE SQUASH
PICCHI-PACCHI STYLE

Zucchine Centinaia al Picchi Pacchi

SERVES 4

K nown in Italy as *centinaia*, or Zucchini-by-the-Hundreds, chayote is an unusual summer squash that is found more often in private vegetable gardens than in markets. Occasionally it can be purchased in specialty produce stores. Chayote thrives in hot climates; it is similar in shape and size to a pear, with tender skin and mild, sweet flesh. Its Italian name refers to the abundant amount of fruit the vines produce.

My mother remembers this vegetable growing at Villino Riccardo, her childhood summer home just outside Palermo, Sicily, in the foothills of Mount Pellegrino. The chayote grew on a pergola, a trellised arbor of leaves and dappled light from which dangled hundreds of pale green fruit.

Villino Riccardo, situated on a narrow country road lined with small villas, was surrounded by gardens and had as its backdrop the looming presence of the mountain. From a loggia perched high above the house one could see an endless expanse of citrus groves and turquoise sea.

The garden surrounding the house was a paradise on earth; a large, shady fig tree growing just inside the front gate; lemon-scented citronella and blossoms of sweet jasmine climbing, rampant and glorious, over garden walls; thick clusters of dusty purple grapes; a banana tree whose fruit would be fried in hot olive oil; trees with tiny apples; and a pear tree with fruit as small as thimbles and as sweet as sugar. In summer the heavy scent of basil and ripening peaches would fill the garden, and a sparkling fountain would refresh the hot air. There were flowers—intoxicating roses smelling of tea and berries, a stand of winter chrysanthemums with gigantic yellow and white blossoms that would be gathered for pilgrimages to the cemetery; and in February, out of the cool, rain-darkened earth would emerge a carpet of fragrant Parma violets.

In this recipe the chayote cooks in a sweet sauce of fresh tomatoes and onion, and is sprinkled with fresh basil right before serving.

1½ *pounds chayote*
4 *tablespoons extra-virgin olive oil*
1 *onion, peeled and finely diced*
Salt and freshly ground black pepper to taste
2 *large ripe tomatoes, peeled, seeded, and coarsely chopped*
Handful basil leaves

Trim away any bruised portions of the chayote and cut into 1-inch dice.

Place the olive oil and onion in a medium sauté pan. Sauté the onion over low heat until it turns light gold. Add the chayote, and salt and pepper to taste. Toss in the oil and cook for about 5 minutes.

Add the tomatoes and salt and pepper to taste. Cook over medium-low heat until the chayote is just tender and the tomatoes have thickened into a sauce. Before serving, tear the basil leaves into fragments and sprinkle over the top.

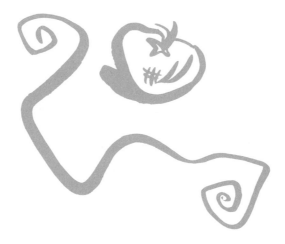

EGGPLANT AND ZUCCHINI PLATTER

Piatto di Melanzane e Zucchine

SERVES 6

A beautiful wreath of eggplant slices surrounds a mound of zucchini coins. The dish is made quickly, since the eggplant slices are broiled on baking sheets and the zucchini is given a lightning-quick sautéeing. The secret to success lies in cooking both the eggplant and zucchini until golden, since this transforms their flavor from sweet to deep and richly burnished. It is a magnificent addition to an assorted antipasto buffet.

4–6 firm Japanese eggplants
Extra-virgin olive oil for brushing on eggplants
6 tablespoons extra-virgin olive oil for zucchini
Salt and freshly ground black pepper to taste
1½ pounds zucchini
2 garlic cloves, peeled and finely chopped

Trim the eggplants and slice lengthwise ¼ inch thick. Arrange eggplant slices on a baking sheet and brush with olive oil. Bake in a preheated 375° oven for 10 minutes. Turn the slices over, brush with olive oil, and continue cooking until the eggplant is golden. Remove from oven and arrange lengthwise in a slightly overlapping pattern around the platter. Season with salt and pepper.

Meanwhile trim the zucchini and cut into thin rounds. Heat 6 tablespoons of olive oil in a large sauté pan. When the oil is hot, add the zucchini rounds and sauté over high heat until golden. Sprinkle with salt and arrange in the center of the platter.

Sprinkle the garlic over the vegetables. Serve at room temperature.

FRESH FAVA BEANS WITH NEW ONIONS

Fave con Cipolle Novelle

SERVES 6

Fava beans, sometimes called broad beans, are anything but rare in Italy. They appear in soups, pasta dishes, and side dishes; they are eaten raw, dipped in salt, or accompanied by slivers of cheese. In spring, mountains of the bright green, cushiony pods appear in market stalls as do new onions with their green tops still attached.

This dish is all about the first tender fava beans of the season and crisp, sweet freshly pulled onions. Although fava beans are not generally available in supermarkets, they can be found in markets catering to an Italian or Middle Eastern clientele. Or, if you are a gardener, you may want to try planting them. Select pods that are small to medium sized, fresh, unwithered, and brightly colored.

Fava beans prepared this way are delicious as a first course, or serve them as a delightful lunch along with fresh ricotta salata and good bread.

3 *pounds fava beans in the pod, shelled and peeled*
Salt and freshly ground black pepper to taste
5 *tablespoons extra-virgin olive oil*
1 *small fresh onion, peeled and finely diced, or 2–3 green onions, green tops trimmed, white bulbs sliced into rings*

Cook the fava beans in boiling water to cover until tender. Drain gently so as not to crush the beans and transfer to a shallow bowl. Season with salt and pepper to taste, drizzle with olive oil, and sprinkle with the onions. Carefully toss.

FAVA BEANS WITH
SWISS CHARD AND TOMATO

Scafata

SERVES 4

This dish features a trio of vegetables—fava beans, tender Swiss chard, and tomatoes—sweetened with carrots and given a fresh, herbal touch with celery.

Scafata is traditionally made with biete da taglio, young Swiss chard leaves with a barely developed rib. If you grow chard in your garden, pick it tender and new. At this early stage of development, the flavor is especially delicate, sweet, and clean-tasting.

5   *tablespoons extra-virgin olive oil*
1   *small onion, peeled and finely diced*
1   *carrot, peeled and cut into small dice*
1   *celery stalk, strings removed, cut into small dice*
1¾ *pounds fava beans in the pod, shelled but unpeeled*
Salt to taste
1   *bunch tender Swiss chard, ribs removed, leaves*
        cut into strips
1   *pound tomatoes, peeled, seeded, and finely chopped*
Freshly ground black pepper to taste

Place the olive oil in a medium braising pan. Add the diced vegetables and fava beans. Stir well. Add salt to taste and a few tablespoons of water. Cover and cook over very low heat until the fava beans are tender. If the mixture becomes too dry, add a few more tablespoons of water.

Add the chard and tomatoes and cook, with the lid partly on, until the tomatoes thicken and the water has evaporated. Grind a little black pepper over the top before serving.

GOLDEN FENNEL FANS

Fettine di Finocchi

SERVES 4

simple, tasty way to prepare fresh fennel. The fennel is cut lengthwise into fan-shaped slices held together by the tender core. The slices are sautéed in extra-virgin olive oil until they turn a light golden brown, which intensifies their naturally sweet flavor.

Serve the fans hot as a vegetable side dish, or at room temperature as part of a buffet.

2 *medium bulbs fresh fennel*
6 *tablespoons extra-virgin olive oil*
Salt and freshly ground black pepper to taste

Cut off the stalks and the feathery tops of the fennel and discard. If the outer layer of the fennel bulb is tough or yellowed, discard it. If it is fresh, remove the tough strings and trim away any bruised or yellowed areas. Trim the base of the fennel, removing any darkened areas. Cut the whole fennel bulb lengthwise into ¼-inch-thick slices. The central core serves to hold together the layers of fennel and has a light, licorice-like flavor of its own.

Heat the olive oil in a large sauté pan. Place the fennel slices in the hot oil, a few at a time, and sauté over medium heat until the fennel is golden on both sides. Season with salt and pepper to taste.

Transfer the cooked fennel slices to a serving platter.

GREEN BEANS IN CORAL-COLORED SAUCE

Fagiolini "al Corallo"

SERVES 4

A dish of green beans braised in tomatoes. Braising tenderizes tougher beans, often all that is available in supermarkets, and brings out their sweetness.

Enjoy this dish all summer long, accompanied by bread to dip into the tomato sauce. It makes a good, light luncheon dish served either warm or at room temperature.

6 *tablespoons extra-virgin olive oil*
1 *red onion, cut into medium dice*
1½ *pounds green beans*
1½ *pounds tomatoes, peeled, seeded, and chopped*
Salt and freshly ground black pepper to taste
1 *tablespoon chopped Italian parsley leaves*
5–6 *fresh basil leaves, chopped*

Place the olive oil and onion in a medium braising pan. Cook the onion over low heat until tender, about 12 minutes. Stir frequently. Add the beans, toss, and let them absorb the flavor of the oil for a few minutes.

Add the tomatoes, salt and pepper to taste, and cook at a moderate simmer, with the lid on, until the beans are tender but firm. Cooking time will vary considerably depending on the age and freshness of the beans. Stir occasionally to make sure the tomatoes do not stick to the bottom of the pan.

If the beans are cooked and the tomato sauce is too watery, cook over high heat briefly to thicken the juices.

Before serving, stir in the chopped parsley and basil.

MIXED GREENS WITH BLACK OLIVES

Verdura Mista alle Olive

SERVES 4

The flavor of greens ranges in strength—from the sweetness of chard and spinach to the assertive bite of rapini and mustard. In Italy platters of freshly cooked greens are on display in every local trattoria, beckoning passersby. In this recipe a mix of tender leaves, some mild, others bitter, are sautéed with black olives. I like it best served right after it cools, with lemon juice squeezed over the top.

1 *bunch red chard*
Salt to taste
1 *bunch mustard greens*
1 *bunch spinach*
2 *bunches arugula*
¼ *cup water*
¼ *cup extra-virgin olive oil*
3 *garlic cloves, peeled and finely diced*
½ *cup oil-cured black olives, pitted and quartered*
Lemon wedges

Strip the leaves from the stalks of the red chard. Reserve the stalks for another use. Wash the leaves well under cold running water. Place the chard leaves in a medium sauté pan and add ¼ cup of water and salt to taste. Cook, covered, over medium heat until the chard is tender. Drain the chard in a colander and gently press out excess water with the back of a wooden spoon.

Strip the leaves from the mustard greens and discard the stalks. Cook the mustard greens following the directions for the chard and drain.

Remove the stems from the spinach and wash the leaves well in several changes of water. Cook and drain as above.

Trim the tough stems from the arugula and wash the leaves well. Place the arugula and the water that clings to the leaves in a small sauté pan and add salt to taste. Cover and cook over medium heat for a few minutes until wilted. Drain as above.

Select a large sauté pan and add the olive oil, garlic, and greens. Turn on the heat to medium and toss the greens in the oil and garlic, adding salt to taste. Add the quartered olives and continue to toss over medium heat until the greens and olives are hot. Transfer to a serving platter and surround with lemon wedges.

LEEKS IN PINK MASCARPONE SAUCE

Porri con Mascarpone

SERVES 4

A special-occasion dish that features sweet, tender leeks in a creamy tomato-pink mascarpone sauce. Very pretty and very rich, it lends itself to an elegant first-course presentation.

8 *tender leeks, medium sized, of about the same thickness*
Salt
2 *tablespoons unsalted butter*
3 *tablespoons extra-virgin olive oil*
½ *medium onion, peeled and finely diced*
1 *garlic clove, peeled and finely chopped*
4 *imported Italian tomatoes, seeded and finely chopped*
8 *basil leaves, divided*
3 *ounces mascarpone*
Freshly ground black pepper to taste

Trim the leeks by cutting off the tough green tops and make a shallow cut along their length. Cook the leeks in abundant salted boiling water until tender. Drain well and set aside.

Select a sauté pan large enough to contain the leeks lengthwise. Combine the butter, olive oil, and onion. Cook over low heat until the onion is lightly golden. Add the garlic and cook another 1 to 2 minutes. Add the tomatoes and 4 basil leaves. Cook, covered, over low heat for 10 minutes. Stir in the mascarpone. Add the leeks and toss gently in the sauce. Cut the remaining basil leaves into julienne. Transfer the leeks and sauce to a serving dish. Sprinkle with the basil and grind fresh black pepper over the top.

RED CHARD WITH GARLIC AND CAYENNE PEPPER

Bieta con Olio, Aglio, e Peperoncino

SERVES 4

ed chard is one of the most beautiful greens. It has rhubarb-colored stalks and russet or deep green leaves that are softly ruffled and veined in dark red. Red chard is at its most savory when sautéed directly in olive oil, without any preliminary cooking; it becomes imbued with the richness of olive oil and garlic, and the heat of red chile pepper.

1 *bunch red chard, about 1¼ pounds*
4 *tablespoons extra-virgin olive oil*
4 *garlic cloves, peeled and chopped*
½ *teaspoon ground cayenne or to taste, or a few drops of*
      Little Devil Olive Oil (see page 52)
Salt to taste
Lemon wedges, optional

Wash the chard well and let drain in a colander. Trim a bit off the stem ends of the stalks and strip off the leaves. Cut the stalks into julienne and cut the leaves into strips. There should be a little moisture clinging to the greens.

Combine in a large sauté pan the olive oil, garlic, and cayenne pepper or Little Devil Olive Oil. Sauté over low heat for about 5 minutes. Add the chard stems and salt to taste. Toss, cover, and cook over low heat for about 5 minutes, stirring occasionally. If the stalks are thick, increase the cooking time to 10 minutes. Add the leaves, another sprinkling of salt, and stir. Cover and cook for an additional 10 minutes, or until the chard leaves are tender and the stems are tender but firm. If there is excess moisture in the bottom of the pan, raise the heat and boil away the water during the last few minutes of cooking.

Serve hot or at room temperature. If serving at room temperature, garnish with lemon wedges.

RAPINI WITH GARLIC BREAD CRUMBS

Cime di Rapa al Pangrattato

SERVES 4

Wild greens are very much a part of rustic Italian cooking. Rapini, a bitter green that resembles broccoli in its early stages of growth, has all the intensity and vigor of the edible wild plants that are gathered in the Italian countryside.

The contrast of bright green rapini and crisp bread crumbs imbued with the warmth of garlic makes for good, simple country eating. This dish is equally delicious made with tender stalks of broccoli.

> 1 *large bunch tender rapini, about 1 pound*
> *Salt*
> ¼ *cup homemade coarse bread crumbs (see page 363)*
> 5 *tablespoons extra-virgin olive oil, divided*
> 3 *garlic cloves, peeled and chopped*
> *Salt and freshly ground black pepper to taste*

Trim the stem ends of the rapini and discard any leaves that are yellow or withered. Using a paring knife, strip the peel from the stalks. Plunge the rapini into abundant salted boiling water and cook until just tender, a matter of only a few minutes if the rapini stalks are slender. Drain well.

Meanwhile prepare the bread crumbs. In a small saucepan combine 2 tablespoons of the olive oil, the bread crumbs, and the garlic. Sauté over low heat until the bread crumbs and garlic color lightly. Season with salt and pepper to taste. Transfer to a small bowl.

Place the remaining olive oil in a medium sauté pan. Add the rapini, lined up neatly, and salt to taste. Sauté over medium-low heat until the rapini is hot and has absorbed the flavor of the olive oil, about 3 to 4 minutes.

Transfer to a serving dish and sprinkle with the coarse bread crumbs.

GRILLED WILD MUSHROOMS WITH OREGANO

Funghi Selvatici all'Origano

The flavor of wild foods grilled over wood is atavistic and elemental. In this recipe big shiitake mushrooms capture the essence of true wild mushrooms. They are brushed with olive oil, sprinkled with salt and pepper, and grilled over fragrant hot coals. The sharp perfume of dried oregano sprinkled over the hot grilled mushrooms is the only embellishment. The mushrooms, with their velvety, dense flesh and dark, thin juices, make a meal in themselves when served with good bread.

Select shiitake mushrooms with very large, fleshy caps, at least 3 inches in diameter.

2 very large shiitake mushrooms per person
Extra-virgin olive oil
Salt and freshly ground black pepper to taste
Dried Mediterranean oregano

Cut off the stems of the mushrooms and discard them. Wipe the caps with damp paper towels. Lightly brush both sides of the mushrooms with olive oil. Season with salt and pepper to taste.

Heat up a grill. Use either an outdoor grill and natural wood coals; or, second best, a stovetop cast-iron ridged grill. Lightly rub the grill with a cloth moistened with olive oil. When the grill is very hot, place the mushrooms on the grill, with the gill side up. Grill until the mushrooms begin to soften slightly. Turn once and grill the other side until just tender and moist. This will take only a few minutes. If the mushrooms appear dry, brush them with a little more olive oil. Be careful not to overcook the mushrooms, since part of their appeal lies in their moist and ever so slightly resistant texture.

Transfer the mushrooms to a platter and sprinkle with oregano. Let the mushrooms rest for a moment before serving. Serve with bread to sop up the juices.

DOUBLE RED GRATIN

Tiella Doppio Rosso

SERVES 4 TO 6

his simple layering of bright red peppers and juicy tomatoes is inspired by Provençal cooking, and yields a dish worthy of summer. The flavors of many foods are best appreciated at room temperature. This gratin is at its best served cold; the juices turn to a honeyed jelly, and the chilled tomatoes and thick strips of luscious roasted peppers bring the temperature outside down by several degrees.

3 *large red peppers*
4 *large ripe tomatoes*
Extra-virgin olive oil
Salt and freshly ground black pepper to taste
½ *cup coarsely chopped Italian parsley leaves*
½ *cup chopped basil leaves*
2 *tablespoons chopped fresh oregano or 2 teaspoons
    dried oregano*
1–2 *tablespoons capers*
2 *tablespoons bread crumbs*

Roast the peppers over a gas flame or under the broiler. Cut peppers in half, core, seed, and remove the white membranes. Cut peppers into thick slices. Core the tomatoes and thickly slice them.

Oil a rustic baking dish large enough to contain the ingredients in several layers. Arrange a layer of tomato slices on the bottom of the dish. Season lightly with salt and pepper to taste, and sprinkle some of the herbs and capers on top. Cover with a layer of pepper strips. Season lightly with salt and pepper, and sprinkle with herbs and capers as described above. Continue layering ingredients, topping the final layer with bread crumbs. Moisten the gratin with a drizzling of olive oil.

Bake for 25 minutes in a preheated 375° oven, or until the gratin is tender and juicy. Let cool to room temperature. Serve this dish hot, warm, or at room temperature. It is at its most refreshing served cold.

FRIED YELLOW PEPPERS WITH MINT

Peperoni Fritti alla Menta

SERVES 4 AS A SIDE DISH
OR 8 AS AN ANTIPASTO

Frying very sweet yellow peppers over high heat concentrates their sweetness to a remarkable degree. When the peppers are seasoned with red wine vinegar, mint, and garlic, nothing could be simpler to prepare or more lively in flavor.

Serve these peppers as part of an assortment of antipasti or as a side dish with grilled tuna.

4 *firm, fleshy yellow peppers*
6 *tablespoons extra-virgin olive oil*
Salt to taste
2–3 *tablespoons imported red wine vinegar*
2 *garlic cloves, peeled and sliced paper thin*
¼ *cup coarsely chopped mint leaves*

Cut the peppers in half lengthwise. Pop out the cores and seeds. Remove any stray seeds and cut away the white membranes. Cut the peppers into strips about ¾ inch wide.

Place the olive oil in a large sauté pan. Turn on the heat to high and add the pepper strips. Cook over high heat, stirring occasionally. When golden brown areas develop on the pepper strips, reduce the heat to medium low. Add salt to taste and cover the pan. Cook until the peppers are tender but still a little crisp. Add the vinegar and stir once or twice.

Off the heat sprinkle with the garlic and mint. Let the peppers cool to room temperature before serving.

POTATO TORTA WITH TOMATOES AND FRESH MOZZARELLA

Torta Tarantina

SERVES 4

Thinly sliced potatoes are layered with tomatoes and fresh mozzarella, and seasoned with garlic and dried oregano. The torta is baked until the top layer of potatoes turns a glorious golden brown. This is a highly flavorful dish imbued with the wild, strong aroma of oregano, garlic, and tart-sweet tomato.

4 *tablespoons extra-virgin olive oil, divided*
1 *pound potatoes, peeled and sliced paper thin*
3 *ounces fresh mozzarella, cut into small dice*
5 *Roma tomatoes, peeled and diced*
Salt and freshly ground black pepper to taste
3 *garlic cloves, thinly sliced*
Dried Mediterranean oregano

Use a little of the olive oil to coat the bottom of a 9-inch shallow, round baking dish. Arrange one layer of potato slices on the bottom of the dish. Sprinkle with some of the mozzarella and diced tomatoes. Season with salt and pepper to taste. Sprinkle with garlic slices and dried oregano. Drizzle with some of the olive oil. Continue layering ingredients, ending with a layer of potatoes seasoned with a little salt and drizzled with olive oil.

Bake in a preheated 425° oven for 50 minutes, or until the top is golden and crusty and the potatoes are tender. If the top layer becomes very brown and the potatoes are not fully cooked, cover the dish with foil and cook until the potatoes are tender.

DICED POTATOES WITH ARUGULA AND HERBS

Patate alle Erbe

SERVES 4

Potatoes, peeled and diced while still warm, are tossed in extra-virgin olive oil and showered with chopped arugula, basil, and Italian parsley. Serve this as a summery side dish with grilled foods or as an accompaniment to sandwiches. It is just as delicious eaten at room temperature as when it is warm.

Black olives make an ideal accompaniment to the earthy flavors of potato and herbs. If desired, serve the potatoes with lemon wedges.

> 1½ *pounds boiling potatoes*
> *Salt and freshly ground black pepper to taste*
> 6   *tablespoons extra-virgin olive oil*
> 1   *small bunch arugula, leaves coarsely chopped*
> 10 *basil leaves, coarsely chopped*
> 3   *tablespoons chopped Italian parsley*
> 1   *small garlic clove, finely chopped*
> *Oil-cured black olives for garnish, optional*

Boil the potatoes in a generous amount of water. When the potatoes are tender but still very firm, drain them. When cool enough to handle, peel the potatoes and cut them into ¾-inch dice. Place the potatoes on a serving dish and season with salt and pepper to taste. Drizzle with olive oil and toss. Sprinkle the arugula, basil, parsley, and garlic over the potatoes and toss again. Garnish with black olives if desired.

DEVIL POTATOES

Patate al Diavolicchio

SERVES 4

*F*rom the rugged, austere region of Basilicata in southern Italy comes this recipe for sliced potatoes drizzled with spicy hot red chile pepper oil.

If any dish can symbolize the triumph of the human spirit over adversity, this is it, a dish that is as simple as it is delicious.

> 1½ *pounds boiling potatoes of about equal size*
> ¼ *cup extra-virgin olive oil*
> 2 *small fresh red chile peppers, seeded and minced, or* ½
> *teaspoon crushed dried red chile pepper*
> *Salt to taste*
> 2 *tablespoons chopped Italian parsley*

Boil potatoes in salted water to cover by 2 inches. When the potatoes are tender but firm, drain them. When the potatoes have cooled enough to handle, peel them and slice into rounds about ¼ inch thick.

Meanwhile place the olive oil and chile peppers, either fresh or dried, in a small sauté pan. Warm over very low heat for about 5 minutes.

Arrange the potato slices on a serving platter in a slightly overlapping pattern. Salt the potatoes and drizzle with the warm oil and chile peppers. Sprinkle with parsley.

BAKED LAYERED POTATOES AND WILD MUSHROOMS

Funghi e Patate al Forno

SERVES 4 AS A SIDE DISH

Thinly sliced potatoes are layered with shiitake and crisp, white mushrooms, garlic, and fresh basil, drizzled with extra-virgin olive oil, then baked. The potatoes become impregnated with the woodsy, mysterious aroma of mushrooms, and the juices turn dark and rich, scented with basil and garlic.

Serve this golden, crusty gratin as a light main dish. It is also delicious served as a side dish with grilled fish.

¾ *pound potatoes*
½ *pound mushrooms*
¼ *pound shiitake mushrooms*
4 *tablespoons extra-virgin olive oil*
3 *garlic cloves, thinly sliced*
8 *basil leaves, coarsely chopped*
Salt and freshly ground black pepper to taste

Peel the potatoes and slice them paper thin. Wipe the mushrooms clean with damp paper towels. Trim the stems. Slice them medium thick. Wipe the shiitake mushrooms clean with damp paper towels. Cut cut off the stems and discard. Cut the caps into thin strips.

Use a little of the olive oil to coat the bottom of a 9-inch round, shallow baking dish. Arrange a layer of potato slices on the bottom of the dish. Sprinkle some mushrooms of both kinds over the potatoes. Sprinkle with garlic and basil. Season with salt and pepper to taste. Drizzle with some of the olive oil. Continue layering the ingredients, ending with a layer of potatoes seasoned with a little salt and drizzled with more olive oil.

Bake in a preheated 425° oven for 50 minutes, or until the potatoes are tender. If the top layer is very brown and the potatoes are not fully cooked, cover the dish with foil and continue cooking until the potatoes are tender.

GOLDEN RADICCHIO

Radicchio Dorato

SERVES 4

*I*n this recipe radicchio heads are cut in quarters lengthwise, dipped in beaten egg and bread crumbs, then lightly fried until crisp and golden brown. The contrast between the crisp coating and the tender, slightly bitter radicchio is irresistible.

2 *large or 4 small heads of radicchio*
2 *eggs*
¼ *cup unbleached all-purpose flour*
1 *cup bread crumbs*
Olive oil for frying
Salt to taste
Lemon wedges

If the radicchio are large, cut the heads into quarters lengthwise. If they are smaller, cut them in half lengthwise.

Crack the eggs into a shallow soup bowl and beat lightly with a fork. Spread the flour on a plate and the bread crumbs on another. Dredge a piece of radicchio in the flour, dip it in the beaten egg, letting the excess drain back into the bowl, and then in the bread crumbs, making sure all sides are evenly coated. Repeat until all the pieces of radicchio are breaded.

In a medium sauté pan, heat enough olive oil to come up about ½ inch. Do not let the oil become too hot or the bread crumbs will darken before the radicchio has had a chance to soften. Fry the radicchio quarters a few at a time, turning the pieces with tongs so as not to pierce the crust. When the bread crumb coating turns an even golden color, lift the radicchio from the pan and let the excess oil drain back into the pan. Place the radicchio on paper towels to absorb the excess oil. Season with salt to taste.

To serve, transfer the radicchio to a clean platter and surround with lemon wedges.

RADICCHIO WITH CREAM AND PARMESAN

Radicchio al Forno con Panna e Parmigiano

SERVES 4

In this elegant presentation, radicchio is baked with fresh cream and Parmesan cheese, grated and cut into fine slivers. It is briefly placed under a broiler until the cream thickens slightly and turns a pale shade of pink. The cream sweetens the radicchio and softens its bitter edge. To add an elusive, smoky quality to the finished dish, grill or roast the radicchio instead of boiling it.

4 *medium heads radicchio*
Salt
3 *tablespoons unsalted butter, plus additional for the baking dish*
Freshly ground black pepper to taste
¾ *cup fresh cream*
4 *tablespoons freshly grated imported Parmesan cheese*
4 *tablespoons paper thin shavings imported Parmesan cheese*
Freshly ground black pepper to taste

Cut the heads of the radicchio in half lengthwise. Plunge them into abundant salted boiling water. When the water returns to a boil, lift out the radicchio with a Chinese strainer and drain in a colander. Use the back of a wooden spoon to gently press out excess water. Transfer the radicchio halves to paper towels to absorb moisture.

Over low heat, melt the butter in a large sauté pan. Add the radicchio in 1 layer and season with salt and pepper. Turn the radicchio over in the pan to allow it to absorb the flavor of the butter. Cook for about 4 to 5 minutes.

Very lightly butter a low-sided dish large enough to contain the radicchio in 1 layer. In the dish arrange the radicchio, cut side down. Pour the cream over the top. Sprinkle with grated Parmesan cheese and top with the Parmesan cheese shavings.

Bake in a preheated 425° oven for 20 minutes, or until the cream thickens and begins to bubble. Transfer the dish to the broiler and broil just until the Parmesan cheese topping turns golden brown.

YELLOW WAX BEANS
WITH BLACK OLIVES

Fagiolini Gialli con Olive

SERVES 4

Wax beans are colored a delicate light yellow tinged with spring green. In this recipe smoky black olives set off the sweetness of the fresh beans and summer herbs.

1 *pound tender wax beans*
Salt
3 *tablespoons unsalted butter*
2 *tablespoons extra-virgin olive oil*
½ *medium onion, peeled and finely diced*
1 *large garlic clove, peeled and lightly crushed*
20 *small black olives, such as Gaeta or Niçoise*
Freshly ground black pepper to taste
2 *tablespoons grated imported Parmesan cheese*
1 *tablespoon coarsely chopped Italian parsley*
6 *basil leaves, torn into small fragments*

Trim the ends of the wax beans. Cook the beans in abundant salted boiling water until tender but firm. Drain well and set aside.

Combine in a medium sauté pan the butter, olive oil, onion, and garlic clove. Cook over low heat until the onion softens. Add the wax beans, black olives, and salt and pepper to taste. Toss over low heat and let flavors develop for about 5 minutes. Before serving, sprinkle with the Parmesan cheese, parsley, and basil, and toss lightly.

BANANA SQUASH WITH ROSEMARY AND SAGE

Zucca Gialla al Rosmarino e Salvia

SERVES 4 TO 6

Winter squash—whether a plump piece of baked banana squash, a rich, smooth pumpkin soup, or the crusty diced butternut squash featured in this recipe—brings brilliant color and a sugary taste to the subdued palette of winter foods. Rosemary and sage—herbs associated with cool weather—balance the light, sweet squash flavor. The texture of each golden cube, slightly firm on the exterior to meltingly tender within, is most satisfying.

1½ *pounds butternut or other winter squash*
6 *tablespoons extra-virgin olive oil*
2 *large garlic cloves, peeled and lightly crushed*
2 *sprigs rosemary, leaves finely chopped*
3–4 *leaves fresh sage, finely chopped*
Salt and freshly ground black pepper to taste

Cut the squash in half and scoop out the seeds. Cut each half into strips about 1 inch wide. Use a paring knife to cut away the peel. Cut the strips crosswise into 1-inch dice.

Place the olive oil in a large sauté pan along with the garlic cloves. Turn on the heat to medium and sauté the garlic until it turns light gold. Stir occasionally so that the garlic colors evenly. Add the diced squash to the hot olive oil and stir well.

Sprinkle with the chopped rosemary and sage, and stir again. Cook the squash until it is tender but still holds its shape and has developed a golden brown crust, about 12 to 15 minutes. Stir from time to time to prevent the squash from sticking. Drain the squash on paper towels to absorb excess oil and quickly transfer to a serving platter. Sprinkle with salt and pepper to taste, and toss lightly.

MILAN-STYLE ZUCCHINI

Zucchine alla Milanese

SERVES 4

Crisp zucchini, strips of tomato, arugula leaves, and highly aromatic fresh thyme make this dish exceptionally flavorful. If using very small zucchini, simply cut them in half lengthwise.

1½ *pounds small, tender zucchini*

8–10 *canned imported San Marzano tomatoes, drained and seeded*

3 *small bunches arugula*

6 *tablespoons extra-virgin olive oil*

3 *large garlic cloves, peeled and chopped*

6 *sprigs thyme, leaves chopped*

Salt to taste

Wash the zucchini well. Make sure the surface of the skin feels smooth and free of grit. Trim the ends. Cut the zucchini into batons. Cut the tomatoes into ¼-inch-thick strips. Trim the stem ends of the arugula and cut into strips.

Place the olive oil in a large sauté pan. When the oil is hot, add the zucchini and toss over high heat. Cook the zucchini until tender but crisp and very lightly flecked with gold. Lower the heat and add the garlic and thyme. Cook for a few moments.

Add the tomatoes and arugula, and season with salt to taste. Raise the heat to high and toss the ingredients until the liquid from the tomatoes evaporates, a matter of a few minutes.

ZUCCHINI WITH BASIL AND PECORINO ROMANO CHEESE

Zucchine con Basilico e Pecorino Romano

SERVES 4

Zucchini, tangy Pecorino Romano cheese, and fresh basil create a dish that is a staple in my home. When made with small, tender zucchini, the flavor is unbeatable.

1½ *pounds small firm zucchini*

4 *tablespoons extra-virgin olive oil*

3 *garlic cloves, peeled and chopped*

Salt and freshly ground black pepper to taste

3 *tablespoons freshly grated imported Pecorino Romano cheese*

10 *basil leaves*

Wash the zucchini well. Feel the surface of the skin to make sure it is smooth and free of grit. Trim the zucchini and slice into thin coins.

Place the olive oil in a large sauté pan and turn the heat to high. Add the zucchini and toss in the oil until it is lightly golden in spots but still crisp, about 4 minutes. Turn the heat to medium low, add the garlic and salt and pepper to taste. Cook until the zucchini is tender but still has a trace of crispness, and toss.

Transfer the zucchini to a serving platter. Sprinkle the grated Pecorino Romano cheese over the zucchini. Tear the basil leaves into fragments and scatter them over the top.

FRIED ZUCCHINI BLOSSOMS ON WILD FENNEL

Fiori di Zucca Fritti

SERVES 4

ucchini blossoms are a special treat from the garden. I love to serve the fried blossoms on a fragrant bed of wild fennel branches—the contrast of the saffron-colored petals peeking out from the golden batter against the feathery green fennel leaves is quite beautiful. If fennel does not grow wild where you live, sprinkle herbs over the top or add chopped herbs to the batter for a pretty herbal touch.

1   *cup unbleached all-purpose flour*
½   *cup water, or ¼ cup water and ¼ cup beer*
16   *zucchini flowers*
Olive oil for frying
Salt
Sprigs of tender wild fennel

Combine in a shallow bowl the flour and water (or water and beer). Stir until smooth. Set aside.

Gently clean the zucchini blossoms by dipping them into a bowl of cold water. Carefully remove the pistils from the zucchini blossoms. Dry the blossoms on a clean dish towel.

In a medium skillet pour olive oil to a depth of ½ inch. Heat the oil until it is hot but not smoking. Dip the zucchini blossoms into the batter and let the excess batter drip back into the bowl. Carefully lower the blossoms, a few at a time, into the hot oil. Fry the blossoms until golden on both sides. Lift out of the olive oil and place on paper towels. Salt lightly and let drain.

Line a serving dish with feathery wild fennel and arrange the fried zucchini blossoms on the fennel leaves. Serve immediately.

Desserts

essert recipes featuring fruits are in keeping with the themes of freshness and seasonality in this book. Unfortunately, nowhere is the loss of quality in the produce in our markets as poignant as in the decline of flavor of fruits, especially the fruits of summer. I remember vividly as a child eating apricots picked from our tree in the small southern California town where I grew up. The fruit was fully ripened and soft, charged with a flavor and fragrance that were the essence of heat, fruit, and flowers.

Supermarket fruits must be chosen with great care, since they are often picked before they are ripe. Many fruits never even find their way to supermarkets, such as honeyed muscat grapes, small white peaches with the sparkle of sugar in their flesh, and jamlike figs. Aside from your own backyard and those of neighbors, farmers' markets are probably the best source for flavorful seasonal fruits. A drive out to the countryside in search of stands selling sweet little strawberries or to a local farms where you can pick your own blackberries can be a memorable outing. I remember in particular a farm where we picked our own berries for a dollar a basket. We gathered the biggest, plumpest berries we could find and then sat under the shade of a tree and ate them all.

With the growing demand for fruit that really tastes like fruit, the quality and selection are beginning to improve. The recipes for fruit desserts in this book are very simple, so it is especially important to search out the best fruits available. Select fruits carefully and let them ripen fully before you use them. Macerating fruits in liqueurs can improve their flavor. Maraschino liqueur adds a magical bouquet to fruits that may be less than perfect. A few drops of balsamic vinegar can bring out the full sweet flavor of strawberries. Citrus juices can also be used to enhance fruits.

The recipes in this chapter feature marinated fruits; fruits with fresh, mild cheeses; fruits as toppings for ice cream or breads; fruits cooked in wine; and fruits juices frozen in granitas or used to flavor custard.

For the final recipe I chose an assortment of refreshing fruits and raw vegetables to be served at the end of the meal. In its simplicity this recipe embodies the philosophy of eating found in the pages of the book.

STRAWBERRIES WITH LEMON AND SUGAR

Fragole al Limone e Zucchero

SERVES 4

T hose giant strawberries in supermarkets look big and beautiful, but so often they disappoint with their pale color and sour flesh. This recipe works wonders on less than perfect strawberries. With small, deep-red fruit purchased from a farmers' market, the results will be sublime.

Serve this dish cold for a refreshing dessert.

2 *heaping baskets ripe strawberries*

4–5 *tablespoons sugar, depending on the sweetness of the berries, or to taste*

4 *tablespoons freshly squeezed lemon juice*

Wash the strawberries well under cold running water. Drain. Hull the strawberries with a sharp paring knife. Thickly slice the berries and place them in a bowl. Add the sugar and lemon juice, and stir gently until the sugar dissolves. Cover and refrigerate for at least 30 minutes, or until the juices start to form. The strawberries can be kept refrigerated for several hours before serving.

ORANGE JEWELS

Gioelli d'Anancia

SERVES 4

A combination of regular oranges and ruby-red blood oranges makes for a welcome and beautiful dessert. Here the oranges are given a specially indulgent treatment. Each segment is separated from its membrane, and the segments are served in their juice. The contrasting orange and red glistening fruit look lovely bathed in the crimson juices.

I saw this dish being prepared in Italy by a skillful waiter as he carried on a conversation with two businessmen at his table. Talking and smiling the entire time, he carefully sliced the fruits over a dish, arranged the segments on plates, and poured the strained juices over the top.

Preparing this dish tableside is a step best left to professionals!

4 *medium oranges*
4 *medium blood oranges*

Using a paring knife, carefully peel the oranges completely, removing all the white pith. Working over a bowl, use a knife to cut into the oranges, freeing each segment from the membrane. Let the segments drop into the bowl as you work.

Use a fork to mash the empty membranes against a plate to extract all the juices. Lift the segments out of the bowl and arrange on individual serving plates. Strain the juices and pour over the fruit.

FRESH FIGS WITH ANISETTE AND MINT LEAVES

Fichi all'Anisetta

There is a moment in late summer when the weather turns sultry and all the hard green knobs of fruit on the fig tree turn dark purple and plump overnight. Nothing tastes better than the first fig picked from the tree, its rosy, jamlike flesh studded with a minute network of beading. Eating figs out of hand is one of the pleasures of summer.

If you have been blessed with an abundance of ripe figs, there are many ways to enjoy them. They go extraordinarily well with fresh, lemony cheeses, such as goat cheese or ricotta salata. A dollop of lightly sweetened mascarpone or a drizzle of thick, fresh cream makes a luscious accompaniment to ripe figs. Figs can be combined with other fruits in fruit salads or can be made into ice cream or preserves.

In this simple presentation, ripe figs are drizzled with a touch of anisette, a rich, licorice-like liqueur, and then sprinkled with mint leaves. Almond biscotti would make an ideal accompaniment.

Ripe figs
Anisette liqueur
Mint leaves

Wash the figs gently in cool water and dry on a clean dish towel. If desired, peel the figs. Cut off the stems. Cut the figs in half and arrange on serving plates, about 3 or 4 figs per person, depending on the size of the figs. Drizzle with anisette and sprinkle with mint leaves.

PRICKLY PEARS

Fichi d'India

SERVES 4

When the fruits of the prickly-pear cactus are ripe and sweet, the best way to enjoy them is simply to peel them open like the petals of a flower and arrange them on individual plates. The magenta flesh, dotted with tiny edible seeds, is full of refreshing juices, with a flavor and texture akin to watermelon. Prickly pears prepared in this fashion are served in Rome in late summer.

If prickly-pear cactus grows wild where you live, you can gather the fruits yourself. They are covered with fine spines, so make sure to wear heavy gloves when you handle them, and clean them meticulously. The prickly pears sold in markets are cleaned, but you may still want to protect your hands when handling them just in case there may be any stray spines.

8–12 *prickly-pear cactus, spines removed*
Lime wedges, optional

Cut a slice off the top of each prickly pear and reserve. Cut 3 or 4 lengthwise slices down the outside of the prickly pear, leaving each slice attached at the base to form petals like a flower. Replace the reserved slices over the top. Chill well and serve very cold, garnished with optional lime wedges.

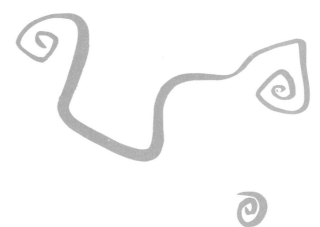

WATERMELON WITH BITTERSWEET CHOCOLATE SHAVINGS

Anguria al Cioccolato

SERVES 6

Practically nothing can rival biting into a wedge of sweet, crisp watermelon. This recipe is for those times when you want a more sophisticated presentation.

Watermelon and dark chocolate have a surprising affinity for each other. The watermelon, very sweet and light, the chocolate, bittersweet yet mellow, both enhancing one another as the flavors merge.

4-pound piece of ripe watermelon
3 tablespoons brandy
2 tablespoons sugar
1½ ounces bittersweet chocolate

Remove the rind from the watermelon and cut the flesh into bite-sized dice, removing the seeds as you work.

Combine the brandy and sugar in a small bowl, and stir until the sugar dissolves.

Place the watermelon in a shallow bowl and drizzle with the brandy mixture. Cover with plastic wrap and refrigerate for 1 hour.

Slice the chocolate into thin shavings. Remove the watermelon from the refrigerator and sprinkle with the chocolate shavings. Stir gently. Spoon the watermelon and juices into dessert goblets.

SUMMER BERRY SALAD WITH MARASCHINO

Insalata del Bosco al Maraschino

SERVES 4

*E*veryone, at one time or another, usually in childhood, has reached out greedily to pick ripe berries growing wild along a country road. Probably no berry since has tasted so good. In this summery salad, which evokes the feeling of wild fruits, berries are marinated in Maraschino, a clear cherry liqueur with a sweet, flowery bouquet that magically intensifies the flavor and perfume of fruits. A few rose petals would make a lovely, fragrant garnish. Make sure the roses are unsprayed.

1   *basket strawberries, stemmed and sliced*
1   *basket blackberries*
1   *basket raspberries*
¼   *cup Maraschino liqueur*

Combine the berries in a shallow bowl. Drizzle with the liqueur and toss very gently. Let macerate for at least 30 minutes.

GRILLED FIGS WITH HONEY AND WALNUTS

Fichi alla Griglia

*I*n this simple recipe, figs are lightly grilled, drizzled with warm honey, then sprinkled with chopped walnuts. It is the perfect dessert to serve with a dinner cooked on the grill, and is especially nice eaten in the garden on a summer evening.

Ripe figs
High-quality honey
Finely chopped walnuts

Serve 3 to 4 figs per person. Place the figs on a grill over gentle heat and warm them through. Turn them over several times while cooking, and use tongs so as not to pierce them. Light grill marks will appear.

Meanwhile warm the honey in a small saucepan.

Arrange the grilled figs on individual serving plates. Drizzle with enough honey to lightly cloak the figs and sprinkle with a light dusting of chopped walnuts.

FRUIT SALAD FROM THE ORCHARD

Macedonia del Frutteto

SERVES 6

This combination of peaches, plums, and figs conjures up images of summer and perfumed languor. Together they create a lush and colorful dessert, the golden and ruby-colored flesh of peaches and plums contrasting with the rosy figs. Before serving the fruit, top them with a sprinkling of walnuts.

4 *peaches*
4 *plums*
8 *figs*
½ *cup white wine*
2 *tablespoons sugar*
3 *tablespoons coarsely chopped walnuts*

Dip the peaches in boiling water for 2 to 3 seconds. Peel and pit them. Cut the peaches into dice. Cut the plums into small wedges. Cut off the stems of the figs. Peel them, if desired. Cut the figs into quarters lengthwise. Place all the fruit in a shallow serving dish.

In a small bowl, combine the white wine and sugar. Stir until the sugar dissolves. Pour the wine mixture over the fruit and gently toss once or twice. Cover and refrigerate for at least 1 hour. Before serving, sprinkle with walnuts.

BAKED APPLES WITH CARAMELIZED SUGAR AND MASCARPONE

Mele al Forno con Zucchero Caramellato

SERVES 8

A very easy-to-make, beautiful dessert of apples baked with white wine and citrus zest, drizzled with caramelized sugar. It is one of my favorites. This dessert can feel very rustic if served in simple white bowls. For a more sophisticated presentation, core the apples before cooking, and fill the centers with chopped nuts and butter. Serve with a big spoonful of mascarpone on the side.

1 *lemon*
1 *orange*
8 *Golden Delicious apples*
1½ *cups sugar, divided*
2 *cups dry white wine*
⅓ *cup water*
Mascarpone, optional

Using a zester, remove the zest from the lemon and orange in long, fine strips.

Make a shallow cut circling the upper third of each apple. This prevents them from splitting. Arrange the apples in a baking dish just large enough to contain them.

In a bowl combine ½ cup of the sugar with the wine and the lemon and orange zests. Pour this mixture over the apples. Bake in a preheated oven at 350° until the apples are tender, spooning the juices over the apples as they cook.

In a small saucepan, combine the rest of the sugar with the water. Stir and cook over low heat until the sugar dissolves. Raise the heat to high and boil until the mixture becomes lightly syrupy and golden brown. Pour the syrup over the apples. Serve the apples warm accompanied by a dollop of mascarpone, if desired.

GOLDEN DREAM PEARS

Pere al Sogno Dorato

SERVES 4

The beauty and flavor of this dish are greatly disproportionate to its ease of preparation. Pears are stuffed with a crunchy filling of amaretti cookies, toasted almonds, and Maraschino liqueur, and baked, not poached, so the flavor of the pears comes through pure and sweet.

The stuffed pears are delicious served plain following a country-style dinner. When accompanied by a dollop of mascarpone or a scoop of excellent-quality vanilla ice cream, they make an elegant dessert appropriate for the most festive occasions.

4 *medium-small pears, ripe but firm*
4 *tablespoons butter, at room temperature, plus extra*
   for the baking dish
1 *tablespoon sugar, plus extra to sprinkle over the pears*
1 *egg yolk*
4 *pairs amaretti cookies, coarsely crumbled*
4 *tablespoons coarsely chopped lightly toasted almonds*
1 *teaspoon Maraschino liqueur*
Mascarpone or vanilla ice cream

Peel and core the pears. Cut them in half lengthwise. Scoop out a little of the pear flesh to make small cavities for the stuffing.

Place the butter and 1 tablespoon of sugar in a small bowl, and mix with a wooden spoon. Add the egg yolk and stir well. Add the cookies, almonds, and liqueur, and stir until the ingredients form a rough paste.

Butter a baking dish large enough to contain the pears in one layer. Arrange the pears in the dish. Mound the filling into the cavities of the pears. Sprinkle a little sugar on the cut surface of the pears. Bake in a preheated 375° oven until the pears are barely tender. Do not overcook, since the texture of the pears can easily turn mushy. A toothpick inserted in the pear should meet with gentle resistance.

Spoon any juices that have formed in the pan over the pears and serve. If desired, place a dollop of mascarpone or a scoop of ice cream alongside the pears.

ORANGE CUSTARD

Coppe di Arancia

SERVES 4

Creamy custard makes a comforting end to a light meal. Finished under a hot broiler to color the tops, these golden custards are infused with the flavors of orange and vanilla.

3   *egg yolks*
1½   *cups whipping cream*
⅓   *cup sugar, plus extra for sprinkling*
1   *teaspoon vanilla extract*
Juice of ½ a small orange

Select a baking pan large enough to hold 4 custard cups. Add enough water to measure one third up the sides. Place the pan on top of the stove and bring water to a boil.

Meanwhile place the egg yolks in a bowl and whisk lightly.

Combine the cream and sugar in a small saucepan and heat just long enough to dissolve the sugar. Let cool and pour into the bowl containing the egg yolks, whisking the mixture as you add the cream. Add the vanilla and orange juice and stir.

Divide the mixture among 4 custard cups. Place the pan with the hot water in the oven, preheated to 325°, and arrange the custard cups in the water. Bake for 15 to 20 minutes, or until just set. Remove the custard cups from the water. Set the oven on broil. Sprinkle a little sugar over the tops of the custards. Transfer them to the broiler for just a minute to brown the tops. Serve tepid or cold.

COFFEE-FLAVORED RICOTTA

Ricotta al Caffè

SERVES 6

F inely ground espresso coffee beans and brandy turn fresh white ricotta into an elegantly dark, bittersweet cream. The longer the ricotta and coffee mixture rests before serving, the stronger the flavor. This dessert looks especially inviting served in small custard cups.

A variation of this classic recipe appears in the pages of Elizabeth David's book on Italian cooking. She suggests serving the coffee-flavored ricotta with fresh cream and thin wafers, which sounds heavenly. In that case, spoon the coffee ricotta into dessert goblets. Pour fresh cream over the top, sprinkle with almonds, and serve with crisp cookies on the side.

3 *cups ricotta, drained of excess water*

½ *cup cream*

¼ *cup freshly ground espresso coffee beans*

5 *tablespoons sugar or to taste*

3 *tablespoons brandy*

Chopped toasted almonds

Beat together until smooth the ricotta and cream. Stir in the ground espresso coffee beans, sugar, and brandy. Cover and refrigerate for at least 2 hours.

Spoon the mixture into very small bowls or goblets. Sprinkle with chopped almonds.

ZABAGLIONE WITH MARSALA-SOAKED RAISINS

Zabaglione con Uva Passa

SERVES 6

White wine zabaglione is mixed with fresh whipped cream and plump, Marsala-soaked raisins. Served in small, rich portions, this dessert is especially good when accompanied with crunchy Italian anise cookies.

2 *tablespoons raisins*
Small piece of lemon peel
Cinnamon to taste
Marsala
3 *egg yolks*
3 *tablespoons sugar*
½ *cup dry white wine*
Freshly whipped cream to taste

Place the raisins in a small bowl. Add the lemon peel, cinnamon, and enough Marsala to generously cover the raisins. Let macerate for at least 1 hour. When the raisins are plump, lift them out of the Marsala.

In a saucepan beat together the egg yolks and the sugar. Add the white wine and stir until combined. Place the saucepan with the egg mixture over a larger pot of simmering water. Stir without stopping. The mixture will begin to foam and swell in size. When it becomes thick and creamy, stir in the raisins and let cool. Fold in enough whipped cream to lighten the zabaglione mixture. Spoon into small dessert goblets and chill.

Serve with crisp Italian cookies.

CHERRIES IN RED WINE ON COUNTRY BREAD

Bruschetta alle Ciliegie

SERVES 4

Buttered grilled bread becomes a base for a compote of cherries cooked in red wine and sugar. This tart-sweet dessert makes a unique offering at the end of a rustic meal. Or serve it as a very special brunch dish.

¾ *cup sugar, or to taste, depending on the sweetness*
   of the cherries
1 *cup rich red wine*
1 *piece lemon rind*
1½ *pounds cherries, pitted*
4 *thick slices country bread*
1½ *tablespoons unsalted butter, at room temperature*

Combine the sugar, red wine, and lemon rind in a medium saucepan. Stir until the sugar dissolves. Add the cherries and stir. Bring to a boil, then simmer for 15 minutes.

Lightly grill or toast the bread and spread with a little butter. Place the bread on 4 individual dessert plates. Spoon the cherries and juices over the bread. Serve warm.

CROSTINI WITH RICOTTA AND FRUIT TOPPING

Crostini con Ricotta e Frutta

SERVES 2

This spread for crostini is made of fresh fruit puree and fluffy white ricotta, served with a drizzle of golden honey over the top.

Serve these dessert crostini after a country-style dinner, along with sweet wine such as Moscato di Pantelleria or Vin Santo. They are also delicious at breakfast served with a cup of strong cappuccino, or as an afternoon snack for a child.

1   *ripe peach or pear, or 3 ripe apricots*
4   *ounces fresh ricotta, about ½ cup*
1   *recipe Crostini (see page 366), using 4 slices of bread*
Fine-quality honey

Peel and pit the fruit and puree in a blender or use a fork to mash it into a puree.

Blend together the ricotta and fruit puree until the mixture is smooth. Prepare the Crostini and spread with the ricotta mixture. Drizzle honey over the top.

WHOLE GRAIN BREAD WITH MASCARPONE AND STRAWBERRIES

Pane Integrale con Mascarpone e Fragole

SERVES 1

slice of dark, nutty-tasting whole grain bread topped with fresh mascarpone and sliced strawberries makes a wonderfully indulgent treat. As you bite into the bruschetta you experience each flavor separately—the warm taste of the grains, the pure, creamy flavor of mascarpone, the tart-sweetness of strawberries, the crunch and sparkle of sugar. Then they all merge into one delightful flavor. Serve it for breakfast with cappuccino, or as a summer afternoon snack. It also makes a fine dessert for a picnic lunch. The mascarpone and strawberry topping served on crostini go very well with afternoon tea.

Find a source for fresh mascarpone produced by artisan-style cheese makers in your area or mascarpone imported from Italy.

Whole wheat bread from the supermarket is too light and airy to use in this recipe. Equally unsatisfactory is whole wheat bread from health food stores, which is often heavy and stodgy in texture. Find a bakery that produces a European-style whole grain bread with a good crusty exterior.

2 *ounces mascarpone*
1 *slice 7-grain bread, sliced about ½ inch thick*
5–6 *ripe strawberries, stemmed, hulled, and sliced*
Sugar to taste

Spread the mascarpone on the bread. Pile the strawberry slices on top of the mascarpone and sprinkle with sugar to taste.

ICE CREAM AND BLACKBERRIES

More e Gelato

One late September in Italy, when the temperatures were soaring, I had this dessert of ivory-colored ice cream topped with soft, gleaming black fruit. The sharp, sweet flavor of the berries merging with the frozen sugared cream made for a refreshing summer treat.

> *Ripe blackberries*
> *Sugar to taste*
> *Vanilla ice cream*

Toss the berries in sugar to taste. Fill tall ice cream goblets half full of vanilla ice cream. Spoon the berries over the top. Serve immediately.

VANILLA ICE CREAM WITH MARINATED CHERRIES

Gelato con Amarene

A touch of liqueur turns this innocent dessert into a sophistacated treat. The cherries are served topped with fine vanilla ice cream and a dollop of fresh, unsweetened whipped cream.

> *Ripe dark cherries*
> *Sugar to taste*
> *Maraschino liqueur to taste*
> *Vanilla ice cream*
> *Freshly whipped cream*

Pit the cherries and sprinkle with sugar and the liqueur. Stir and let rest for several hours in the refrigerator.

To serve, spoon the cherries and their juices into dessert goblets. Top with scoops of ice cream and a small dollop of whipped cream.

LEMON GRANITA AND BRIOCHES

Granita di Limone e Brioche

SERVES 6

My mother's grandmother ordered lemon granita brought to her house during the hottest days of summer. It was delivered in big glass mugs, on a tray, along with fresh brioches, carried by a boy from the *caffè* down the street. The lemon granita and the tender breads were the family's breakfast when it was too hot to eat.

Lemon granita for breakfast is cooling and reviving, but it is also wonderful piled into a tall glass as an afternoon pick-me-up.

If you have a Meyer lemon tree in your yard, use the juice when making this granita. Meyer lemons are less tart and more fragrant than lemons from the market.

3 *cups water, divided*

½ *cup sugar or to taste*

1 *cup freshly squeezed lemon juice, preferably from Meyer lemons, strained of seeds and pulp*

Lemon blossoms, optional

6 *individual brioches*

Stir together 1 cup of water and the sugar until the sugar dissolves. Add the remaining water and the lemon juice. Stir well. Transfer the mixture to a pie tin and place in the freezer.

After about 30 minutes, ice crystals will begin to form. Stir the mixture well, breaking up the ice crystals. Return it to the freezer and continue to break up the crystals at 30-minute intervals. The finished product will be slushy, with small icy granules.

If not serving the granita immediately, transfer it to a glass or plastic container with a tightly fitting lid.

To serve, spoon the granita into chilled goblets or metal ice cream dishes. Garnish with lemon blossoms, if available. Serve with brioches.

ASSORTED RAW FRUITS AND VEGETABLES

Sopratavola

SERVES 4

*I*n southern Italy, various fruits and raw vegetables are served together at the end of a meal. The combination of fruits and vegetables may seem unorthodox, but it is a cooling and refreshing custom.

Not all fruits and vegetables are suitable. The vegetables you select should have a light, mildly sweet, or even mildly peppery flavor and a high water content.

Pink melon wedges, clusters of red grapes, pale green celery stalks and fennel wedges, romaine leaves, and scarlet radishes with leafy green tops, arranged in a big bowl all fulfill their function to refresh the eye as well as the palate.

4 wedges pink honeydew melon, seeds and fibers removed
1 small celery heart, stalks separated, base of stalks trimmed
Handful of radishes with fresh green leaves
1 bunch crisp, seedless grapes, cut into small clusters
1 small fennel bulb, trimmed of all but the small, tender
*   feathery tops, cut into wedges*
Leaves of 1 tender romaine heart

Arrange fruits and vegetables in a big bowl and refrigerate until ready to serve.

A Glossary of Ingredients

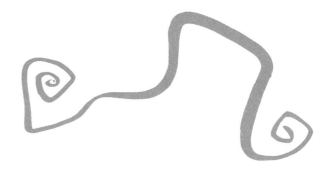

Bread Crumbs

To make bread crumbs use good-quality bread with no added flavoring. Place chunks of dried bread in a food processor or blender and process to the desired size, coarse or small. Transfer crumbs to a jar with a tight-fitting lid and store in the cupboard. To toast the bread crumbs, place them in a dry sauté pan over medium heat. Stir often until the bread crumbs are golden. Immediately transfer to a bowl to cool.

Butter

I call for unsalted butter in the recipes. Store it in the freezer, since it is highly perishable. Without the salt, which acts as a preservative and hides traces of rancidity, the pure, sweet butter flavor comes shining through. It imparts a fresh, creamy quality to cooked dishes.

Capers

Capers are the unopened buds of a shrub that thrives in hot climates. If left to bloom, the buds blossom into pretty pale pink flowers. Capers are generally sold packed in brine, but are also preserved in salt. To use capers in salt, rinse them well, then soak them in a bowl of cold water. Small capers are considered superior to large ones both in flavor and texture. Capers add lively little bursts of flavor to salads, pasta dishes, meats, and fish.

Cheeses

CACIOCAVALLO   A southern Italian cheese, caciocavallo is mild and delicate when young, becoming sharper as it ages. The cheese is often formed into a figure eight with a small knob on the top and a larger bulb at the base. A smoked variety is also made. If caciocavallo is unavailable, substitute a mild imported provolone.

FONTINA   Produced in the Aosta Valley in northern Italy, fontina has a nutty flavor like that of a creamy Gruyère. Depending on the season during which it is produced, it can be either delicate or more full-flavored. Fontina is used both as an eating cheese and in cooking. Avoid fontina produced outside of Italy, since it tends to be bland.

GORGONZOLA   Gorgonzola is a blue-veined cheese made from whole cow's milk. The Gorgonzola called for in this book is the dolcelatte, or "sweet-milk" variety, not the sharper piccante type. It has a buttery, creamy quality that offsets its rich, strong flavor. Taste Gorgonzola before buying it. If the flavor is too strong, the cheese is overripe. Gorgonzola makes a magnificent table cheese, and is also used in pasta sauces and salads.

MASCARPONE   A double cream cheese, mascarpone has the texture of heavy whipped cream. It is used in desserts, in delicate pasta and vegetable dishes, and it is served with fruit at the end of a meal. Mascarpone is imported from Italy, but it is also produced in the United States by small, artisan-style cheese makers.

MOZZARELLA   Originally made in Italy from water-buffalo milk, this fresh cheese ideally should be eaten a few days after it is made. In the United States, fresh mozzarella is made from cow's milk. The texture is firm but very moist, the flavor light and fresh. It is stored packed in water to prevent the surface from drying out. If you plan to keep mozzarella a few days, immerse the cheese in water and refrigerate it until needed. The solid, rubbery mozzarella wrapped in plastic sold in supermarkets is no substitute for the fresh kind. Fresh mozzarella is often called for in the recipes in this book. Find a company in your area that produces fresh Italian cheeses or buy imported mozzarella.

PARMESAN   Parmesan cheese is a member of the family of cow's milk grating cheeses referred to as Grana. The two principal Grana cheeses are Parmigiano-Reggiano and Grana Padano. Parmigiano-Reggiano is considered the finest of the Grana cheeses. It has a full and buttery flavor, a moist texture, and a golden color. It is also quite expensive. Grana Padano has a milder flavor and is less moist, but is still a fine-quality grating cheese. It costs considerably less than Parmigiano-Reggiano and makes a satisfactory alternative. Use either Parmigiano-Reggiano or Grana Padano in recipes calling for grated Parmesan cheese. Use it in cooking, slivered and sprinkled over salads, and as a table cheese. Buy it by the piece. Wrap it tightly and keep it refrigerated. Do not buy domestic Parmesan cheese either by the piece or grated. It is an unsatisfactory substitute.

PECORINO ROMANO   A sheep's milk cheese aged for grating, Pecorino Romano has a very tangy, salty quality that enlivens vegetable flavors. In regional cooking, it is used primarily in dishes from central and southern Italy. It has a drier texture than Parmesan cheese, and the color is whitish rather than golden. Purchase Pecorino Romano by the piece. Wrap it tightly and keep it refrigerated. Aged Pecorino is used primarily as a grating cheese and is not eaten on its own.

RICOTTA   A fresh cow's milk cheese, ricotta has a soft, fluffy texture and mild flavor. It is very versatile in cooking, as it complements both sweet and savory foods. Ricotta makes a healthy, nutritious snack when spread on a slice of bread.

RICOTTA SALATA   Ricotta salata is a sheep's milk ricotta that has been salted to draw out a certain percentage of its moisture content. It has a soft but firm texture and a lemony flavor. A variety of salted ricotta is also available for grating. It has a very firm, dry texture and sharp flavor. When buying ricotta salata, make sure to differentiate between the two types of cheese.

SCAMORZA   A cheese from central and southern Italy, scamorza was originally made from buffalo milk, but nowadays is usually made from cow's milk. It has a medium-firm texture. Generally pear shaped, it is also sold in novelty shapes such as that of a small pig. Scamorza can be broiled, grilled, or baked, as well as eaten fresh. If unavailable, substitute smoked mozzarella.

CROSTINI

Select good-quality Italian or French bread with a 2- to 3-inch diameter. Serve crostini with various toppings as appetizers, as an accompaniment to vegetable side dishes, or in soups.

Extra-virgin olive oil or unsalted butter
A good-quality baguette or other thin loaf, cut into as many
    ¼-inch-thick slices as needed

Place enough oil or butter in a large sauté pan to lightly coat the bottom and turn on the heat to low. Fry the bread slices on both sides, one layer at a time, until golden, adding more oil or butter as needed.

Alternately, melt the butter in a small saucepan. Lightly brush the butter or oil on both sides of the bread slices and arrange on a baking sheet. Place in a preheated 400° oven and bake until slices are golden on both sides. These can be made in advance and served at room temperature.

SMALL CROSTINI

These crunchy Italian croutons are sprinkled over creamy soups or tossed into salads.

1 *small loaf good-quality bread*
8 *tablespoons extra-virgin olive oil*

Cut the bread into ½-inch-thick slices, and then cut slices into dice. Place the olive oil in a large sauté pan and turn on the heat to medium. Sauté the bread cubes in the hot oil until they are golden and crusty. Drain on paper towels. These can be made hours in advance. Store small crostini in paper bags for up to several days.

Lemons

I use lemon juice often in my cooking. It is one of my favorite ways to make flavors sparkle and come alive. A squeeze of lemon seasons leafy salad greens, mild cheeses, raw vegetables, beans, and marinated dishes.

The juice can also be sweetened to flavor fresh fruits or be frozen into a granita. Look for lemons with thin skins that yield to gentle pressure, a sign that they are juicy. Never use bottled lemon juice. Eureka lemons are the kind most commonly sold in markets and have a sharp, clean, aromatic flavor. Meyer lemons, a special variety that is sweeter and more perfumed, are available only to home gardeners. Plant a Meyer lemon tree in your backyard or find a neighbor who has one laden with fruit.

Extra-virgin Olive Oil

Probably the most important ingredient called for in these recipes, olive oil enhances the flavor of vegetables without overwhelming them. Extra-virgin olive oil, never to be confused with so-called pure olive oil, is the first pressing of the olives. Its flavor can be peppery, nutty, or fruity; the viscosity ranges from light to medium to heavy; and the color from light gold to a deep golden green. There is a wide selection of extra-virgin olive oils available in markets and specialty food shops, and prices can range from modest to wildly expensive. Since availability fluctuates, taste a variety of brands until you find several whose flavor and price appeal to you.

Extra-virgin olive oil lasts for up to six months when kept in a cool, dark place. I keep a bottle of extra-virgin olive oil near the stove for easy access during cooking, and I use it frequently enough not to worry about it turning rancid. Use it daily in cooking and you, too, will never have to worry about the lifespan of a bottle of olive oil.

Pure Olive Oil

An inferior grade of oil used primarily for frying. Never substitute it for extra-virgin olive oil in a recipe.

Olives

Green olives are the unripened fruit of the olive tree. As they ripen, the olives change color until they become black. There are so many types of olives to choose from that it is an adventure in itself to become acquainted with them all. When possible, taste olives before you buy them. Look for fleshy olives with a pleasing flavor. Depending on the variety, the taste can range from mild to intensely pungent. Olives can be cured in salt or brine, or they can be oil-cured and are sometimes flavored with herbs, garlic, or other seasonings. Canned olives lack the fleshy texture and deep flavor that make olives so satisfying and should never be substituted in recipes.

Olives add tremendous depth of flavor to vegetable cooking—from the rich, meaty quality of oil-cured black olives to the tang of green olives cured in brine. Olives are perhaps the most popular antipasto of all. A small dish of well-chosen olives makes a simple, appetite-provoking beginning to a meal. Good bread and wine are natural accompaniments.

Pasta

Imported dried pasta is superior to domestic brands. It has a stronger flavor and the ability to stay al dente longer. Buy a range of pasta shapes, from small ones for soup to thick strands to toss with sauce. Experiment with new shapes to experience how they react to different sauces. It is the only way to understand fully why there are traditional pairings of pasta shapes and specific sauces.

Fresh pasta is a tender dough made with egg, rolled into thin sheets, and cut into widths of varying thickness. It is the only pasta tender enough to use for lasagne and stuffed pasta dishes. Its porous surface and egg-enriched taste complement cream, butter, and other delicate flavors. For a complete guide to pasta, see *Pasta Fresca*.

Black Pepper

The perfume and heat found in the flavor of freshly ground whole black peppercorns is indispensable in cooking. Grind black pepper directly over a dish just before serving to appreciate its full bouquet. Invest in a good-quality pepper mill and throw away any containers of ground black pepper that lurk in your cupboard.

Red Chile Peppers

Red chile peppers, fresh or dried, lift the flavors of vegetables and mild foods like pasta and beans. Fresh red chile peppers are fully ripened and have a spicy, but sweet and rounded flavor. It is advisable to wear gloves when handling them. When fresh red chile peppers are unavailable, substitute dried red chile peppers or chile pepper flakes. Take care not to burn the chile pepper flakes in cooking, since they can turn acrid.

Saffron

These small, rusty-gold threads are the stigmas of the purple crocus. Saffron is picked by hand and therefore commands a high price. Luckily, just a pinch is needed to imbue foods with its brilliant color and musky perfume. It is sold either powdered or in strands. Saffron complements the flavor and fragrance of rice especially well.

Salt

Salt is the most basic seasoning in cooking. Use a pure salt such as sea salt or a kosher salt without additives. In cooking, salt helps draw out flavor and acts as a balance to the many sweet, light flavors found in a variety of vegetables. Pure salt is stronger and truer in flavor than processed salt, so less is required. A mistake made by many people who try to cut back on their salt intake is to add a little at the last moment. Instead, season with salt early in the cooking and gradually add a bit more at each stage. This gives the salt a chance to penetrate the food instead of remaining on the surface. The salt you do use will have a greater impact.

Canned Tomatoes

The very best canned tomatoes are the plum-shaped San Marzano variety from Italy, picked when fully ripe and packed whole. The tomatoes have dense, velvety flesh and a flavor that is fresh and fruity. They require only brief contact with heat to break down into a remarkably fresh-tasting sauce. Canned San Marzano tomatoes contain none of the preservatives, citric acid, and firming agents that mar the domestic brands and turn them unpleasantly sharp and acidy. You may be frustrated in your attempts to find true San Marzano tomatoes; they are not consistently available in this country. If unavailable, substitute any variety of canned whole imported tomatoes packed free of additives. If all else fails, try the Pomì brand of chunk tomatoes imported from Italy and sold in 35-ounce cartons. They contain no additives and are generally found in stores specializing in Italian products. Use canned tomatoes when fresh, ripe tomatoes are out of season or in the place of the ubiquitous supermarket tomato, all too often a shadow of the real thing.

Sun-dried Tomatoes

Buy plump sun-dried tomatoes packed in olive oil. The air-dried kind sold in plastic bags are all seeds and no flesh and do not reconstitute successfully. Try making your own, an easy and economical way to have a supply of high-quality sun-dried tomatoes in your pantry (see page 46). Use some of your dried tomatoes to make sun-dried tomato paste (see page 47). The paste is delicious tossed with hot pasta or added to soups and sauces. It also makes a good substitute for *estratto*, an uncooked paste made from pureed tomatoes unavailable in the United States (see page 212 for Pasta with Cauliflower and Sun-Dried Tomato Paste).

Vinegar

Many supermarkets and most specialty food shops carry a wide range of vinegars. The vinegars used in this book include imported red wine and white wine vinegars, and balsamic vinegar. Use high-quality aged red wine vinegar with a pleasing sharp-mellow flavor and mild white wine vinegar. Balsamic vinegar, made only in Italy, is aged in wood over a period of years and is particularly sweet, deep, and mellow. Use balsamic vinegar sparingly, since it can be overpowering, especially when used with fresh leafy greens. Drizzle a little balsamic vinegar into the hollow of a pitted avocado half for a simple, delicious dish.

BIBLIOGRAPHY

Alberini, Massimo, and Giorgio Mistretta. *Guida all'Italia Gastronomica.* Milan: Touring Club Italiano, 1984.

Andolina, Paola. *Cucina di Sicilia.* Palermo: Dario Flaccovio Editore, 1990.

Biondi, Lisa. *Le Quattro Stagioni in Cucina con Lisa Biondi.* Milan: AMC Editrice, 1981.

Boni, Ada. *Italian Regional Cooking.* New York: Bonanza Books, 1969.

Brown, Edward E., and Deborah Madison. *The Greens Cookbook.* New York: Bantam Books, 1987.

Bruning, H. F., Jr., and Umberto Bullo. *Venetian Cooking.* New York: Macmillan, 1973.

Clifton, Claire. *Edible Flowers.* New York: McGraw-Hill, 1983.

David, Elizabeth. *Classics: Mediterranean Food, French Country Cooking, Summer Cooking.* New York: Alfred Knopf, 1980.

————. *Italian Food.* London: Penguin, 1976.

Di Stefano, Bianca. *Cucina Che Vai, Natura Che Trovi.* Palermo: Edikronos, 1981.

Donati, Stella. *Il Manuale delle Verdure.* Milan: Gruppo Editoriale Fabbri, 1986.

Gosetti, Fernanda. *Il Nuovo Orto in Tavola.* Milan: Mondadori, 1974.

Hazan, Marcella. *The Classic Italian Cook Book.* New York: Alfred Knopf, 1976.

————. *Marcella's Italian Kitchen.* New York: Alfred Knopf, 1986.

————. *More Classic Italian Cooking.* New York: Alfred Knopf, 1978.

Johnson, Cathy. *The Wild Foods Cookbook.* New York: Penguin Books, 1989.

Johnston, Mirielle. *The Cuisine of the Sun.* New York: Random House, 1979.

Lodato, Nuccia. *Le Ricette della Mia Cucina Siciliana.* Florence: Edizioni del Riccio, 1978.

Martini, Anna. *The Mondadori Regional Italian Cook Book.* Milan: Mondadori, 1982.

Monanni, Nunzia. *Pasta e Riso all'Italiana.* Milan: Rizzoli, 1987.

Olney, Richard. *Simple French Food.* New York: Atheneum, 1977.

Root, Waverly. *The Best of Italian Cooking.* New York: Grosset and Dunlap, 1974.

————. *Food.* New York: Simon and Schuster, 1980.

————. *The Food of Italy.* New York: Random House, 1971.

Ross, Janet, and Michael Waterfield. *Leaves from Our Tuscan Kitchen.* New York: Ballantine Books, 1987.

Simeti, Mary Taylor. *Pomp and Sustenance.* New York: Alfred Knopf, 1989.

Simonetta. *A Snob in the Kitchen.* New York: Doubleday, 1967.

Taylor, Norman. *Taylor's Guide to Vegetables and Herbs.* Boston: Houghton Mifflin, 1987.

Tropea, Ivana. *Le Ricette della Mia Cucina Romana*. Florence: Edizioni del Riccio, 1977.

Valli, Emilia. *Le Verdure*. Bologna: Edizioni Calderini, 1988.

Zaffina, Giovanna. *Le Ricette della Mia Cucina Calabrese*. Florence: Edizioni del Riccio, 1977.

La Cucina Italiana, a monthly magazine.

Sale e Pepe, a monthly magazine, Mondadori Editore.

A Tavola, a monthly magazine, Rizzoli.

INDEX

Bread (*cont.*)
    strawberries, 357
  see also Crostini
Bread, grilled (bruschetta),
  129–144
Bread crumbs, 363
  garlic, rapini with, 324
  golden radicchio, 332
Broccoflower, 16
  with provolone, 308
Broccoli, 14–15
  cold composed vegetable
    platter, 246–247
  with garlic and red chile
    pepper, 307
  sauce, polenta with, 238–
    239
  and tomato salad, 108
Broccoli:
  con aglio e peperoncino, 307
  gran misto freddo, 246–247
  insalata di pomodoro e, 108
  polenta con, 238–239
Brodo:
  di manzo, 158
  di pollo, 157
  vegetale I, 155
  vegetale II, 156
Broth:
  beef, 158
  chicken, 157
  vegetable, I, 155
  vegetable, II, 156
Bruschetta (grilled bread),
  129–144
Butter, 363

Caciocavallo, *see* Cheese,
  caciocavallo
Caffè, ricotta al, 353
Cannellini, see Fagioli cannellini
Cannellini beans, *see* Bean(s),
  cannellini
Capers, 363
  mixed salad with pine nuts
    and, 97
Caponatina, eggplant and
  almond, 48–49
Caponatina alla Siciliana,
  48–49

Capperi, insalata mista ai
  pignoli e, 97
Caprino(i):
  e erbe, panino con, 148
  fichi e, 69
  ai finocchi, 72
  formaggio dorati, 281
Carciofi:
  bazzoffia, 253–254
  bocconcini di verdura, 282–
    283
  crema di, pasta fresca con,
    216–217
  gatto di patate e, 266–267
  dell'Hotel Gritti, 63
  insalata cotta e cruda, 118–
    119
  panino con pesto di olive e,
    145
  pesto di, bruschetta al, 143
  ripieni di ricotta e pignoli,
    274–275
  alla Sarda, 303–304
  tiella di patate e, 306–307
  al timo, 304–305
Carciofini:
  fritti, 90
  al limone alle erbe, 77–78
  ripieni, 88–89
  risotto con, 234–235
Cardi al forno con olive e
  acciughe, 309–310
Cardoons with black olives
  and anchovies, 309–
  310
Carote(i):
  ai funghi porcini, 312
  insalata cotta e cruda, 118–
    119
  insalata di verdura fresca e
    mozzarella, 113
  insalata mista tenera, 96
  insalata russa, 112
  con panna e basilico, 312
  piccanti, antipasto di, 81
  pinzimonio, 60
  ragù alla primizia, 252–
    253
Carrots, 15–17
  cooked and raw salad,
    118–119

Carrots (*cont.*)
  with cream and fresh basil,
    311
  with porcini mushrooms,
    312
  raw vegetable and
    mozzarella salad, 113
  raw vegetables with olive
    oil dipping sauce, 60
  Russian salad, 112
  spicy, antipasto of, 81
  spring vegetable stew,
    252–253
  tender mixed salad, 96
Cauliflower, 16
  mixed vegetable fritters,
    282–283
  pasta with sun-dried
    tomato paste and,
    212–213
  salad with lemon dressing,
    110
Cavolfiore:
  bocconcini di verdura, 282–
    283
  insalata di, all'agro, 110
  pasta al, e estratto, 212–213
Cavolfiore verde con provolone,
  308
Ceci:
  insalata alla campagnola,
    123
  zimino di bietole, porcini e,
    174–175
  zuppa di scarola e, 179
Celery, 16–17
  assorted raw fruits and
    vegetables, 360
  black and green olives
    with, 42
  lady in white, 68
  pears, and Parmesan, 73
  pink risotto with, 232–
    233
  raw vegetables with olive
    oil dipping sauce, 60
Cetriolo:
  insalata del Signor Arancio,
    107
  insalata sbattuta, 103
  insalata tricolore, 109